MUTINY ON THE RISING SUN

The Atlantic world. Map designed by Bill Nelson.

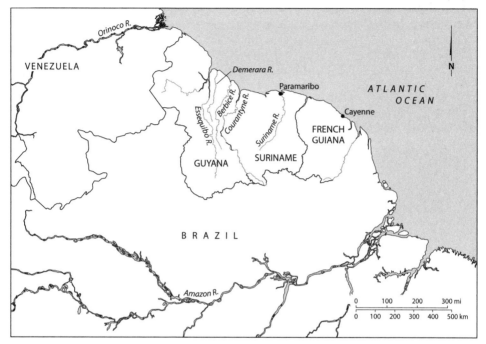

The Guianas. Map designed by Bill Nelson.

Mutiny on the Rising Sun

A Tragic Tale of Slavery, Smuggling, and Chocolate

Jared Ross Hardesty

NEW YORK UNIVERSITY PRESS

New York

NEW YORK UNIVERSITY PRESS
New York
www.nyupress.org

References to Internet websites (URLs) were accurate at the time of writing. Neither the author nor New York University Press is responsible for URLs that may have expired or changed since the manuscript was prepared.

Cataloging-in-Publication data is available from the publisher.

ISBN: 9781479812486 (cloth)
ISBN: 9781479813148 (library ebook)
ISBN: 9781479810215 (consumer ebook)

New York University Press books are printed on acid-free paper, and their binding materials are chosen for strength and durability. We strive to use environmentally responsible suppliers and materials to the greatest extent possible in publishing our books.

Manufactured in the United States of America

10 9 8 7 6 5 4 3 2 1

Also available as an ebook

For my grandparents

CONTENTS

NOTE ON TEXT, DATES, AND TERMINOLOGY

Mutiny on the Rising Sun draws from a vast archive of original manuscript sources. During the eighteenth century, spelling, capitalization, punctuation, and grammar were not uniform. As such, when quoting from original English-language documents, I retain the original formatting. The book also uses Dutch archival documents. Since those have been translated into English, quotations from them are formatted following modern conventions. Likewise, many of the names found in the Dutch sources have been modified for accuracy.

Moreover, at the time of the mutiny in 1743 and until 1752, the British Empire remained on the Julian Calendar, while the Dutch (and most of Continental Europe) followed the Gregorian Calendar. Because of discrepancies in timekeeping, by the middle of the eighteenth century, the Julian Calendar was eleven days behind the Gregorian. When working on a case that spanned both calendars, this can create confusion. For example, the mutiny took place on either 1 June 1743 (Julian Calendar) or 12 June 1743 (Gregorian Calendar), depending on where persons lived and what calendar they followed.

To address this issue, in this book I render all dates by the Julian Calendar—also called "Old Style" as opposed to the Gregorian's "New Style." This decision is not to privilege the British over the Dutch but rather to standardize dates as they would have been understood by most of the colonial Americans involved with the case. Nevertheless, in chapters 5 and 6, which narrate the end of the mutiny and its aftermath, exact dates matter. In those chapters, dates are still rendered in the Old Style, but often followed by their New Style date in parentheses. When distinguishing between the two calendars in chapters 5 and 6, I use the abbreviations "OS" for Old Style / Julian and "NS" for New Style / Gregorian. Everywhere else, dates are in the Old Style.

The Julian Calendar differed in another way. The new year began on 25 March as opposed to 1 January. Most contemporaries made note of this, labeling all dates between 1 January and 24 March with both years, writing, for example, "15 January 1742/3." To simplify, this book considers 1 January the new year, although if the author of a manuscript document used both years, that will appear in the citation.

Finally, a significant portion of this book deals with issues of race and slavery. Only when absolutely necessary do I use eighteenth-century nomenclature for people of African and Indigenous descent. When discussing Native people, I am as specific as possible and use ethnic identifiers, avoiding broad terms like "Indian" and "Native American." Indigenous people in the Guianas are referred to as "Amerindians," and that term appears in the text. Terminology also matters for discussing slavery. For that reason, I generally use the term "enslaved" to refer to those captives held in bondage. Nevertheless, while I eschew calling enslaved people "slaves" as much as possible, doing so is sometimes difficult for stylistic reasons.

Introduction

John Shaw stood at the helm of the schooner *Rising Sun* enjoying the cooler night air. After more than a week in the heat and humidity of Paramaribo, it was a welcome relief. It was eleven o'clock on the night of 1 June 1743 and Shaw, the ship's boatswain currently on watch, prepared to mark the passage of another day. Everything was calm and unremarkable. The captain, Newark Jackson, had just retired to his cabin.[1] The ship was on its proper course, making a zig-zag pattern—tacking—by sailing northeast and then southeast to fight against the current and the wind.[2] Hugging the northeastern coast of South America, the schooner lumbered eastward away from Dutch Suriname and toward French Cayenne.

The *Rising Sun* and its crew had just spent the previous week trading in Suriname's capital Paramaribo. It was business that should not have been conducted. The schooner, having voyaged from the British West Indian colony of Barbados, entered Suriname under false pretenses. Claiming to need supplies and repair, the ship received permission to dock from the colony's governor, Jan Jacob Mauricius. Not a fool, Mauricius knew the schooner carried contraband and was there to offload its cargo in defiance of the law. International treaties, however, prevented the governor from denying distressed ships safe harbor. He commanded them to moor at Fort Zeelandia, Suriname's seat of government, finish their repairs, buy their necessities, and make haste in leaving.[3]

They did not leave immediately. The crew lingered for a week, selling the ship's illicit cargo, while the captain and supercargo, or merchant, George Ledain visited old friends and trade associates. After days of malingering, Mauricius became so annoyed with the crew that he stationed five soldiers on board the *Rising Sun* to prevent any further contraband trade.[4] Somehow, the illegal commerce continued. Jackson, meanwhile, kept telling the governor that the ship was in need of ever more repairs and the sailors ended up caulking the entire vessel while in Paramaribo. Even if the ruse was not particularly clever, one had to admire the crew's dedication to it.

Finally, on 31 May 1743, the *Rising Sun* departed Paramaribo and used the Suriname River's current to leave quickly.[5] On their way out, they deposited the five soldiers at Fort New Amsterdam, where the Commewijne River flows into the Suriname. The ship then caught the tide out for a rapid exit, stopping at Braam Point at the mouth of the Suriname River to take on wood and spend the night.[6]

Early the next morning, the *Rising Sun* departed Suriname entirely and started to tack eastward toward Cayenne, the second and final destination before returning to Barbados. The day was totally uneventful. The captain, supercargo, and John Shaw were all veterans of the Suriname trade and had been on this route many times before. The ship's mate, William Blake, was a skilled pilot and navigator, while the three "Portuguese" sailors Jackson hired in Barbados to assist with the voyage, Ferdinand da Costa, Joseph Pereira, and Thomas Lucas, collectively boasted decades of experience at sea. Although the trading venture was illegal in three different empires, it was at least routine and uneventful.

Or it should have been. As Shaw stood watch at the *Rising Sun*'s helm, one of the Portuguese sailors on duty with him, Pereira, engaged him in conversation. Pereira inquired about the ship's compass and where each of the points on that compass led. The boatswain thought "no harm" of the conversation and explained that the uppermost point went to Orinoco in the Spanish colony of Venezuela. Tiring of the conversation, Shaw asked Pereira to fetch him a dram of rum. The sailor went down in the hold and returned ten minutes later with no dram but with more of the same questions. Shaw offered the same answers and Pereira returned below deck.[7]

Fifteen minutes later, all hell broke loose. Shaw heard a "Great Noise" coming from the ship's cabins. "Murder! Murder!" the cries rang out.

Pereira and Ferdinand da Costa had snuck into Jackson's and Ledain's cabins and stabbed them. Meanwhile, Thomas Lucas attacked John McCoy, Ledain's clerk, in his berth, stabbing him nine times. The captain and merchant slipped out of their cabins, but as Jackson began ascending the ladder above, Lucas saw him and stabbed him three more times. Jackson made it on deck, and Ledain, following Jackson up the ladder, suffered five more stab wounds. As Lucas was distracted stabbing the captain and supercargo, McCoy, slashed to tatters, crawled deep into the hold of the ship.[8]

The screams jolted the ship's mate, William Blake, out of his slumber. As he went on deck to see what was happening, one of the three mutineers stabbed him in the shoulder.[9] He curled into a ball on the deck and looked over to see Ledain nearly dead and in a pool of his own blood and gore. The merchant whimpered "I am dead" and perished a few minutes later. Jackson, likewise lying on the deck, was clinging to an axe that Da Costa dropped when he followed Ledain up the ladder.[10] The captain responded to Ledain's cry, shouting, "I am dead! I am dead!"[11] Lucas ordered Jackson killed. Da Costa snatched the axe from Jackson's hands and began chopping.[12]

Pereira, meanwhile, had stolen Jackson's cutlass from his cabin and turned his attention to John Shaw. He began slashing the boatswain wildly, cutting him all over his body.[13] When Pereira turned his attention back to Jackson and Ledain, Shaw was able to slip below deck. There, watching in horror and confusion, were fifteen enslaved Africans, most of them children. The *Rising Sun*'s voyage to Suriname was not just any smuggling run but an illicit slave trading voyage, and now the remainders of that venture stood as terrified and unwitting witnesses to a bloody mutiny.[14]

Shaw cowered in his bunk as the murders continued above. For the mutineers, it was time to start disposing of bodies. Two of them gathered around Jackson, still clinging to life despite multiple stab wounds and the tremendous pain inflicted by Da Costa's axe. They picked the captain up, one at his feet and the other at his shoulders. They swung his body to gain momentum and threw him overboard.[15] Jackson screamed as he plunged into the dark abyss.[16]

Mutiny on the Rising Sun reconstructs the origins, events, and eventual fate of the *Rising Sun*'s smuggling voyage. Using the events of that horrible night in June 1743 as a starting point, it narrates a "human history of smuggling." Sources surrounding the case allow us to study Newark Jackson, George Ledain, the mutineers, the other men on board the schooner, business associates on land, the widows who dealt with the mutiny's fallout, and the enslaved people the *Rising Sun* trafficked. All these people lived in a world where smuggling stood at the center of their lives. The case of the *Rising Sun* illustrates how larger forces created the conditions for smuggling, but individual actors, often driven by raw ambition and little regard for the consequences of their actions, designed, refined, and perpetuated this illicit but routine commerce.

The records from the mutiny ultimately shine a bright light on an eighteenth-century international smuggling ring. The *Rising Sun* was a small part of a system of illegal commerce that underpinned the economy of colonial America and the early modern Atlantic world. By the middle decades of the eighteenth century, smuggling formed a cornerstone of the Atlantic trade system and was central to the economy of Britain's North American colonies. Engaging in illicit trade in this period, however, was openly and widely practiced, making it much different from the black markets and underground economies of the twenty-first century. The Atlantic empires of Britain, France, Spain, Portugal, and the Netherlands sought to control the flow of many everyday household commodities, such as sugar, molasses, coffee, cotton, and chocolate. Policy makers and imperial officials had deep-seated fears that if these goods circulated outside of imperial boundaries or ended up in the hands of the enemy, the imperial state would be denied tax revenue and suffer irreparable harm. Proactively, metropolitan officials and their colonial officers attempted to control the flow of commodities and manufactured goods in and out of their colonies. Nevertheless, enforcement of these controls was nearly impossible, and merchants, especially those from the North American colonies, found these measures easy to evade. Even by conservative estimates, half of all commerce in the Atlantic world during the eighteenth century was illegal and could be classified as smuggling.[17]

As a human history of smuggling, this book examines how illicit trade shaped the lives and experiences of people like those on board the *Rising Sun*. In the eighteenth century, smuggling, in the words of one historian, "became the way for local populations" of every social class "to act locally and think globally."[18] Men and women, rich and poor, people of all races and ethnicities alike engaged in buying and selling contraband. Smuggling brought goods from across the globe to local consumers, profoundly shaping the economic, social, cultural, and political order. Most significantly, slavery lay at the heart of this world of smuggling. Slave labor produced and processed lucrative and commonly smuggled tropical commodities, such as sugar, molasses, and cocoa. At the same time, captives were themselves used as trade goods and exchanged for the very products produced by fellow enslaved people.

While illicit trade was a subversive act that challenged imperial governments, the way that smugglers trafficked and became dependent upon the stolen labor of enslaved people ultimately reinforced the status quo. Placing the events of the *Rising Sun* in the wider world of Atlantic slavery demonstrates that it was a small piece in the larger history of the rise of racial capitalism. Smuggling may have undermined empires, but, like most other early modern commercial practices, it still relied on the exploitation of bound African and Indigenous bodies. That immiseration, in turn, generated the wealth that laid the foundation for a modern industrial, capitalist economy.[19]

For this particular smuggling ring, the most important slave-produced commodity was cacao, or, as we know it in its refined form, chocolate.[20] The cacao tree is indigenous to the Americas. Native Americans first domesticated the plant more than four thousand years ago. They learned how to process cacao beans and incorporated it into their everyday life and religious practices. It became especially important in Mesoamerica. The Mayans used the plant's beans as a form of currency, while the Mexica, or Aztecs, consumed vast quantities of the crop in a drink they called "chocolatl."[21] Spanish explorers encountered cacao early in their explorations of the Americas and developed a taste for it. Soon, its popularity spread across the Atlantic, and by the end of the seventeenth century Europeans and Euro-American colonists consumed chocolate in ever increasing quantities.[22]

British and British Americans proved to have an especially large appetite for chocolate, and demand far outstripped supply. Production proved to be a problem with the finicky crop. It will grow only in tropical regions, twenty degrees north or south of the equator, under particular conditions. Susceptible to a variety of diseases and infestations, cacao trees need to be managed by a skilled horticulturalist.[23] There were areas of the British Empire where cacao could be grown. Indeed, when the English conquered the Caribbean island of Jamaica in 1655, it was home to vast cacao groves the Spanish had planted, but ignorance and neglect caused a sharp decline in cacao production until there were few trees left.[24]

By the 1730s and 1740s, there was very little cacao production within the empire and certainly not enough to satiate consumer demand. Smuggling proved to be a solution to this problem. The North American merchants and ship captains involved with the smuggling ring had to leave the British Empire to find cacao. These actions not only violated the law but also demonstrated how interconnected the British North American colonies were with the wider world.

Much of this story takes place in the Dutch colony of Suriname. Part of the region of South America collectively called the Guianas or the Wild Coast, Suriname, along with modern-day Guyana, French Guiana, and parts of Brazil and Venezuela, was first explored by Europeans, most famously Sir Walter Raleigh, in the sixteenth century.[25] Seeing the potential of the region's lush tropical jungle and river system for large-scale, slave-based agriculture, European nations began colonizing the

Guianas in the early seventeenth century. Suriname became a focal point. The Dutch captured the colony, initially settled by the English, in 1667.[26] They transformed Suriname into a major producer of sugar and, by the 1730s, cacao.

As cacao production—using enslaved labor—increased, so did trade from British North America. New England and New York merchants and ship captains, who had been trading illegally in Suriname since the late seventeenth century, expanded their businesses, purchasing not only the sugar and molasses they desired but now also cacao.[27] They helped fuel the consumption of chocolate across the English-speaking world as Surinamese cacao ended up in the British West Indies, London, and Boston. That, in turn, literally created markets for new goods and changed tastes. The *Rising Sun* played a part in this larger process, ultimately making the mutiny a story in the early history of globalization.

As significant as smuggling was to the creation of new tastes and the movement of commodities like cacao, it was also a secretive activity, meant to be hidden away from the prying eyes of customs officials and imperial authorities. How, then, do we tell the history of something that was clandestine and deliberately concealed? This mutiny—resulting in the deaths of at least seven people and directly and indirectly shattering the lives of countless enslaved Africans—reveals a world obscured by the intentionally enigmatic nature of smuggling. In that sense, the mutiny on the *Rising Sun* was what historians call a contingency. It was always possible a mutiny could happen on the schooner, but few could have predicted it. And when it did occur, the actions of the surviving crew—further contingencies—ensured that what transpired would ultimately be recorded, preserved, and left to posterity to read. Looking at those records and tracing the people involved reveals an otherwise hidden world.

To reconstruct the final voyage of the *Rising Sun*, this study draws from source material generated all around the Atlantic following the mutiny. Dutch authorities in Suriname interrogated two of the mutineers, leaving a rich record of their trial. These Dutch records, in many ways, form the cornerstone for understanding a case that had the greatest consequences in the English-speaking world. Moreover, documents, such as probate records, commercial correspondence, account books, and newspapers from Britain and its American colonies, provide a significant amount of detail about the case, especially its repercussions. All told, the mutiny on the *Rising Sun* generated manuscript evidence in New England, Barbados, Suriname, the Netherlands, and Great Britain all while garnering significant attention in print. This transnational archive provides intimate details of the *Rising Sun* and its world, allowing us to tell this human history of smuggling and follow a cast of characters across the middle decades of the eighteenth century.

When reading the documentary evidence about the case, however, it is important to keep two pieces of context in mind. First, the records reveal a world very different from our own. Eighteenth-century America was an incredibly violent place where the use of force structured everyday life. Violence courses through this entire episode, from the terror used against enslaved people to conflicts between sailors to how the state punished criminals. And, of course, the mutiny itself was exceptionally brutal.[28] Moreover, the merchants, planters, sailors, and government officials who appear in this story held radically different conceptions of what was moral and ethical. Ideas and institutions that modern people find abhorrent, such as racism, slavery, and smuggling, were commonplace and socially accepted in the eighteenth century.[29] While there was certainly criticism of these practices, systemic violence against the victims and profits for the benefactors marginalized and silenced critics. Thus, planters, slave traders, and smugglers could be and were considered virtuous, upstanding members of their communities. Related, parts of the story that we today might find morally ambiguous, such as sailors organizing a mutiny to make an independent life for themselves, were readily and harshly condemned by contemporaries as immoral.

Second, as rich as the records related to this case may be, they are incomplete and biased. Often, basic details, such as how and when Captain Newark Jackson arrived in Barbados prior to the departure of the

Rising Sun, are unclear or totally unknown. This fragmentary archive not only makes it difficult to reconstruct certain lives, events, and moments but also reflects the prejudices and realities of the time. Court testimony, one of the key pieces of evidence for the mutiny, could be coerced with the threat (or use) of state violence, and defendants lied in an attempt to save themselves from punishment.[30] Official documents often erased the voices and experiences of whole groups of people, such as Amerindians, sailors, and the enslaved, while printed accounts of the mutiny reduced the mutineers to caricatures. Finally, the way Dutch officials, merchants involved with the case, and printers narrated the mutiny focused on the extraordinary violence of the event and not the everyday lives of the people involved. Put another way, the surviving documents allow us to describe Newark Jackson's murder in grisly detail, but they do not permit us to know his age when he died. Nevertheless, these records are all we have of the case, and we can use them judiciously to uncover information about the *Rising Sun*.[31]

All these evidentiary issues are central to understanding the experiences of the enslaved people on board the *Rising Sun*. Indeed, there is never a direct mention that the voyage of the *Rising Sun* was a slave trade venture. It rests entirely on circumstantial evidence laid out in the text and appendix I, "On Circumstantial Evidence." There are only a handful of documents that mention the enslaved people, but the texts are woefully incomplete and ultimately reify the terror of slavery. To ignore those documents or, more precisely, avoid them for fear of perpetuating slavery's horrors, however, would be to miss one of the most important contexts for understanding what transpired on the schooner.[32] In the end, it is possible to reconstruct the experience of these captives with empathy while placing the terror enacted upon them in its proper context.[33]

Reading the documents related to the *Rising Sun*, even with all these caveats, allows us to better understand what transpired on the schooner, the smuggling ring it was part of, and the significance of illicit commerce and global entanglements for early Americans. As such, *Mutiny on the Rising Sun* focuses on *how* smuggling functioned in the early modern Atlantic, *who* was involved, and *why* illicit trade shaped everyday lives and commercial practices.[34] Nevertheless, a human history of smuggling must be focused on the individuals involved. To reconstruct these lives, the book examines Captain Newark Jackson, the men who organized the smuggling ring, the enslaved people trafficked by the schooner and who constituted the cargo, and the crew, including the mutineers. The fifth chapter narrates the end of the mutiny, highlighting the capture and trial of the mutineers, while the sixth examines various aftermaths of the mutiny and fate of the survivors. An epilogue takes the case and its meaning to the present, exploring how people in the twenty-first century are reckoning with the legacies of smuggling and slave trading in early America.

Ultimately, the case of the *Rising Sun* opens a unique window on early American life. It connects early Americans to people across imperial and national boundaries, demonstrating that the colonization of what became the United States was more of an entangled enterprise than an exceptional, solitary errand in the wilderness.[35] Americans forged those connections in many ways, but a primary vehicle was illicit trade. Smuggling was ubiquitous, fundamental to the everyday lives of people living in the eighteenth century, and helped pioneer the consumption of new products such as chocolate. Nevertheless, slavery and human trafficking often lay at the heart of the entire operation. Without access to commodities produced by slave labor or the ability to buy and sell people, the relentless growth of the Atlantic economy, whether through legal or illegal trade, was impossible. In short, this smuggling ring starkly reveals how reliant commerce was on the exploitation of racialized others. If smuggling entangled early Americans with people across the Atlantic, racial capitalism made those entanglements profitable.

1

The Captain

As Captain Newark Jackson plunged to his death, mortally wounded and screaming, there were probably many thoughts running through his mind. Was he focused on his immediate situation and the pain of his injuries? Was he thinking of his fellow crew members? The enslaved children below deck? Or were his thoughts further afield, thinking of faraway places and far distant memories? Was he thinking of his wife Amey and their three children now left to fend for themselves? His numerous businesses in Boston buried under a mountain of debt? Were there any regrets? Certainly, he lamented hiring the three men responsible for his death. But what about deeper regrets, ones that would have most likely required much more time for reflection than Jackson had in his final moments? Did he regret his involvement in the smuggling ring? And what of trading in slaves, the cargoes of flesh and humanity that brought so many risks?

Much like his final sentiments, little is known about Newark Jackson's life. He moved to Boston in the early 1730s and was already married to Amey (née Smith). Beginning in the late 1730s, the couple had three children, Elizabeth, Newark Jr., and Amey Jr. Jackson was a ship captain and merchant, often dealing in exotic and new products such as chocolate. To acquire many of those goods, he violated imperial trade laws by doing business in Dutch Suriname, French Cayenne, and places unknown. That made a Jackson a smuggler.

This picture of Jackson's life is woefully incomplete. Exploring his world, actions, and behavior, however, gives a fuller picture of his life and experiences. And doing so paints a human face on a smuggler and slave trader. Perhaps the most important context for understanding Jackson's life was his blind ambition, although it was certainly not as calculated as it may first seem. Aspects of Jackson's life—his move to Boston, his associations there, his business practices—all suggest a man striving to make something of himself in a chaotic, unregulated, and exploitative world. He used all the tools available, from long-distance trade to marketing new products and joining institutions that brought proximity to power.

As much as Jackson found a modicum of security and success, however, this behavior had a dark side. Much of his business activity required him to flagrantly violate the law, as he traded outside of the British Empire and evaded customs officials. Indeed, his reputation seems to have hinged on the fact that he was a successful smuggler, a ship captain other merchants could rely upon to cross legal and geographic boundaries and acquire the commodities they desired. To finance his many business endeavors, Jackson burdened himself and, following his murder, his family with what was ultimately an unsustainable amount of debt. Even more poignantly, as Jackson strove to find comfort for himself and his family, he left a trail of human misery behind him. Much of the wealth he amassed came from shipping slave-produced commodities, the ownership of enslaved people, and the trafficking of African captives. Their despair directly contributed to Jackson's success.

In some ways, it is easier to account for the things we do not know about Newark Jackson than those that we do. We have no idea what Jackson looked like, for example. Nor do we know where Jackson was born or where he lived before moving to Boston in the early 1730s, although circumstantial evidence suggests he was from Essex County, possibly Marblehead or Gloucester.[1] Jackson's first appearance in the archival record was not until the early 1730s. The earliest documentation comes exclusively from Boston newspapers. In July 1731, Jackson appeared in the *Boston News-Letter*. The newspaper contained the notice that, among many other ship captains, Jackson had "Cleared Out" of the port and was heading to North Carolina.[2]

Over the next few years, Jackson appeared in similar shipping records printed in Boston's newspapers, but the most important document for understanding Jackson's move to Boston is from early 1735. The previous year, shipwright Benjamin Darling caulked and repaired a ship for Jackson. It seems that Jackson paid only thirty of the forty-one pounds that he owed Darling, causing Darling to sue him for the remaining eleven. Jackson lost and had to pay. Such lawsuits over debt were commonplace in colonial America, but what stands out about the case is the summons issued for Jackson to appear at the Court of Common Pleas. In it, court officials described Newark Jackson as being "of Boston."³

The phrase "of Boston" had significant meaning in the eighteenth century. Years after Jackson's murder, a young John Adams took to his diary to contemplate the meaning of the phrase. Adams himself was not from Boston, but had moved there to practice law. The question of belonging weighed on his mind. He described that "when a man is called of such a Town," it meant that he was a "legal Inhabitant of that Town, entituled to all the Privileges, and compellable to bear all the Burdens of that Town."⁴ Thus, by 1735 court officers recognized Jackson, regardless of where he was born, as a legitimate resident of Boston eligible for all the opportunities Boston afforded its inhabitants and obligated to the town's common good. No matter where he came from, he now fully belonged to Boston.

At the time of Jackson's arrival, Boston was one of colonial America's most bustling port cities. Founded a century earlier, Boston had grown dramatically in the previous three decades and more than sixteen thousand residents called the town home. Not only was Boston the capital of the Province of Massachusetts Bay, but it also exercised effective political dominion over the rest of New England and much of British-controlled Atlantic Canada. The first generations of Bostonians conceived and constructed this system of power, transforming Boston into a city-state that harnessed the resources of an ever-burgeoning hinterland. Those resources, channeled into trade connections across the Atlantic and all over the Americas, in turn allowed Bostonians to carve out a certain degree of independence from the English Crown and create a political and economic system that best served New England's settler population, constructing a commonwealth in the forests of North America.

In the two generations before Jackson arrived in Boston, however, the old commonwealth model began to change. Fiercely autonomous Bostonians began to feel more comfortable as subjects of the British Empire. They relished the possibilities of trade with the mother country. And given that Boston was three thousand miles and a three-month voyage from London, they could enjoy the benefits of that association, such as military aid and access to manufactured goods, while still exercising a certain degree of independence, especially when it came to commerce.

With these increased connections to Britain, Boston boomed. The town became home to extensive rope making and distilling industries and the second most productive shipyards in the British Empire.[5] All these industries sustained Boston's main business, overseas trade. From the moment of the town's founding, Bostonians sought opportunities to build trading networks. The problem, however, was that the region's stony soil and cold climate made it impossible to produce valuable agricultural commodities, such as sugar, cotton, and tobacco. Nevertheless, beginning in the 1640s, Bostonians found a work-around. Instead of producing those commodities themselves, they began provisioning the places that did.

The most important market cultivated by Bostonians was the West Indies, especially the island of Barbados. There, English settlers experimented with and found success growing sugarcane using slave labor. Needing every acre of farmable land for sugar production, planters turned to importing food, livestock, and timber to sustain the enslaved labor force and plantation production. New England turned out to be perfectly suited to supporting this endeavor. The region produced sizeable agricultural surpluses, maintained large herds of livestock, had plenty of timber, and was home to a robust fishing industry that trawled the rich fishing banks of the North Atlantic.

Boston merchants began provisioning West Indian plantations—and by extension one of the most exploitative slave labor systems in world history—and never looked back. The West Indian trade became the backbone of Boston's overseas trading system. In addition to provisioning plantations, Bostonians built the ships that traded with the Caribbean, filling holds with valuable sugar and molasses after selling their own region's surplus. These tropical commodities could then be taken anywhere, including metropolitan Britain, where they would be exchanged for manufactured goods. Manufactures could then be sold across the Atlantic, allowing Bostonians to corner old markets and cultivate new ones. All these entrepreneurial activities brought prosperity to Boston itself, enriching the town's merchant class, sustaining industry that supported this trade, and transforming the town into an attractive destination for migrants.[6]

When Jackson arrived in Boston in the early 1730s, he probably would have been awed. The town was a global marketplace. Once again, the experience of fellow migrant John Adams proves instructive. After moving to Boston, the young lawyer visited the home of a wealthy merchant and recorded all he saw. "Turk[ish] Carpets," a "Marble Table," and a "beautiful Chimney Clock," Adams marveled, describing the merchant's home as the "most magnificent of any Thing" he had ever seen.[7] The material world Adams encountered was the direct result of Boston's overseas trade. Such wealth and the dreams of it helped entice young men to try their luck in the town.

Ostentation aside, however, 1730s Boston may not have been the most attractive destination for an ambitious man like Jackson. For the previous generation, the town had been losing influence in the West Indian trade as more southerly port cities, namely New York and Philadelphia, developed their own merchant fleets that engaged in the provisioning trade. Both those cities also had more fertile hinterlands that produced larger harvests and more desirable commodities such as wheat. Boston was able to be competitive by continuing to ship fish, timber, and livestock, but its total share of the trade declined.[8] Closer to home,

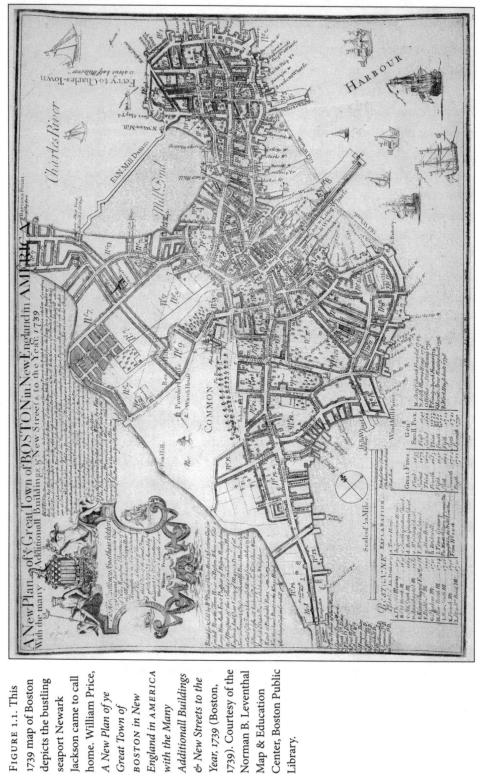

FIGURE 1.1. This 1739 map of Boston depicts the bustling seaport Newark Jackson came to call home. William Price, *A New Plan of ye Great Town of BOSTON in New England in AMERICA with the many Additionall Buildings & New Streets to the Year, 1739* (Boston, 1739). Courtesy of the Norman B. Leventhal Map & Education Center, Boston Public Library.

other New England port cities, such as Salem, Massachusetts, Newport, Rhode Island, Portsmouth, New Hampshire, and New London, Connecticut, began to directly compete with Boston. Provisions and labor were cheaper in those places, their own merchant communities undercut Boston and opened shipyards, and Boston merchants shifted operations to those places. By the end of the decade, orders for new ships from Boston's shipyards declined by half, while other industries, such as distilling, declined by as much as 66 percent. Meanwhile, there were currency shortages throughout the region, and when Massachusetts responded by printing paper money, it only caused inflation.[9] While the trend was not readily apparent in the 1730s, over the next few decades Boston's population declined as residents left for other places and sought better prospects.[10]

Nevertheless, Jackson still found opportunities in Boston. These economic issues disproportionately affected Boston's working classes, while merchants continued to thrive. As a ship captain, Jackson brought with him a skill set that the town's business community valued. Unlike artisans and other urban laborers, he was not entirely dependent on his wages. When hired to command a voyage, he was allotted a certain amount of the ship's cargo space and allowed to trade on his own account. Traveling to faraway places gave Jackson direct access to trade goods and knowledge of local markets on both ends of the voyage, giving him an advantage. Boston's prospects on the whole may have been declining, but for a young, enterprising, and ambitious man with the right skills and connections, there was still a world of possibilities.[11]

Newark Jackson's life in Boston can be traced through business activities, most significantly his work as a ship captain. Although there is little information about Newark Jackson as a ship captain, the available evidence suggests he was competent and capable. Ship captains had responsibilities on land and at sea. Outside of locating and managing the ship's actual cargo, the captain was in charge of every other part of preparing for a voyage. Jackson would have had to purchase provisions for the crew and equipment for the ship, including block, tackle, sails, rope, muskets, and tools.

An enterprising ship captain would see these tasks as opportunities to cultivate relationships with local artisans and merchants. One Boston ship captain and contemporary of Jackson's, Moses Prince, went so far as to call the artisans he conducted business with "my tradesmen."[12] Ship captains could then draw upon those connections every time they needed to outfit a voyage or engage in other business enterprises. Jackson seems to have maintained good relationships with artisans and merchants. Eighteenth-century Boston was a litigious, debt-ridden community. In nearly fifteen years of outfitting voyages, however, only one artisan ever sued Jackson for outstanding debts.[13] The paucity of debt suits against Jackson is remarkable and demonstrates that, with the artisans and merchants he contracted with at least, he was an honest broker. His ability to service his debts in turn allowed Jackson to readily find work, outfit voyages, and find backers and supporters in other commercial endeavors.

In addition to outfitting voyages, ship captains also had to hire crews. Bustling maritime hubs like Boston were home to many sailors, but even then recruiting could be difficult. Jackson probably struggled to recruit enough seamen. To compound the issues, merchants and shipowners often intervened in the recruitment process, requiring captains to hire friends and kin as officers.[14] Such challenges in recruiting may explain why Jackson, despite the risks, was willing to hire the three sailors who ultimately murdered him in 1743.

Both provisioning and recruiting required Jackson to assume a considerable amount of risk. Even though the shipowners and investors ultimately paid for supplies, equipment, and sailors' wages, Jackson had to forward the money and be reimbursed later. Waiting for merchants to pay was usually not an option. Sailors could demand a certain percentage of their wages up front, and if Jackson could not produce the money when demanded, they had plenty of other opportunities for work. Likewise, being able to purchase supplies in the moment allowed a ship to be more quickly outfitted. Yet doing so meant Jackson assumed great financial liability that may or may not be covered. In October 1742, Jackson sued merchant Nathaniel Cunningham after waiting nearly a year to be reimbursed more than sixty-five pounds. Jackson had served as captain for a voyage on board Cunningham's ship *Integrity*. Perhaps Cunningham did not understand the irony of his ship's name. Even after Jackson successfully completed the venture, the merchant "unjustly" refused to pay not only the costs of provisioning but also Jackson's wages.[15]

Once at sea, Jackson would have been free of the pressures of outfitting and recruiting. Ship captains exercised absolute control over their vessels and were mostly in charge of the ship's cargo and maintaining discipline on board. Nevertheless, Jackson tended to captain smaller vessels, meaning for many voyages he would have also been the navigator and pilot of the ship. His crews were likewise small, probably no more than three or four sailors and possibly a mate in his earliest voyages.

Moreover, captains had an incredible amount of power over the sailors serving under them, especially when out to sea. They could—and were expected to—mete out violent punishment when their charges stepped out of line. Since ancient times, sailors were thought to be far too independently minded and foolhardy to go unwatched. By virtue of spending long periods away from land in a profession that created a rough equality between everyone on board, they held dangerous ideas about equality and had no use for hierarchy. Failure to keep them in line could result in violence, up to and including mutiny.[16] Nevertheless, Jackson was not a particularly draconian or abusive captain. One of his murderers later told authorities in Suriname that "he had no complaint" against his superior.[17]

Unlike his experiences and practices as a ship captain, there is much better record of Jackson's trading activities. According to the port entries and departures contained in Boston's newspapers, Jackson undertook ten separate voyages between July 1731 and August 1736.[18] Beyond the newspapers, in spring 1736 Jackson appeared in Suriname's shipping records, and customs officials in Barbados recorded his arrival there in March 1738. Between March 1738 and May 1743, however, there are no additional port entries or departures. Nevertheless, existing documentation demonstrates the way Jackson's career changed over the course of the 1730s.

Earlier in the 1730s, Jackson mostly engaged in the coastal trade, confining himself to the coast of North America, trading in low-value commodities, and occasionally voyaging to Europe to sell those goods. Such ventures would not have been unusual for a young ship captain establishing his reputation. Over an eighteen-month period, from October 1732 until April 1734, Jackson's movements can be tracked. On 30 October 1732, the *Weekly Rehearsal* noted that Jackson had just returned from New London, Connecticut.[19] There, he most likely acquired agricultural products and perhaps livestock that would be gathered in Boston and shipped elsewhere.

After spending about six weeks in Boston, Jackson took his first documented trip to Europe, departing Boston for London in December 1732.[20] In London, he most likely sold a cargo of salt cod and timber. In exchange, Jackson would have filled his hold with the goods of the world. London, the bustling capital of the British Empire, was also its "central mart."[21] New England merchants like Jackson traded in London to purchase goods unavailable in the colonies, including cloth, fine wines and spirits, furniture, tools, and exotic fruits and spices. Jackson's cargo, however, while useful, was not particularly valuable. It would not have covered the cost of a cargo of expensive manufactured goods. Thus, Jackson purchased goods on credit, either on his or on his employer's account, to fill his hold.[22]

Jackson departed the capital sometime in early 1733 but did not return immediately to Boston instead sailing to North Carolina.[23] Jackson voyaged there numerous times in the early 1730s. He most likely purchased naval stores used to waterproof ships.[24] Boston, home to such a large shipbuilding industry, had an insatiable demand for these goods that exceeded local production capacity. By traveling directly from London to North Carolina, Jackson engaged in an old New England trading practice sometimes called the carrying trade.[25] He sold at least part of his cargo of manufactured goods from London there. North Carolina, despite an extensive naval stores industry, was a relatively marginal colony and outside of most major trading circuits. Under such conditions, manufactured goods from Britain would have brought higher prices than in Boston, helping to offset the trade deficits created by trading in London. Stopping in North Carolina also increased profit margins and allowed Jackson to purchase more naval stores.[26] Jackson returned to Boston in early April 1733.[27]

Upon his return from North Carolina, Jackson made two trips to Newfoundland in July and September 1733.[28] By 1733, Bostonians had been trading to Newfoundland for the better part of a century.[29] Although not the most lucrative, the trade provided a constant and reliable market for Boston merchants and ship captains. When Jackson went to Newfoundland, he most likely carried provisions such as salt, food, timber, livestock, naval stores, and rum to supply fishing communities. In exchange, Jackson would have filled the hold of his ship with salt cod from some of the richest fisheries in the world.[30]

For New England merchants and ship captains, the Newfoundland trade offered important—and sometimes illegal—opportunities. Newfoundland fishing communities welcomed New England merchants as they offered the best prices on goods necessary for survival. Profits generated in Newfoundland allowed New Englanders to offset the trade imbalance with Britain. The waters and villages of Newfoundland also became a site of illegal trade. Cod fisheries required thousands of tons of salt a year to cure fish. Much of that salt came from southern Europe and the West Indies. When ship captains, many of them New Englanders, purchased salt in Portugal, Spain, southern France, or the Caribbean, they also bought other products, such as port wine and brandy, which were hard to obtain and heavily taxed in the British Empire. New England ships likewise carried tea, sugar, molasses, and manufactured goods purchased in the Dutch and French West Indies when headed to Newfoundland. The waters off the coast of Newfoundland were an unregulated market for all these goods.[31] Perhaps Newfoundland was the site where Jackson began his career trading contraband.[32]

Jackson's final documented voyage of this eighteen-month period can be directly tied to his Newfoundland ventures.[33] On 11 April 1734, the *Boston News-Letter* printed that Jackson had entered the port of Boston from Lisbon, Portugal. New England merchants had been trading with Lisbon and other ports in southern Europe since the 1630s.[34] These ports provided access to the salt necessary for curing fish. They also had an insatiable appetite for salt cod. Such an arrangement created the perfect opportunity for those engaged in the carrying trade. Jackson most likely took a mixed cargo of fish, timber, and naval stores to Lisbon and there exchanged it for salt and other southern European staple commodities, such as wine and citrus fruits. The salt would have then found its way to Newfoundland or other North Atlantic fisheries to cure more cod. Much of that now-salted cod would have been sold to Portugal. By inserting themselves as middlemen in the production and sale of salt cod, New England merchants like Jackson enjoyed not only profits from turning low-value commodities like salt and fish into more valuable salt cod but also fees for transporting those goods.[35]

Over an eighteen-month period, Newark Jackson had traveled all over the North Atlantic. He had visited other port cities in New England, provided needed goods to remote colonies, such as North Carolina and Newfoundland, and conducted business in two European capitals. Completing all these voyages was a success in and of itself and allowed Jackson to prove himself to Boston merchants as dependable and capable.

Gaining this experience and reputation accounts for why, by the mid-1730s, Jackson's sailing career began to change. Now "of Boston," he engaged in the much more lucrative Caribbean trade. It was also in this moment that he began to regularly trade across imperial boundaries and appeared in Suriname for the first time. The documents describing Jackson's maritime activities also changed in this moment. As he increasingly participated in riskier, illicit commerce, Jackson largely disappeared from printed shipping notices and only occasionally appeared in official port entry records.

In early 1736, the *New England Weekly Journal* announced that Jackson was "outward bound," or preparing to leave, for the "West Indies."[36] Often when ships left for the Caribbean, the newspaper noted where they were headed specifically. Indeed, in the same notice containing Jackson's intentions, other captains departed for Barbados, the Leeward Islands, and Saint Christopher (Saint Kitts). Two weeks later, another newspaper likewise noted he was traveling to the "West Indies."[37] Such a vague description was probably intentional, as the next place Jackson surfaced was Suriname.

On 20 March 1736, Jackson arrived in Paramaribo from Boston on the *Merry Christmas*, a small New England–built schooner, to trade. While port authorities did not thoroughly detail Jackson's cargo, it was probably similar to what the ship captain typically carried. Suriname's planters desired salted fish, especially the cheaper grades of cod and mackerel that would be used to feed enslaved Africans. He likewise may have carried salt, flour, whale oil, timber, and naval stores. Much like the fish, all these commodities would have been important for keeping Suriname's plantation machine running.[38]

According to the colony's clerk, Jackson also arrived with "1 horse" aboard his ship.[39] The inclusion of the horse in Jackson's cargo and in the government's record of his arrival was important. In 1704, Suriname's government approved an ordinance allowing British North American ships to trade in Suriname provided they brought horses for sale. Suriname was in desperate need of horses both for transportation and to power sugar, grist, and lumber mills. New England merchants were happy to provide them, even breeding a shorter, muscular horse called a "Suriname horse" specifically for the trade. By the end of the eighteenth century, New England had exported more than thirty-one thousand horses to Suriname.[40]

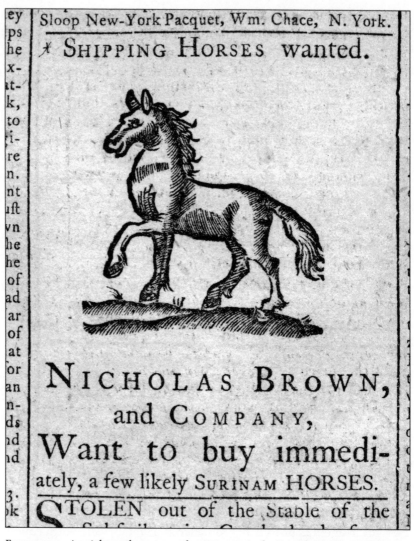

Sloop New-York Pacquet, Wm. Chace, N. York.

* SHIPPING HORSES wanted.

NICHOLAS BROWN, and COMPANY, Want to buy immediately, a few likely SURINAM HORSES.

STOLEN out of the Stable of the

FIGURE 1.2. An eighteenth-century advertisement in the *Providence Gazette* looking for horses to sell in Suriname. Nicholas Brown and Company advertisement for shipping horses, *Providence Gazette*, 7 January 1764, RHi X17 3363. Courtesy of the Rhode Island Historical Society.

Even with the horse exception, however, trade in Suriname was not unrestricted. Dutch authorities prohibited foreign merchants from selling manufactured goods from Great Britain and luxury items from Asia into Suriname and forbade them from exporting certain commodities, including sugar, coffee, and cacao, from the Dutch colony. Likewise, colonial officials placed a 5 percent duty on all imports and exports brought by North American ships, which was double that for goods exported to the Netherlands.[41]

By conducting business in Suriname, Jackson not only had crossed imperial boundaries but also was in violation of British imperial law. Nevertheless, trade between New England and Suriname was lucrative enough for both sides to disregard the law. For Suriname planters and merchants, their need for North American commodities, equine or otherwise, incentivized trading forbidden items, such as sugar, cacao, and tea from Asia, to New Englanders. It also encouraged officials in the colony to turn a blind eye or, in some cases, actively aid and abet this illicit trade. Likewise, New England ship captains had few qualms exporting manufactured goods from the Netherlands—not prohibited under the 1704 statute in Suriname, but forbidden by British trade restrictions, called the Navigation Acts—to sell in the British colonies. Knowing how desirous Suriname planters were for their business, they also brought prohibited commodities, such as navigation instruments and enslaved Africans, and found a ready market. Newark Jackson happily immersed himself in this system of illegal trade.

Although the potential for riches was a powerful motive for engaging in risky, illicit trade, Jackson probably had other motivations. As a counterfactual, Jackson could have easily remained in the legal coasting trade with occasional trips to Europe. While it did not promise quick riches from lucrative, exotic commodities like the Suriname trade, it would have provided a constant income with much less risk. One scrupulous customs official or a chance encounter with a Royal Navy vessel could have destroyed Jackson's career. Yet Jackson deliberately chose to engage in smuggling—a risky business that ultimately cost him his life.

Searching for motives beyond a desire for wealth and Jackson's own blind ambition allows us to better understand Jackson's *mentalité*, or worldview.[42] As one historian of smuggling in colonial Venezuela has described, foreign smugglers would have understood what they were doing but "asserted [the] right to navigate and trade freely." Jackson would have acknowledged that he lived in a world with multiple, overlapping legal systems, each with their own idiosyncrasies that he had to respect only in certain circumstances.[43] As a subject of Great Britain, Jackson was obligated to follow only British trade laws. When he traded outside of the British Empire, those laws were no longer enforceable as the British state did not have jurisdiction. While trading in Suriname, then, men like Jackson could argue that only citizens of the Dutch Republic fell under the colony's trade restrictions. Meanwhile, since Suriname was outside the British Empire, he did not have to follow British trade restrictions either.

If these seem like convoluted, self-serving justifications for breaking the law, they were. As with most people engaged in illegal trade, Jackson's actions "evinced a weak allegiance to their home nations and a greater preference for independent, nonstate voyaging."[44] Suriname especially proved to be lucrative as there was not a large, native merchant class in Paramaribo, allowing ship captains like Jackson to deal with agents from their homeland or directly with planters. In both cases, ship captains had to pay middlemen very little and increased profits for themselves and their employers.[45] Moreover, while Jackson probably thought of himself as a loyal British subject, his actual political allegiance was much more local. He, like many other Boston merchants and ship captains, identified with his hometown. Unlike the British Empire, Boston did not impose any trade restrictions. Indeed, providing Boston access to Suriname's molasses and cacao provided an important service to the town's distillers and consumers, who otherwise would have had to pay more for such exotic commodities.[46] In that local context, smuggling was a form of patriotism.

Regardless of motives, Jackson spent quite a bit of time in Suriname. During his 1736 voyage, he arrived on 20 March and did not depart until 15 May, remaining in the colony for nearly two months.[47] Jackson's weeks-long stay was not that unusual. Most New England ship captains visiting Suriname stayed an average of eighty days in Paramaribo. Although the capital of a bustling plantation colony, Paramaribo was still relatively isolated, meaning visiting captains and sailors "must have made quite an impact" on the provincial city.[48]

While Jackson's impact on Suriname is largely unknown, the experiences of John Greenwood, a Boston-born painter who lived in Suriname from 1752 until 1758, help illustrate Jackson's time in Suriname. Greenwood departed Boston in the early 1750s as economic conditions worsened in the town and the artist struggled to find clients. The son of a ship captain involved in the Suriname trade, Greenwood decided to embark for the Dutch colony before continuing to Europe, where he planned to further study painting. He ended up spending over five years in Suriname, and while most of his paintings no longer exist, he found plenty of work painting portraits of planters and their families. Like so many New Englanders in Suriname, Greenwood amassed a small fortune and departed for Europe in 1758 with nearly "3000 guineas" or 3,150 pounds sterling.[49]

Greenwood kept a diary of his time in Suriname, documenting the portraits he painted, sketching the flora, fauna, and landscape of the tropical colony, and keeping records of myriad experiences. He also composed a short history and description of Suriname at the end of the diary. Jackson's experiences would have mirrored Greenwood's. For ship captains like Jackson waiting to finish business, there were many "Amusements," including billiards and a version of golf. Visitors could likewise distract themselves with "Comedies, Tragedys or something like them" at Paramaribo's theater. For the more socially inclined, there was a "Consort" every Monday night and a monthly ball. There were numerous social clubs, like the Orange Society, which allowed "as many as will Enter"—including a "Common Shoemaker with Bag, wig & Sword"—and the more exclusive French Club.[50]

The social lubricant for all these festivities was alcohol. Greenwood recorded the prodigious amounts of booze consumed by free people, local and foreign, in Suriname. Drinking began early as men "from 9 o'Clock in ye Morning till Noon" downed drams of gin. Women, according to Greenwood, preferred red wine to water.[51] Overindulgence was not that unusual for white colonists living in Caribbean plantation societies. Drinking helped create social bonds between whites, important in slave societies like Suriname where enslaved Africans outnumbered whites twenty-five to one, allowed planters to ostentatiously display their wealth by consuming fine imported wines and liquors, and, banally, gave those who did not work a way to pass the time.[52]

In addition to recording all these social activities, Greenwood also described the darker side of Suriname society, something any visitor, including Jackson, would not have missed. He recorded the awful treatment of enslaved people, making special note of when colonial officials gruesomely executed them. In March 1753, local courts condemned seventeen enslaved people to death for poisoning their enslaver. Greenwood witnessed a teenage girl—who allegedly administered the poison—be slowly burned at the stake. The executioner also strung up another conspirator by driving an iron hook through his ribs. As the man twisted, the executioner grimly mocked, "Can't you lie still in your Hammock?"[53] Planters believed such public displays of violence were necessary to terrorize enslaved people into obedience and deter further resistance.

As such grisly tortures and dark humor suggest, Suriname was a land of death. Greenwood recorded the numerous diseases that afflicted the colony's inhabitants, from yaws to various poxes to vague "fevers." Like in most other parts of the Caribbean during this period, disease killed large numbers of people, European and African. Foreign merchants venturing there, including Jackson, risked their lives. Indeed, in 1752, shortly after arriving in Suriname, Greenwood recorded British ship captains who ventured to the colony. He gave up fairly quickly, describing only six ships, including the one that brought him. Nevertheless, of those six captains, Greenwood recorded that two of them "Died here."[54] Jackson was lucky not to have died of disease on one of his voyages to Suriname.

Perhaps the best evidence that Greenwood left of what life was like for New England ship captains in Suriname was not his writings but rather a painting, *Sea Captains Carousing in Surinam*. Painted at some point during Greenwood's time in Suriname, *Sea Captains* depicts a scene from the private upstairs room of a Paramaribo tavern. All the white men in the image are New England ship captains, members of a "maritime fraternity" of provincial Britons living in Suriname.[55] In the room, pandemonium and debauchery reign. The captains are drinking profusely—one to the point of vomiting—gambling, and dancing. Enslaved people are also present in the image, serving the partygoers.

At first glance, Greenwood tells a morality tale. This interior scene can be interpreted as an exposé of the debauched lifestyles of the wealthy and allegedly genteel behind closed doors.[56] *Sea Captains*, however, has a twist. Greenwood painted it not to condemn the behavior of New England ship captains but most likely at their behest. Two of the men in the painting are Rhode Island merchants William Wanton and Esek Hopkins, who also commissioned the painting. While it seems absurd that a merchant would pay for such a self-damning portrait, it was also meant to be amusing. Once back in Newport, the painting would have reminded the sitters of the enjoyment they had in Suriname. It was also an artifact of their success. These were men able to complete voyages to Suriname and commission works of art. The painting, in short, drips with arrogance and self-congratulation.[57]

Captain Newark Jackson would have been comfortable carousing in Suriname. His life and experiences demonstrate the same cool arrogance that drove Wanton and Hopkins to commission the painting. And the wine glasses, decanters, punch bowls, and other drinking paraphernalia in Jackson's estate inventory likewise suggest a man who enjoyed a good drink and a better party.[58] While Jackson himself left little trace of his time in Suriname, it is easy to see the amusements and activities he would have enjoyed while there.

When Jackson departed Suriname in late May 1736, he told Suriname officials that he was headed for Newfoundland. Shipping

FIGURE 1.3. John Greenwood, *Sea Captains Carousing in Surinam*, ca. 1752–58. Oil on bed ticking, Museum Purchase 256:1948. Courtesy of the Saint Louis Art Museum.

records, however, show that before heading to Newfoundland in August 1736, Jackson first returned to Boston.[59] By listing Newfoundland as his destination, Jackson deployed a sleight of hand, one showing his collusion with other British ship captains trading in Suriname and possibly colonial officials. Jackson probably sold most of his cargo from Suriname in Boston. Whether he sold any of it in Newfoundland when he arrived there a few months later is unknown. Having Dutch officials list Newfoundland as his destination, however, allowed him to claim he was transshipping his cargo when he arrived in Boston and gave him the cover necessary to sell contraband in his hometown.[60]

After his whirlwind voyage to Suriname and Newfoundland, Jackson appeared one last time in the shipping records before his final voyage in 1743. In March 1738, port authorities in Barbados noted Jackson's arrival from Boston on board the sloop *Industry*.[61] Once again, Jackson engaged in the West Indies trade, although this portion of the voyage was legal. Important details emerge from this brief record. First, officials in Barbados recorded that Jackson was part owner of the *Industry* along with Boston merchant Joseph Dowse.[62] While it is unclear when Jackson came into partial possession of the *Industry*, his interest in the ship nevertheless marked a major turning point in his career. Although Jackson would continue captaining ships that belonged to others, such as the *Rising Sun*, ownership of a vessel marked Jackson's transition from dependence on wages to possession, however small, of the means of maritime trade. The *Industry* was a sign of not only Jackson's increasing wealth but also his growing significance in Boston's commerce.

Jackson used all the trade relationships he made to open markets for himself and his business partners. Exploiting those new opportunities in turn built trust and networks with other merchants, which then opened ever more possibilities. By the time of his murder in 1743, Jackson had inspired enough confidence and built a solid enough reputation to be hired to illicitly traffic a cargo of captive Africans from Barbados to Suriname.

MAP 1.1. Places visited by Newark Jackson, 1732–1743. Map designed by Bill Nelson.

Indeed, Jackson's ambition and reputation also help explain why he chose and was ultimately hired to captain the *Rising Sun*. On the surface, it is unclear why he received or took the job in the first place, although he did have experience in the Suriname trade. For his part, it was not a particularly lucrative proposition. By the early 1740s, Jackson was part owner of his own ship and engaged in many different types of commerce. Taking a job as a captain in another person's employ was, in many ways, a demotion. Moreover, one of the benefits of captaining a ship was the commission, a fee paid by the shipowner for handling and selling the cargo. With George Ledain on board and in charge of the cargo, Jackson would have received not a commission but a lower wage.

Nevertheless, the voyage still offered opportunities for Jackson. As a trustworthy captain, he could have demanded his wages be paid in specie or gold and silver coinage, a real benefit for a person living in cash-strapped Boston.[63] He could at least be paid in bills of exchange—a type of financial instrument similar to a modern check, but drawn upon a private individual or firm—drafted by leading London merchants rather than worthless paper currency from New England.[64] Likewise, employers offered captains and ship officers space in the hold for their "private venture" or goods that they were allowed to buy and sell on their own account without paying freight fees. By captaining a ship to Suriname, Jackson was able to purchase products for his own shop in Boston and ship them home with little overhead.

Finally, the planned smuggling run on the *Rising Sun* was fast (by eighteenth-century standards at least). Had the mutiny not occurred, it would have taken about three weeks. As he had many times before, in spring 1743, Jackson traveled to the West Indies to trade. Whether he agreed to captain the *Rising Sun* and ferry its human cargo to Suriname in Boston or Barbados, he could have easily added three weeks to his sojourn. It meant extra money and direct access to cacao. Odiousness of the slaving venture aside, the willingness of his employers to bet on Jackson under such self-serving circumstances was a sign, after more than a decade of reputation building, that he had made it.

A growing and glowing reputation allowed Jackson to dabble in many different business ventures. It was not unusual for ship captains to retire from the sea and take up trading from home. By 1743, it was clear Jackson's career was headed in that direction. His chocolate business was one possible avenue to a second career on land.

Jackson was one of the first Bostonians to sell chocolate.[65] While New Englanders had consumed the good in limited quantities during the seventeenth and early eighteenth centuries, widescale distribution and consumption did not begin until the 1730s and 1740s.[66] By that time, there was a burgeoning consumer society in the colonies.[67] Tropical commodities such as chocolate were central to new habits of consumption, and Jackson, through his smuggling activities, had direct access to cacao. Chocolate production in the colonies was largely an American invention. While colonists certainly mimicked European practices, chocolatiers like Jackson were pioneers in milling, processing, manufacturing, marketing, and selling chocolate.[68] The captain had to design his own manufacturing and distribution process for chocolate. Innovation, as Jackson's story illustrates, was the child of ambition.

Twice in 1740, Jackson published advertisements for chocolate in the *New England Weekly Journal*. There, the first words, bolded and capitalized, informed readers that the chocolate was "MADE AND SOLD" by Jackson and available at his shop near "Mr. Clark's Shipyard" in Boston's North End. He also offered chocolate for both individuals and wholesalers, placing him on the ground floor of what would eventually become a major regional industry.[69]

At the time of his death in 1743, Jackson owned a shop that sold chocolate. The three men who assessed Jackson's estate after his death set aside an entire section of the inventory for goods and property found "In the Shop." It covered nearly a page of the five-page inventory. Like many merchants and ship captains, Jackson's shop offered a variety of goods. He sold cloth, cutlery, tools, dishware, sugar, and spices. Yet alongside silver ribbon, gold necklaces, and iron bowls, Jackson also offered chocolate. In early 1744, when the inventory was taken, there was more than thirteen pounds of it in the shop. To make the sweet treat, the shop contained a "Chocklat mill" and other items to process raw cocoa beans. Some of the sugar and spices in the shop would have also been used in the chocolate-making process.[70]

In the eighteenth century, almost all chocolate was consumed as a hot drink.[71] The chocolate bars that Jackson's shop produced would be ground down and mixed with hot milk or water to make a decadent

MADE AND SOLD,
BY *Newark Jackson*, near Mr. *Clark's* Shipyard, at the North End of *Boston*, choice good Chocolate, by Wholefale or Retale, at a reasonable Rate.

FIGURE 1.4. Newark Jackson placed this advertisement for chocolate in the *New England Weekly Journal* on 25 March 1740. Courtesy of the American Antiquarian Society.

beverage sweetened with sugar and spiced with cinnamon, clove, orange, nutmeg, and other spices. He produced chocolate bars for customers to purchase and prepare at home, but Jackson also owned thirty half- and quarter-pint tin cups for serving drinking chocolate.[72] While browsing Jackson's selection of cloth, ribbon, and other wares, patrons could enjoy a nice hot chocolate. Making this possible was Jackson's easy access to cacao through the Suriname trade. It allowed him to offer a unique experience to his patrons and attract customers to what would have otherwise been a fairly ordinary store.

Slave labor made Jackson's chocolate. At the time of his murder, he owned three enslaved people, named Warham, Boston, and Siller. Warham and Boston were men, while Siller was a woman.[73] Jackson put them to work in his budding chocolate business, a labor-intensive undertaking. Premodern chocolate production was "at times intense and at other times tedious. Often it was both." Transforming cocoa beans into chocolate required roasting, shelling, sorting, grinding, blending, molding, setting, and then packaging. Additional work would have been needed to make drinking chocolate for shop patrons.[74] While Jackson could have hired free laborers and artisans to help process cacao, doing so would have cost him dearly. Boston faced a critical labor shortage in the early and middle decades of the eighteenth century. The town was a center of manufacturing, especially shipbuilding and distilling. Any new industry would have had to compete with those already established for workers. Jackson, like so many other Boston merchants and artisans, turned to slave labor for his workforce.[75]

Beyond his chocolate making, Jackson was an active community member. Most significant was his association with Boston's Christ Church (Old North Church), an Anglican church and part of the Church of England, the official state church in the British Empire, established in 1723 in Boston's North End. He seems to have joined the congregation shortly after his arrival in Boston in the mid-1730s and became increasingly more invested until the time of his death. His name peppers church records as he purchased a pew, donated money for repairs, and contributed to building the church's famous steeple.[76] As the owner of pew "N°. 13," he was located at the front of the church near the pulpit.[77]

Jackson's connection to Christ Church is also highly suggestive of his attitude and outlook on life. Puritans, or radical Protestants who sought to reform—or purify—the Anglican church of its Catholic trappings, founded the New England colonies. They did so to build a Godly commonwealth in North America. That also made them dissenters to the mainstream Anglican faith. For the longest time, Puritans in New England forbade the Church of England in the region, but pressure from the imperial government forced the acceptance of Anglicans by the late seventeenth century. Nevertheless, the Puritan, or Congregational, church remained the dominant faith and was officially supported with taxes from colonial governments. As Boston's ties with Great Britain grew, however, so did the Anglican faith. Merchants, mariners, and migrants, especially, were drawn to the faith, and it seems Jackson fit this mold.

Not to downplay Jackson's religiosity, but he probably affiliated with Christ Church for reasons that were not entirely pious.[78] In his 1738 will, Jackson requested to be buried in the churchyard at King's Chapel, Boston's other Anglican church and the "mother church" of

Old North. Both Christ Church and King's Chapel hosted congregations of Boston's leading merchants. Associating with these institutions and, in the case of Christ Church, literally positioning himself front and center by purchasing a pew near the pulpit brought Jackson, an outsider, to the attention of these leading men, a deliberate act to generate social capital.[79]

By embedding himself in these two religious institutions, Jackson proved himself a member of a greater Anglican community, which in turn allowed him to cultivate economic connections. When Jackson's executors took stock of his estate, they listed all of his debts owed. His creditors were a veritable who's who of Boston's Anglican and merchant community. The largest creditors, merchants Henry Caswell and James Smith, were also active members of King's Chapel. Others included the super-wealthy Peter Faneuil, an Anglican and patron of Episcopal causes in Boston.[80] For Jackson, social networks became credit networks, providing him with the capital, social and economic, to engage in various mercantile endeavors.

More immediately, Jackson's membership at Old North created prospects for employment and investment. It is not a coincidence that Jackson's pew was kitty-corner to that owned by George Ledain. Every Sunday, if not more often, the men would have been in close contact with each other. Proximity most likely brought opportunity. Jackson's affiliation with the church presented him an opening to acquaint himself with Ledain and possibly find work.

What drove Newark Jackson? Obviously, without a diary or letters it is impossible to know Jackson's thoughts nearly three centuries after his death. Nevertheless, cliché aside, Jackson was a man of his times. Like so many other early American men, he strove to achieve a competency or, in the words of one historian, a "comfortable independence" that required the ownership of revenue-producing property.[81] Every colonist defined competency "according to status, background, and capacity."[82] It seems Jackson was especially ambitious. He wanted and, indeed, achieved many things. By the time of his death, he owned multiple businesses and luxury furnishings, dressed himself, Amey, and the children in fine clothes, and regularly consumed expensive and exotic—by eighteenth-century standards at least—commodities like coffee and chocolate.

And yet, striving for a competency had a dark side. As one of the most important—and most anxiety-inducing—values driving economic activity in the American colonies, the desire for financial independence encouraged men to engage in risky, often illegal behavior. Indeed, the "obsession with competency" bothered men like Jackson more than the "legitimacy of commerce."[83] Such angst around success, especially for ambitious social climbers like Jackson, provides a deeper psychological reasoning as to why he willingly flouted imperial trade restrictions and smuggled.

Paradoxically, Jackson's desire for financial independence—or at least the appearance of it—drove him deeply into debt. Historians have long demonstrated how the eighteenth-century mercantile economy functioned on an elaborate system of credit and debt.[84] Jackson was very much part of this world, but his debt stands out. At the time of his death he owed over 1,021 pounds to creditors. As a merchant, Jackson also gave credit and over 451 pounds was due unto his estate in 1743, leaving a balance of 570 pounds owed to creditors.

Nevertheless, it seems that the initial assessment left much of Jackson's debt unaccounted. Numerous creditors came out of the woodwork in the months following his death looking to be paid. As it turned out, Jackson had a 450-pound line of credit with the merchant firm of Peter Faneuil and James Boutineau. Other, smaller—in this context at least—debts of 20 or 30 pounds also emerged.[85]

So many outstanding debts appeared that Jackson's executors, Thomas Greenough and Jackson's widow Amey, took out newspaper ads seeking his creditors and debtors. They published one of these in November 1743, months after first accounting the estate.[86] Likewise, Jackson had mortgaged much of the real estate he owned. All told, Jackson's estate, worth more than 2,433 pounds when he died, was nearly insolvent. In theory, had Jackson's life not ended so suddenly, he would have gradually transitioned from being a debtor to a net creditor in early Boston's credit nexus. In the end, however, such a change was not guaranteed and required taking substantial risks to accumulate the capital necessary to service his debts.

In addition to the massive accumulation of debt, slavery underpinned all of Jackson's business activities. In other words, he willingly destroyed the lives of others to advance his own. He, much like other eighteenth-century men, accepted African slavery as "natural and inevitable" and "seldom concerned himself with reflecting on its morality."[87] While this behavior was normal and accepted in the eighteenth-century colonies, it does not mitigate the fact that Jackson owned people as property. His competency, in short, was built on the misery of the enslaved.

And Jackson's death upended the lives of the people he owned. Not only did they provide labor for the Jackson household, but they were also an investment that increased in value over time and, as Amey Jackson would later learn, were readily saleable.[88] As Amey attempted to service her husband's debt, she ultimately had to sell the three enslaved people who lived in the household.[89] Indeed, in the same advertisement seeking creditors and debtors, Amey and Greenough appended a note informing readers of a "young Negro Woman about 17 years old to be sold. And a Negro Man about 20 Years old."[90]

Daring, adventurous, and ambitious, Newark Jackson took to the sea on what should have been a routine smuggling run in spring 1743. And yet, as later events proved, it was anything but predictable. His untimely end, however, created a record that reveals an ambitious man, who moved to a major Atlantic seaport looking for opportunities, engaged in risky business practices, associated with leading institutions and figures in his community, and pioneered the sale of new products. Yet his social striving had a dark side as Jackson accumulated unsustainable debts, exploited slave labor, and trafficked in human beings.

Understanding Jackson in these contexts, however, suggests he was not unique. He was one of many enterprising men in colonial British America who risked everything and exploited others as they attempted to climb the social ladder. Central to Jackson's social striving was his employment in the smuggling ring. Finding work as captain of the *Rising Sun*, he joined a cartel committed to enriching themselves from illegal trade.

2

The Cartel

As Newark Jackson plunged into the water, George Ledain lay dead, a mangled, bloody mess on the deck of the *Rising Sun*. Joseph Pereira approached Ledain's lifeless body, speaking in Portuguese to the other mutineers. He picked Ledain's body up under the shoulders, dragged the merchant to the deck railing, and shoved the dead man into the sea.[1]

Ledain's ignominious watery burial stood in stark contrast to his life. That night on the *Rising Sun*, the mighty did indeed fall. By the time of the mutiny, George Ledain had become a fixture in Boston's merchant community. After marrying the daughter of a Boston shipbuilder and settling in the town in the late 1720s, Ledain enjoyed success as a ship captain over the next decade and built a network of contacts all over the Atlantic. These connections allowed him to engage in lucrative trading activities, trafficking smuggled goods and African captives. To show off his wealth, he wore fine silk clothes, fancy wigs, and "lac'd" hats.[2]

Ledain also stood at the center of an international smuggling ring. He was one of the three men who facilitated an illicit trade that hired Boston ship captains to sell New England produce and enslaved Africans from Barbados to Dutch Suriname. In return, the captains purchased molasses, sugar, coffee, and, most important for this story, cacao. Standing beside Ledain were Gedney Clarke, a Barbadian merchant, who was the chief organizer of the ring, and Edward Tothill, a New York–born, Dutch-speaking friend of Ledain's who lived in Suriname and served as the local agent.

A desire for profit and power—greed—drove men like Ledain, Clarke, and Tothill to create a smuggling ring, conduct illegal trade, and traffic in human beings. Nevertheless, once set in motion, this commercial endeavor required constant upkeep. The three ringleaders had to hire captains, purchase cargoes, and sell the products of trade. Despite the illicit nature of this commerce, there are plenty of records detailing the lives of these three men, evidence to suggest why, beyond a desire for profit, they would engage in this particular illegal trading venture and how they organized its operations. All of these point to the way that the desire for wealth from Atlantic trade had incredible creative potential but also blinded the organizers to questions of morality, fairness, and openness that, in part at least, resulted in George Ledain's murder.[3]

Three men—George Ledain, Gedney Clarke, and Edward Tothill—stood at the center of the cacao smuggling ring. Surviving documentation, circumstantial evidence, and inference demonstrate the nature of these men's relationship and how they constructed a profitable and pioneering illegal trade network. Each of the men represents a node in the smuggling ring, with Ledain serving in New England, Clarke working in Barbados and as the connection with London, and Tothill acting as the agent on the ground in Suriname.

George Ledain was in charge of New England operations. Ledain's background provides numerous clues about his later career as a smuggler. He was originally from Essex County, Massachusetts, most likely the town of Newbury. Ledain's family had been in Essex County since the 1670s, and he was a descendent of Jerseymen, French-speaking British subjects from the Isle of Jersey in the English Channel. Over the next couple of generations, the Jerseymen of Essex County, while culturally distinct, assimilated, although they remained committed Anglicans and refused to join New England's Congregational churches.[4]

Outside of Ledain's genealogy, there are also details of his family life and personal history. In 1729, he wed Mary Adams and established residence in Boston shortly thereafter.[5] His marriage brought an important connection. Isaac Adams, Mary's father, owned a shipyard in Boston, and it seems Ledain was close to his father-in-law and, after Isaac Adam's death, his brother-in-law, Isaac Jr. For Ledain, as a ship captain and merchant, having access to a shipyard proved incredibly useful.[6] He and

Mary also joined Christ Church, where they baptized their children, George Jr. and Mary Jr.[7]

Like Newark Jackson, George Ledain Sr. had been an active, successful ship captain in the late 1720s and early 1730s. He also had long-standing ties to the West Indies. He first appeared in shipping records in 1731, two years after moving to Boston, in the Bahamas purchasing a load of salt most likely headed for the Newfoundland fisheries.[8] Ledain surfaced again two years later in April 1733. This time Ledain was in Suriname aboard the *Endeavor*.[9] He was in Suriname again in late 1736, captaining the *Mary Ann*, a sloop he partially owned.[10] As these forays suggest, Ledain had been trading in Suriname for years by the time he became involved in the smuggling ring. He would have known Suriname's merchant community, both local and foreign, understood the plantation economy, and had a keen grasp of trade in the Dutch colony.

Ledain had expertise necessary for becoming an important node in the illicit cacao trade and organized the smuggling operation in New England. By the late 1730s he was the partial owner of two ships, the sloops *John and Sarah* and *Mary Ann*, that he could send to the West Indies.[11] He also hired captains and secured cargoes for the voyages to Suriname. Although the exact terms that Ledain offered ship captains do not survive, it seems they were given a certain percentage of the cargo hold, allowed to sell goods belonging to them on their own account, and given a commission for transporting and selling the cargo.

In addition to hiring captains and securing goods to sell, Ledain may have also drawn on his family connections to provide ships. Court records would later describe the *Rising Sun* as a "barquentine or schooner."[12] Dutch authorities failed to classify the ship because it was a type of larger schooner, a topsail schooner, that was two-masted, with the top of the foremast rigged with square sails like a barquentine, another type of sailing ship.[13] While unfamiliar to the Dutch, these square-rigged schooners were commonly used as trading vessels in the British West Indies. Although based in Barbados, the *Rising Sun*, like most West Indian ships,

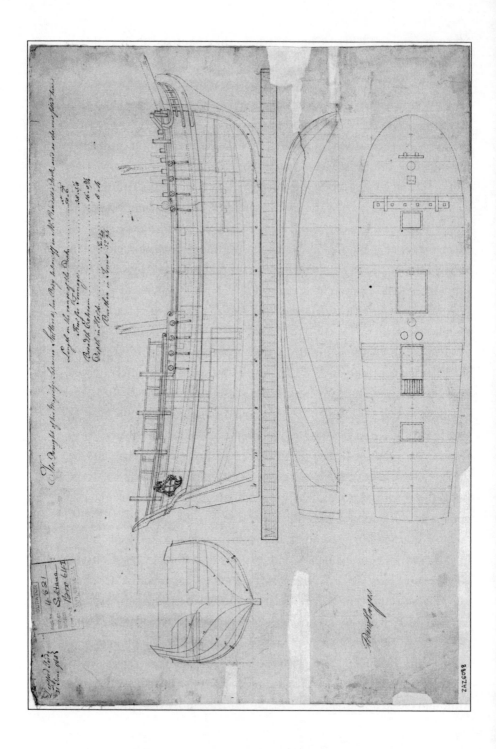

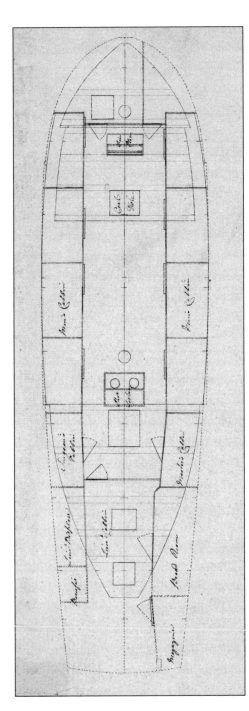

Figures 2.1. and 2.2. Drawings of the New England–built Royal Navy schooner *Sultana*. There are no surviving drawings of the *Rising Sun*, but the *Sultana* would have been of a very similar build and design. The *Rising Sun*, however, was larger. Courtesy of Royal Museums Greenwich.

was likely New England–built. It is possible, given the age of the ship, about "8 to 10 years old," that Ledain commissioned it from his brother-in-law specifically for smuggling.[14]

Waiting to receive those New England ships and captains in Barbados was one Gedney Clarke. Although eventually becoming one of the wealthiest men in the British Empire, Clarke is a bit of an enigma. He rarely emerges in the records, despite maintaining extensive business and familial connections. Rather, he randomly appears in account books and correspondence with leading London merchant firms, major planters in the West Indies and southern mainland colonies, business partners in New York and New England, and family friends. Much of his diminished presence, especially considering his oversized wealth, can be explained by the fact that he generated a significant amount of that wealth through illegal activities such as smuggling and illicit slave trading.

However, there is enough evidence to demonstrate that at the time of the mutiny Clarke was a chief organizer of the cacao smuggling ring. He was the nodal point, commissioning ships, dispatching captains and crews, and serving as the collector and transhipper of cacao and other products. Much of the cacao gathered would be shipped by Clarke from Barbados to the London merchant firm Lascelles and Maxwell. By centralizing all the cacao shipments, sending them from Barbados, and entrusting them to the care of a respected, esteemed merchant house, Clarke legitimated illicit commerce.

Hidden behind this legitimate face, however, were Clarke's personal connections to all aspects of the illegal cacao trade. Although he lived in Barbados, he was born in Salem, Massachusetts, to an established, wealthy family, which explains his connection to fellow Essex County native George Ledain. In addition to Ledain, he maintained close commercial ties to other merchants from New England, trading the region's produce for Barbadian sugar and molasses. Clarke moved to Barbados in 1733 and wed Mary Fleurian, the daughter of a planter and merchant.

This strategic marriage gave Clarke access to the leading families of Barbados. At the same moment Clarke began to construct his cacao smuggling network in the mid-1730s, then, he also found himself connected to some of the most powerful, wealthy, and ingenious players in the British Empire.[15]

None of these movers and shakers were more important for Clarke than Henry Lascelles. Lascelles had served as the customs collector in Bridgetown, Barbados, from 1715 until 1734 and remained on the island for a few years afterward. There he met Clarke.[16] Lascelles and his brother Edward were from a Yorkshire gentry family and had amassed a significant fortune as planters in the West Indies. By the early 1740s, they owned more than twenty plantations and used their wealth to establish a merchant firm in London that specialized in tropical produce and slave trading. Over time, the family eventually elevated to a peerage (the Earls of Harewood), but in this moment they were traders, investors, and brokers. Clarke's relationship with the Lascelles only deepened over time as he eventually became a formal partner in the family business firm and his son, Gedney Clarke Jr., married Frances Lascelles, the daughter of Edward.[17]

Perhaps the most important part of this early relationship between Clarke and the Lascelles was their willingness to invest in and support Clarke's smuggling activities. When Henry Lascelles returned to London to run the business firm in the mid-1730s, his brother Edward assumed the position of customs collector in Barbados. He turned a blind eye to the commodities his associate Clarke smuggled into the colony. Moreover, the Lascelles directly supported the cacao ring as well. They were partial owners of the *Rising Sun* and found nine other underwriters to provide fifteen hundred pounds worth of insurance for the ship and her cargo.[18] Even more poignantly, after the mutiny the Lascelles continued to invest in Clarke's business ventures, specifically earmarking money to fund trade with the Dutch plantation colonies of Suriname, Demerara, and Essequibo. Clarke's response to this infusion of capital is also important. In his correspondence with the Lascelles, he openly pondered

FIGURE 2.3. Eighteenth-century Barbados, Gedney Clarke's adopted homeland and the smuggling ring's base of operations. Map of Barbados designed by Thomas Jefferys and from Griffith Hughes, *The Natural History of Barbados* (London, 1750). Courtesy of the John Carter Brown Library.

smuggling rum from the Dutch colonies into Great Britain as Barbadian produce to evade British trade restrictions. He was familiar with this course of action from years of trading cacao.[19]

Before cacao and other commodities could be laundered through Barbados, however, they had to be purchased in Suriname. Facilitating that purchase was Edward Tothill. Tothill exchanged the cargoes New England ship captains took to the Dutch colony, whether enslaved Africans or other products, for the tropical commodities of Suriname. Originally from New York, Tothill was the son of Jeremiah Tothill, an English merchant who moved to New York shortly after the English conquered the colony from the Dutch in 1664. Tothill's mother, Janneken de Key, was the daughter of a prominent Dutch family in New York.[20] Edward was the second youngest child and eventually settled in Boston in the 1720s, naturalized, married, had four children, and, like George Ledain, became a congregant at Christ Church.[21]

There were other Boston connections. One of Tothill's cousins married Abraham Wendell, a merchant from Albany, New York, who relocated to Boston. Along with his brother Jacob and son John, Wendell became an established figure in Boston's merchant community. Meanwhile, Tothill's father worked closely with New York City's Huguenot, or French Protestant, merchant community and knew Benjamin Faneuil, whose son Peter likewise moved to Boston. It should not be surprising that when both Wendells and Faneuils became involved in the Suriname trade, they turned to family friend and kinsman Edward Tothill.

Tothill's first wife died in 1737, and although his children were still minors, the merchant had the skills to start a new life in Suriname as an agent.[22] He had grown up speaking Dutch and had connections to powerful New England and New York merchant families. It was the perfect opportunity, and almost immediately after his arrival in Suriname, he began serving the interests of British merchants and ship captains doing business there.[23]

Tothill thrived in his position as an agent, often called a "factor" in the eighteenth century. He married into the planter elite, managed plantations, and purchased a large home and warehouse on Watermolenstraat in Paramaribo.[24] He most likely used this house as a staging ground for smuggling, warehousing tropical goods to quickly facilitate illicit trade. Moreover, Tothill became a man of standing in Suriname. Dutch documents related to the aftermath of the mutiny referred to him as a "Burger," or an upstanding, wealthy member of colonial society.[25] A couple of years later, Tothill became a minor officeholder in Suriname, and when he died in 1749 the inventory of his estate noted he lived a "noble life."[26] After more than a decade of living in Suriname, Tothill had successfully embedded himself in the local community.

And yet Edward Tothill remained true to his New England business partners. In that sense, he can be considered part of a "trade diaspora." Tothill pursued "lucrative commercial endeavors involving the mediation of cross-cultural trade."[27] He facilitated commerce between Suriname planters and New England ship captains and merchants by securing cargoes of tropical commodities and finding buyers for North American produce. A final hallmark of Tothill's status as a merchant living abroad was his role as creditor and moneylender.[28] By 1740, Tothill had lent out more than 4,200 guilders to planters, other notable colonists, and plantations themselves, which, as corporate bodies, could take on debt.[29]

Lending money was not only profitable but also important for the planters of Suriname. Throughout the colony's history, but especially in the 1730s, Suriname faced a financial crisis. Plantation societies in general always struggled with debt and obtaining credit. Most of a plantation's wealth was in the form of land and slaves, leaving little cash on hand. Planters had to borrow significant sums of money to cover costs, especially the purchase of enslaved African laborers, until harvest time. Moreover, to service creditors and cover expenses, planters issued bills of exchange, a financial document that required someone else, usually someone in debt to the plantation or who had purchased a certain per-

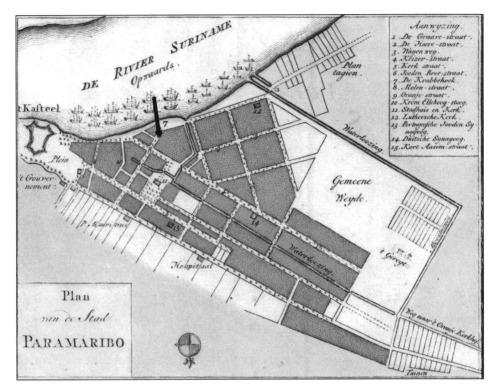

FIGURES 2.4, 2.5, AND 2.6. The arrow on this map of eighteenth-century Paramaribo shows the approximate location of Edward Tothill's mansion on Watermolenstraat. It was near the city's waterfront and main portage, perfectly positioning it for trading contraband. The two modern photographs, taken in 1988 and 1998, respectively, show the large house, the bottom floor of which most likely would have been used as a warehouse. The house was torn down in 2003. Map of Paramaribo from "Plan van de Stad Paramaribo," in Isaak Tirion, *Nieuwe en Beknopte Hand-Atlas* (Amsterdam, 1769). Map courtesy of Princeton University Libraries. Photographs courtesy of KDV Architects, Paramaribo, Suriname.

centage of future produce, to cover expenses. The system sort of worked when plantations were productive, but any fall in production or over-drafting bills of exchange brought it to a halt.

In the 1730s plantation output fell in Suriname, limiting the ability of planters to service debt and access more credit. Enter Edward Tothill. Tothill's "trade and moneylending activities placed" him in a "unique socio-economic position."[30] He was able to channel the resources of New England to Suriname, lending the money planters needed to continue production. Extending credit gave him access to tropical commodities and allowed him to conduct trade, much of it technically illegal under Dutch law, all while enjoying the protection and benefits of a free white man living in Suriname. His status, in turn, allowed him to best serve New England's interests far from home.

As part of his role as a merchant living abroad, Tothill maintained connections to merchants in Boston. In a 1740 letter about a consign-ment of molasses and other tropical goods to John and Jacob Wendell, his cousins by marriage, Tothill included a long postscript lamenting the deaths of his mother-in-law, grandmother, mother, sister, and second wife over the past year.[31] Including such personal information in what was otherwise a formulaic business letter suggests that the relationships Tothill had with New England were deeply personal. These details were key to maintaining his business networks and building trust with trade partners.

These personal connections mattered for the smuggling ring. Records from the mutiny attest that Ledain and Tothill were close friends. Dutch court documents referred to Ledain as Tothill's "goedvriend" or good friend.[32] The term "good friend" had a particular meaning in the eigh-teenth century. Often, the word "friend" would be used to describe any business partner, patron, or connection. In this sense, Gedney Clarke and Edward Tothill were friends because they conducted business together. To be a good friend, however, meant that the friendship came before is-sues of commerce and money. Good friends would never sue each other for debt or place personal advancement ahead of their relationship.[33]

If Gedney Clarke wished to acquire cacao and other products to launder through Barbados, he needed access to a competent factor in Suriname, and that was Edward Tothill. Despite Clarke's New England origins, however, there would have been a hesitancy to trust an opportunistic Barbadian merchant whose most important patrons were major London merchants. Tothill's ultimate loyalties were to Boston and his good friend George Ledain who lived there, not someone like Clarke, whose association brought considerable risk and little immediate benefit. The way to access Tothill and thus Suriname was through George Ledain. It is doubtful any of these players conceived of what might happen to a smuggling ring, by its very nature built on an illicit foundation and alliances of convenience, if the good friend holding it together tragically died.

Ledain, Clarke, and Tothill were all shrewd, inventive businessmen, but why they built their illegal trade network in the first place remains a vexing question. Smuggling cacao and other produce from Suriname through Barbados using New England ships and captains was logistically complicated, financially burdensome, and potentially hazardous. It seems, however, that the men, especially Gedney Clarke, engaged in this behavior to evade new trade regulations and circumvent increasingly scrupulous customs and colonial officials.

Beginning in the 1650s and continuing until the early nineteenth century, the English—and later British—government attempted to regulate commerce with and manufacturing in its colonies. These laws, called the Navigation Acts, aimed to restrict colonial trade to within the empire and limit the amount of industry present in the colonies. Driven by an economic ideology called mercantilism, these laws sought to transform colonies into markets for goods manufactured in Britain and ensure a constant supply of produce from the colonies to the mother country. In short, they created, on paper at least, a hermetically sealed imperial economic system that limited imports, created exports, and allowed the British government to hoard gold and silver. In the mercantilist mindset, these were all positives, as they would prevent foreign domination of the

British economy, give Britain the economic power necessary for waging war, and defend Britain's interests around the globe.

The Navigation Acts, however, had problems. Across the British Atlantic, they limited access to and drove up prices on certain goods, such as cacao, that were not produced within the British Empire. Those imported goods could be acquired only after passing through the hands of numerous middlemen, being heavily tariffed—another cornerstone of mercantilist thought—and finally being transshipped to the colonies. Likewise, the acts drove up the price of produce created within the empire. In Britain, high import duties made foreign sugars prohibitively expensive, while the protected status of British West Indian sugars meant consumers paid higher prices for them than elsewhere in Europe. Colonists, meanwhile, had to compete with metropolitan buyers, which only further boosted prices. Moreover, the acts were near impossible to enforce. As strict as the laws were on paper, eighteenth-century sailing technology and the slow nature of communication meant that it was easy to evade paying the taxes levied and even easier to access the restricted goods elsewhere.[34]

When examining the inability to enforce the Navigation Acts and the problems of access and cost those laws created, the question becomes not so much "why smuggle?" but rather "why not smuggle?" The enforcement that did happen tended to focus on valuable commodities, such as sugar, and ensuring metropolitan Britain was a protected market for colonial produce. Especially for North America colonists who largely fell outside these enforcement strategies, smuggling and trade across empires offered the opportunity to acquire desired products at much cheaper prices. Molasses illustrates this trend. Colonists in New England had an insatiable demand for the cheap sweetener necessary for making rum, the backbone of the region's robust distilling industry. Acquiring foreign molasses occupied a legally gray area. While colonists should not have been trading outside the empire, importing foreign molasses was not illegal per se. As long as colonial ship captains declared the molasses and paid a small duty on it, the trade was largely allowed to continue. Since molasses from the French and Dutch colonies could be upward of 70 percent cheaper than that purchased from the British West Indies, even with the duty it made sense to purchase it from those places. And the duty itself was easy enough to evade.[35] Precise numbers are hard to find, but in 1716 Massachusetts imported 72,000 gallons of molasses from the British Caribbean and nearly 105,000 gallons of foreign molasses. The real amount of foreign molasses, however, was probably significantly higher as large quantities likely went unrecorded to evade customs collectors.[36]

For the longest time, imperial policy makers in London turned a blind eye to smuggling. Guided by an idea later called "salutary neglect," or avoiding the strict enforcement of British laws, especially trade restrictions, in the colonies, officials allowed colonists to conduct business as they saw fit. By allowing the colonies to govern themselves, even if doing so resulted in some lost tax revenues, there would still be a net increase in commerce, which would ultimately benefit the mother country.

Nevertheless, salutary neglect was not a deliberate policy. Certainly, some politicians believed in its central tenets, but for most of those governing the empire in London, there was a desire to better manage and control colonial commerce. Yet throughout much of the first half of the eighteenth century, "administrative inefficiency, financial stringency, and political incompetence" ultimately hamstrung any attempts to more centrally and effectively manage the colonies.[37]

As imperial officials floundered in attempts to regulate the colonies, salutary neglect proved especially harmful to the planters of the British West Indies. West Indian merchants, such as Gedney Clarke, imported foreign sugar, molasses, and rum into Barbados. They then sold it to London as British produce. On the open market, sugar sold at a lower price than it did in Britain. The Navigation Acts, however, created a protected market and ensured high prices for British West Indian sugar in metropolitan Britain. While British West Indian planters benefitted, the acts also incentivized smuggling cheaper foreign sugars. Even with the protections of the acts, however, smuggling ultimately drove down the price of those commodities in London.[38] Lower prices hit the planters, already dealing with issues of soil exhaustion on the long-settled islands, especially hard, undercutting profits.[39]

Seeking redress, the West Indian planters turned to politics. While they may not have been able to compete with French and Dutch plantations, they did have the ear of politicians in London. Often called the "West India interest," this lobbying group was able to persuade Parliament to pass empire-wide laws that protected planters. Beginning in the late 1720s, the West India interest sprang into action, arguing that Parliament had to protect British plantations and crack down on the smuggling of foreign molasses and sugar. At first they were quite ambitious, seeking a total eradication of smuggling, but ultimately settled for a compromise bill, the Molasses Act of 1733. This law, passed by the British Parliament, heavily taxed foreign molasses, sugar, and rum imported into the British Empire, protecting the West India interest's near monopoly on the British sugar market. Although not as ambitious in scope as first desired, the act was still a huge victory for British Caribbean planters who feared foreign competition.[40]

Historians have long dismissed the Molasses Act as being a futile attempt to reign in smuggling, but it nevertheless represented a change in the commercial relationship between Britain's colonies and the mother country.[41] Besides the Navigation Acts, the Molasses Act was an attempt to regulate commerce in a moment when government often proved either too unwilling or unable to enact new laws or enforce ones already on the books. Likewise, the act demonstrated the growing political power of West Indian planters versus other colonists within the empire. Planters had the ear of Parliament. Others did not. In other words, while the Molasses Act of 1733 may have been ineffective, it did have effects.

One of those effects was the creation of the cacao smuggling ring. To understand how, it is important to examine the impact of the Molasses Act on the West Indies. While North American merchants could easily and flagrantly violate the law, it was more difficult in the West Indies, where, by the late 1730s, there was a constant British naval presence and more imperial oversight. Nevertheless, merchants and smugglers found an effective strategy for evading the Molasses Act. They co-opted local customs officials into aiding with smuggling foreign sugar and molasses often by offering a bribe or a cut of the profits from illicit goods.[42] This practice was often not difficult, as many officials, such as Henry and Edward Lascelles, the long-serving customs collectors in Barbados, already aided contrabandists before the passage of the act.

Even this practice came under scrutiny, however, as the British government became more adamant about enforcing the act. And none of those officials was a more zealous enforcer than Robert Dinwiddie. Dinwiddie, later the lieutenant governor of Virginia, started his career as a merchant, but by the 1720s had entered the customs service. He made a name for himself as an effective customs collector and eventually the British Commissioners of Customs appointed him inspector general for West Indian and other colonial ports. In 1738, the commissioners sent him to Barbados to assess the collection of taxes, including those created by the Molasses Act. He was then ordered to remain in Barbados to better collect revenue. Unsurprisingly, he found extensive irregularities in how Barbadians collected customs, which led to the ouster of Barbados's inspector general Charles Dunbar and his staff. He also drafted a long list of accusations against Edward Lascelles. Lascelles survived Dinwiddie's accusations, but they nevertheless led to a more scrupulous and less corrupt customs office in Barbados.[43]

As Dinwiddie rooted corruption out of the customs office, merchants in Barbados faced a stark choice. They could turn their backs on illicit trade, but it would be financially ruinous. By the 1730s, most West Indian planters dealt directly with London buyers, who would purchase their whole crops on consignment. This practice cut island-based merchants, such as Gedney Clarke, out of the British sugar trade. If they tried to compete with major London merchant houses, they would lose.[44] The other option was to take risks and explore new markets and commodities. Illegal trade could continue as long as it did not interfere with the interests of planters.

Gedney Clarke found an opportunity in cacao from Suriname. His New England brethren had been trading to Suriname since the seventeenth century, usually mixed cargos of food, livestock, and timber. Using his New England connections, especially those in Essex County and Boston, Clarke inserted himself into this trade, hired New England ships, purchased New England trade goods, drew on New England's agents in Suriname to acquire cacao (and molasses), and, as he already had been doing, used Barbados as a clearing house for foreign produce.

Policy decisions may have incentivized smuggling cacao and other commodities, but the actual operation of the smuggling ring relied on the decisions and actions of not only Ledain, Tothill, and Clarke but also the men they hired. The ringleaders developed methods for recruiting captains, securing cargoes, and trafficking cacao and other commodities. Despite most of these activities being clandestine and illegal, there is evidence of how this illicit trade network functioned.

A properly functioning illegal trade system required trust, which was in short supply in a trade network separated by geography and potential conflicts of interest, whether between Clarke (and his London financiers) and Ledain and Tothill or between individual ship captains and their employers. A way to generate that trust, however, could be through shared norms, customs, and institutions.[45] Shared religion and religious practice, especially, could provide the common ground necessary for sustaining illicit trade. It should be no surprise that Boston's Christ Church became the space for organizing the cacao smuggling ring.

Founded in 1723, Old North was Boston's second Anglican church and attracted ambitious merchants and ship captains like Newark Jackson and George Ledain. The older Anglican church, King's Chapel, had long been dominated by the wealthiest of Boston's merchants, making it hard to signal one's success to fellow wealthy congregants. So a younger generation flocked to Christ Church, where they associated with one another, heard sermons from the church's first rector, Timothy Cutler, and become actively involved in church life.

FIGURE 2.7. A modern photograph of Christ Church in the City of Boston, colloquially known as the Old North Church. Courtesy of Getty Images.

Newark Jackson and George Ledain were pew owners at Old North, but all the men involved in the smuggling ring were associated with the church.[46] William Wingfield, another captain hired by Ledain and Clarke, was a member of Old North. So was Edward Tothill while he lived in Boston, and he worshipped there during a visit in 1740. Jackson, Ledain, and Tothill all donated money for the construction of Old North's steeple.[47] Ledain was especially active in church life and helped secure a hundred-pound donation from Gedney Clarke to purchase a peal of bells.[48] Clarke followed through the donation, tying with Peter Faneuil, Boston's wealthiest man and famed philanthropist, for the largest single gift.[49]

As their association and donations demonstrate, Old North served as a social nexus for the smuggling ring. By affiliating with the institution, regardless of actual religiosity, the men signaled to one another and the community at large that they were trustworthy and capable of supporting communal goals. For captains like Jackson and Wingfield, it generated the social capital necessary to come to the attention of wealthy merchants and opened the door to employment opportunities. For Clarke, Ledain, and Tothill, it offered not only a more trustworthy pool of captains but also cover for their illegal and often morally questionable activities. Much like they laundered cacao through Barbados to make it a "legal" commodity, they laundered their reputations through Old North, signaling that they were upstanding men of commerce who gave back to the community that supported their activities.[50]

It is also possible to understand the day-to-day operations of the cacao smuggling network. Sources from the *Rising Sun* and a series of lawsuits in the early 1740s between George Ledain and Boston ship captain William Wingfield provide additional information on how the ring operated. The details of the lawsuits will be explored later, but, more immediately, the cases provide information about the nature of the voyages, how the captains conducted business, and the experience of those employed by Ledain and Clarke in the illicit cacao trade.

When Ledain hired Wingfield, he was to take the sloop *Charming Rebecca*, with a cargo of foodstuffs, manufactured goods, and enslaved Africans, to "Kayan"—Cayenne in modern French Guiana—to "sell the . . . cargo, purchase other goods, and then proceed to Barbados."[51] Ledain's instructions ordered Wingfield to go to Cayenne, a struggling French outpost clinging to the northern shore of South America, where planters grew cacao. Given the colony's marginal status, home to only 5,500 people in 1750 and neglected by France, the planters in the colony were quite welcoming of anyone looking to trade.[52] Like other parts of the French Empire in the Americas, it was illegal for non-French vessels to do business there. Nevertheless, colonial officials turned a blind eye and metropolitan authorities could not stop illicit trade.[53] British merchants, especially those from New England, found a warm welcome. As Thomas Wilson, mate of the *Charming Rebecca*, later described, Wingfield developed a close business relationship with at least one planter.[54]

Nevertheless, it is unclear what sort of commerce men like Wingfield did in Cayenne. Planters in the colony did not begin growing cacao until 1735.[55] Cacao trees, on average, take five years to bear fruit. In theory, the cacao Wingfield purchased in Cayenne would have been one of the first crops harvested. How, then, could Cayenne have been such a common destination for cacao smugglers by the early 1740s?

The voyage of the *Rising Sun* offers some answers to this question. Like Wingfield in 1740, Jackson and Ledain's stated destination was "Cayan."[56] Nevertheless, the men went to Suriname. Unlike neighboring Cayenne, Suriname had a booming, productive, and diverse plantation economy. It was also one of the largest producers of cacao in the Americas. And it was illegal for any non-Dutch vessel to transport that commodity out of the colony.[57] The Society of Suriname, the private company that governed the colony, attempted to ensure that trade laws would be upheld by appointing loyal officials and customs inspectors and providing the colony with a ready supply of soldiers to enforce the law.[58] Evading the authorities in Suriname could be challenging. In the context of this smuggling ring, using "Cayan" as a destination became code for smuggling cacao out of Suriname.

As this subterfuge suggests, illegally trading in Suriname required a certain degree of creativity. In 1704, the Society of Suriname legalized trade with merchants from New England, New York, and "neighboring islands." The trade was extremely limited as Dutch officials banned trade in any manufactured goods, luxury goods from Asia, grains, meat, spices, and slaves. That left New Englanders with the option of trading dried fish, foodstuffs, and timber.[59] Likewise, to trade in Suriname, North American ships had to bring horses to the plantation colony in desperate need of animal power.[60] In return, New England merchants were allowed to purchase only molasses, rum, and manufactured goods from the Netherlands. Nevertheless, opening the door to limited legal trade allowed for a wider illicit commerce.

Although New England ships could take advantage of the loopholes in Suriname's trade restrictions, men involved in the cacao smuggling ring often had contraband, including enslaved Africans, on board their ships. These commodities would have caused considerable consternation among colonial authorities, who, in theory, did their best to stop illegal slave trading. If caught, smugglers would have a hard time convincing officials that they were supposed to be in Suriname.

Paperwork showing that Cayenne was the destination, then, was a cover. It helped to assuage the concerns of anxious officials in the Dutch and British colonies. The marginal French colony became a byword for the smuggling of cacao out of Dutch Suriname. And the fact that captains actually traveled to Cayenne, the colony began producing cacao, and some of the smugglers, such as William Wingfield, began purchasing it there only added legitimacy to the practice.

George Ledain pioneered the use of Cayenne as a waypoint for smuggling through Suriname. Between April 1736 and October 1737, port entry records from Barbados and Suriname document three separate voyages for Ledain. He captained the *John and Sarah* for the first voyage and the *Mary Ann* for the latter two. Two port entries are from Barbados and noted that Ledain had just arrived from Cayenne, while his December 1736 departure record from Suriname stated that he was heading to the French colony. In Barbados, Ledain had cacao on board the vessel. Given cacao was not planted in French Guiana until 1735, it would have been impossible for Ledain to purchase cacao there in 1736–1737, although he did probably stop to trade. These methods, in addition to his connection to New England ship captains, made Ledain a key asset to the smuggling ring.[61]

Telling half-truths and falsifying paperwork were some of the many strategies used to deal with snooping local officials and customs authorities. These tactics, commonly used across the Americas and Europe and despite an "infinite number of variations," fell into four broad categories, although merchants and ship captains would often use a combination of them.[62] First, in places like Suriname, where a limited legal trade was allowed, merchants and ship captains would conduct illicit business alongside the legal one. This explains why so many New England ship captains arrived in Suriname with at least one horse to trade.[63] Other times, smugglers would work with local officials and notables, often bribing them, to conduct trade.[64] They would then provide cover for smugglers when they left, signing paperwork that they were headed to places where it was legal to trade. After the passage of the Molasses Act, for example, port officials in Suriname often provided paperwork noting New England ship captains were heading to Portuguese Madeira, where it was legal to trade molasses untaxed. In reality, most of those ships returned to North America or the West Indies.[65] Third and related to the previous, sometimes colonial officials would pretend to arrest or stop smugglers, thus bringing their ship into port, while in reality helping them move contraband.[66]

In addition to listing Cayenne as a final destination, Newark Jackson and the crew of the *Rising Sun* deployed the fourth and final common smuggling strategy: they pretended to be in dire need of supplies and repairs.[67] Under international treaty law, foreign ports could not block entry to any vessel in distress, even if suspicious. This trick allowed

Jackson to dock in Paramaribo on 23 May 1743, claiming shortages of wood and water and needing to caulk the ship. The governor, Jan Jacob Mauricius, had his suspicions from the start and ordered the ship to dock near the fort—and thus under the supervising eyes of officials—and produce their paperwork.[68] Once docked, however, the men could contact Tothill, who, over the next few days—and probably under the cover of darkness—exchanged the captives on board the vessel for cacao and other commodities.

The *Rising Sun*, however, lingered too long. Out of frustration, on 27 May Mauricius stationed five soldiers on board the vessel, having probably received word about the captives on board and fearing illegal sales.[69] Yet the ship was still there on 30 May when the governor ordered them to make haste in leaving.[70] It seems the presence of soldiers had not stopped the illicit commerce. One has to wonder if Jackson, Ledain, and Tothill bribed the soldiers to look the other way while they traded illegally, or perhaps Mauricius himself was on the take, using soldiers to cover his own malfeasance. Finally, on the morning of 31 May, the "repairs" were complete and the men received permission to leave.[71] The crew had to offload the soldiers at Fort New Amsterdam near the mouth of the Suriname River to ensure they had stopped smuggling. By then, however, the deed was done. After dropping the soldiers at the fort, the *Rising Sun* finally headed to Cayenne until other events intervened.[72]

While in Suriname and possibly Cayenne, captains sold their cargoes and purchased cacao and other tropical commodities. They dealt either directly with planters or through agents depending on the goods they were selling and how long they planned to remain. In addition to salt fish, agricultural goods, livestock, naval stores, and enslaved Africans, the ships also carried manufactured goods such as cloth and tools.[73] The *Charming Rebecca* had chintzes and other fabrics on board, while also carrying lanterns and various carpenters' tools such as axes, awls, and saws.[74] These manufactured goods were explicitly prohibited by Suriname authorities, yet contrabandists sold them anyway. They exchanged these goods for cacao. During his voyage, Wingfield purchased 2,056

FIGURE 2.8. Paramaribo's busy waterfront was a hive of economic activity, including smuggling and slave trading. Frederik Jägerschiöld, *Gezicht op de Stad Paramaribo* (1772). Courtesy of the Rijksmuseum, Amsterdam.

pounds, or slightly more than one ton, of cocoa—a substantial amount considering the still relatively limited market for the product.[75]

After doing business in Suriname and Cayenne (with all that place's embedded meanings), the captain had to deliver his cargo of cacao to Barbados. There, waiting, was Gedney Clarke. By importing cacao into Barbados and reexporting it from the same place, Clarke transformed a smuggled, illicit commodity into a legal one, a form of commodity laundering. Indeed, export registers from Barbados begin to record the presence of cacao in the late 1730s despite there being no cacao trees on the island.[76] While the bulk of cacao went to Britain, some also returned to Boston, usually as part of the captain's private venture, and would have been the source of Jackson's cacao for his chocolate business.

There was one final part to this clandestine trade. Once the voyage was complete, the captains returned home to Boston, but not on the ships they used to smuggle. In his petition to the court, Wingfield noted he "came home to Boston a passenger" after his voyage.[77] Likewise, Jackson took command of the *Rising Sun* only after his arrival in Barbados. Clarke and Ledain used these ships in the West Indian trade, so it should not be surprising that they remained there. Yet doing so also allowed them to assert more control over the itineraries of the ships, lowered freight costs since they were not paying for space on the vessels of others, and, given the limited range of the voyages, lessened the chances of the ships being lost on the high seas or seized by customs officials.

While this system of illicit trade appears clever on the surface, it proved near impossible to manage captains and crews and account for contingencies such as, say, a mutiny. Because of these significant risks, as Clarke and Ledain attracted capital for smuggling and found ways to circumvent commercial regulations, they also attempted to reign over the smuggling ring itself with something of an iron fist. This can be clearly seen in the legal battle between Ledain and William Wingfield.

The legal battle between Ledain and Wingfield survives as a series of suits and countersuits filed in Boston concerning Wingfield's 1740 voyage on the *Charming Rebecca*. Ledain, representing himself and Clarke, claimed that Wingfield swindled them out of hundreds of pounds worth of cacao through underhanded dealing. Since they suspected Wingfield was deceiving them, they withheld his wages and commission, which the captain then countersued for, plus damages. Ultimately, in August 1742, the case ended in arbitration, with Clarke and Ledain rewarded more than 352 pounds in Massachusetts currency, a significant sum of money, as damages.[78]

In his defense, Wingfield filed a petition to explain his side of the story. According to the captain, it was actually Clarke who had refused to pay him even after Wingfield went to Barbados to confront him. After that encounter, Wingfield alleged that Clarke "would not pay him one farthing" unless the captain sued the merchant in a "strange and chargeable place." Wingfield knew he could not get a fair hearing in Barbados, where Clarke had extensive ties to the merchant and planter elite, the very men who served as judges and juries in the colony. Instead, he would have to sue George Ledain and Clarke together in Boston.[79]

After Wingfield confronted Clarke and returned to Boston to file suit, he was "detained at home" and unable to work because he had to deal with the lawsuit. Even worse, Clarke used the opportunity to malign Wingfield, calling the ship captain a "villain & knave" for cheating him and Ledain out of a "considerable quantity of cocoa." Ledain then proceeded to spread the rumor around Boston, and while Wingfield could not prove Ledain had ever said anything, "his name & character by which he" lived was "severely & unjustly taken from him."[80] Wingfield, his reputation ruined and out of work, had no option but to pursue lawsuits to not only earn his commission but also restore his honor.[81]

As it turns out, William Wingfield did attempt to undermine Clarke. According to Thomas Wilson, the mate of the *Charming Rebecca*, Wingfield had a conversation with a planter named Mr. Gueran. He told Gueran that he would take cacao from his plantation to Clarke. There, Wingfield would offer to split the profits between Gueran and Clarke. If Clarke did not agree to the terms, Wingfield would sell the cacao on his own account, cutting Clarke out altogether and splitting the profits with Gueran. Somehow Clarke learned of this deal. Likewise, it seems that Wingfield had problems managing his crew. In Barbados, one crew member snuck ashore in the middle of the night with a quantity of cacao from the main hold of the ship and sold it.[82] Wingfield's dereliction of his duties as captain would not have impressed Ledain and Clarke. But it was probably the underhanded agreement with Gueran that infuriated the merchants. In return, they maligned Wingfield's reputation and forced the case into arbitration, where the court made the captain pay the merchants hundreds of pounds in damages.

One fact was clear: if you cheated George Ledain and Gedney Clarke, they ruined your career. Such draconian action makes sense. This was illicit commerce after all. Legal action, including that of Wingfield, opened smuggling to the exact scrutiny smugglers looked to avoid. By dealing with such issues and challenges at an interpersonal level, Clarke and Ledain hoped to remain in the shadows and continue profiting.

One of the most perplexing questions about the mutiny on the *Rising Sun* is why George Ledain was on the ship at all. By 1743, he had largely retired from seafaring, instead preferring to conduct business from the comfort of Boston. Earnings from cacao and captives continued to flow and showed no signs of slowing. Likewise, as British colonial merchants built networks of agents—composed of men like Edward Tothill—in the eighteenth century, there was less of a need for supercargoes on board vessels. Ledain's job was largely redundant of duties that could be performed by Jackson and Tothill.[83]

With that in mind, Ledain's presence on the *Rising Sun* on that awful night in late spring 1743 suggests a commercial relationship in peril. The ordeal with William Wingfield most likely prompted those troubles. Despite resulting in a victory, the case was still fairly damning for Ledain, who showed a certain incompetence in hiring Wingfield. The two-year legal battle in Boston publicly aired the activities of the smuggling ring. It was clear to any observer where Boston's cacao came from and the methods used to procure it. Bostonians may not have minded illegal trade, but they were unrelenting in their quests for riches and would not hesitate to copy the tactics now on public display. In pursuing charges against Wingfield, Ledain said the quiet part out loud, jeopardizing a source of profits.

Gedney Clarke must have questioned Ledain's competence and judgment after the debacle. The best evidence of the growing rift between the two merchants comes from a February 1744 letter from Boston merchant Edward Bromfield to Clarke. Months after the mutiny, Bromfield wrote to Clarke not only about his own business dealings with the Barbadian but also of Clarke and Ledain's joint account, which Clarke understandably wanted to close. Nevertheless, Clarke had difficulty reconciling as Bromfield created the account "as Capt Le Dain ought to have rendered it."

Bromfield's description of the account suggests Ledain and Clarke were out of communication in the months before the mutiny. The Bostonian had to explain why Clarke received a 238-pound bill of exchange drawn on Boston merchant John Allen. As Bromfield described, during the arbitration case against Wingfield, Ledain feared Wingfield would not pay any settlement if he lost, so the court ordered Wingfield to place the money in the care of John Allen. When Ledain and Clarke won, Allen drafted a bill of exchange. Bromfield, despite writing what little he knew of "that affairr," was more informed than Clarke about the outcome of a lawsuit directly involving Clarke's interests that had been resolved eighteen months prior.[84]

In short, it seems that the nine months between the end of the Wingfield case and the departure of the *Rising Sun* from Barbados were a time of turmoil for Ledain and Clarke's business relationship. Perhaps that's why Ledain volunteered to serve as the supercargo on the *Rising Sun*. He understood his commercial relationship with Clarke was at stake and sought to reassure the merchant that their venture was secure. He did that by personally overseeing a voyage. Or perhaps Ledain had lost faith in Clarke and worried he could no longer trust the Barbadian. Regardless, the voyage also allowed Ledain to visit his good friend Edward Tothill in Suriname, further strengthening commercial relations in case his partnership with Clarke fell apart.

Ledain, then, was not only the merchant on board the *Rising Sun* but also its manager, ensuring that everything ran smoothly. His job was not only to ensure that Jackson and the rest of the crew followed instructions and did not skim profits, however. After departing Barbados for Suriname, he was also in charge of an expensive, valuable, and living cargo. Below deck on the *Rising Sun* were a few dozen African captives whom Ledain would exchange for cacao and other merchandise in Suriname. Trafficking enslaved Africans was central to the operation of the smuggling ring, and the group on board the *Rising Sun* held a special significance. Their misery and captivity might have saved the smuggling ring.

3

The Cargo

The blood-curdling screams echoed through the decks of the *Rising Sun* and across the dark, watery void of the southern Caribbean. Listening to the horror and crammed below the decks of the schooner on that night in late spring 1743 were fifteen people. Thirteen of them were children, adolescent boys and girls, and two were young men. All of them were slaves. Even if they did not understand the languages being spoken and screamed, the message was clear enough. Violence and mayhem engulfed a ship that doubled as their prison. There was no escaping the terror.

Identifying these enslaved people and studying their experiences is perhaps the most difficult—and at some points impossible—part of reconstructing the events of the *Rising Sun*. When the schooner departed Barbados earlier in May 1743, it carried a cargo of various trade goods and a few dozen African captives. The trafficking of enslaved Africans to Suriname to exchange for cacao was central to the illicit trade network established by Ledain, Clarke, and Tothill. Coercion underpinned the entire operation.

A smuggling ring built upon slavery and human trafficking created a trail of human misery and tragedy, but unfortunately much of it went unrecorded. Indeed, one of the legacies of racial capitalism was the permanent commodification and deliberate erasure of enslaved people, their lives, and their voices. The paucity of evidence about the captives on board the *Rising Sun* is just one example of this legacy. And the only reason there is record of the fifteen people is because of a fluke. After the mutiny, there were two inventories taken of the ship. The first recorded all the cargo on board, while the second concerned the ship itself, including rigging, sails, and cannon. At the end of the ship's inventory, however, the fifteen enslaved people appeared.[1]

The inventory erases as much as it reveals. In an eighteenth-century inventory, enslaved people were often listed by name, each given a line, and valued separately. In this document, however, only four lines are dedicated to the fifteen enslaved people. One line lists the "13 slaves boys as well was girls," followed by a line with their value, 2,170 guilders.[2] The next two lines list the young men and their values. Only one, Sirius, is given a name, but the inventory makers described both as "Negro" and valued them at 300 guilders each.[3] Those are the only personal details offered by the inventory.

Nevertheless, the presence of enslaved people on the *Rising Sun* creates an opportunity to study the ship's—and, by extension, the smuggling ring's—involvement in the often illicit inter-American slave trade. Despite the paucity of evidence regarding the enslaved people on board the schooner, sources such as the inventory do offer clues. The fifteen people listed in the ship's inventory had been part of a larger cargo of captives dispatched to Suriname. Those still on board at the time of the mutiny—deemed "remainders" in the cruel vocabulary of the slave trade—would have been the captives that Jackson, Ledain, and Tothill were unable to sell. That so many were children is unsurprising given Suriname planters' preference for enslaved adults. Had the mutiny not occurred, the smugglers would have attempted to sell the children again when they arrived at Cayenne. And after the mutiny did occur, the mutineers allowed the enslaved people to live out of not a shared humanity, but a desire to sell them for their own benefit.

Using these small details and a close reading of other evidence, the *Rising Sun*'s living cargo can be better understood. We can see who these enslaved people were and their experience of being on the *Rising Sun* while examining how the illegal slave trade ultimately connected to the production, sale, and smuggling of cacao. Context, then, allows us to empathize with, if not identify, the victims of this horrific trade.

Slavery was the glue that held the smuggling ring together. All the men who participated in the smuggling ring were slave owners. At the time of his death in 1749, Edward Tothill owned ten enslaved people.[4] In addition to his mercantile activities, Gedney Clarke also owned plantations in Barbados, Virginia, and, later, Essequibo and Berbice and hundreds of enslaved people to work them.[5] As discussed, Newark Jackson owned three enslaved people at the time of his death. George Ledain did too. Even William Wingfield, the disgraced captain Ledain and Clarke sued for his malfeasance, owned two slaves, Cato and Venus, when he died in 1774.[6] Slaveholding was a quotidian, normalized, and socially acceptable practice. As such, these men would have never shown any concern or moral qualms about the ownership of human beings. Their lived experience of being slave owners and traders in a world built on the stolen labor of exploited Africans and Indians made the buying, selling, and enslaving of racial others a largely unthinking decision.

Trafficking enslaved Africans was central to the business activities of the men involved in the smuggling ring. After Newark Jackson's death, to cover his debts his widow Amey sold two of the enslaved people they owned. When advertising them, Amey described their ages. The young man, either Wareham or Boston, was twenty years old, while Siller, a "young Negro Woman," was seventeen.[7] Their ages suggest that Jackson had purchased them as part of his trading activities in Suriname. They, like the young people on board the *Rising Sun* during the mutiny, were possibly the remainders of an earlier slaving voyage Jackson undertook.

George Ledain was likewise in the habit of buying and selling enslaved people. Most publicly, in May 1740 he advertised a "parcel of very likely" slaves for sale in the *Boston Weekly Post-Boy*.[8] It is unclear where Ledain acquired the enslaved people, but given he had been active in the smuggling ring for a couple years, he most likely received them from Gedney Clarke. He also placed this advertisement shortly before he hired William Wingfield in June 1740, consigning a "Woman & two Children Negro Slaves" for Wingfield to sell in Suriname or Cayenne.[9]

Perhaps the most active slave trader, however, was Gedney Clarke. These activities were not isolated to the cacao smuggling ring and spanned his entire career. His slaving came to fill an important niche in the slave economies of North America and the Caribbean. In the British Empire, the large, dynamic plantation societies in the West Indies like Barbados and Jamaica had an voracious demand for enslaved Africans. Merchants and ship captains engaged in the transatlantic slave trade preferred these places as destinations. In practice, however, it meant the transatlantic trade underserved other colonies, such as Virginia and South Carolina. They too had a high demand for enslaved African labor and turned to West Indian merchants to supplement the supply of captives. Likewise, colonies outside the British Empire contended with their own issues acquiring enough enslaved Africans. Although imperial officials in those places prohibited foreign slave traders, British merchants saw an opportunity and built slave smuggling networks. Gedney Clarke engaged in both types of slaving.[10]

Around the time he started the cacao smuggling ring, Clarke began doing business in Virginia. Clarke's sister Deborah was the second wife of William Fairfax, a royal customs official who in 1732 became the agent for his cousin's five-million-acre tract of land in northern Virginia. Clarke purchased a plantation in the Fairfax lands and, in exchange for corn, tobacco, and other produce, sold enslaved Africans. This trade continued throughout the 1740s, and Clarke's customers included Lawrence Washington, the older brother of the famous George.[11]

Clarke also became involved in the slave trade to South Carolina. In 1739, a slave rebellion shook the colony, leading to a ban on slave importation for the next five years.[12] Within months of the law's expiration, Clarke was waiting in the wings to supply enslaved Africans. He maintained a robust correspondence with Robert Pringle, a London-born merchant who resided in Charleston and was one of South Carolina's leading businessmen in the 1740s.[13] In May 1744, Pringle wrote Clarke with excitement. The act prohibiting the slave trade was set to expire, and Pringle believed that as soon as it did enslaved Africans "will sell to Good advantage."[14] Less than a week before the slave trade ban's expiration on 29 June 1744, Pringle wrote again, telling Clarke he did "not hear of any Negroes com-

ing this way." He attempted to entice Clarke, explaining that the "first . . .
to arrive will come to a Good Markett."[15] Using connections like Pringle
to learn of market conditions, Gedney Clarke began a robust slave trade
to South Carolina that lasted until his death in 1764.[16]

While Clarke's slave trade to Virginia and South Carolina was legal, he
also illicitly trafficked African captives from Barbados to places outside
the British Empire. Clarke invested in illegal slaving to the Dutch colonies
in the Americas, including Suriname and neighboring Essequibo, Berbice, and Demerara. These latter three colonies, to the immediate west of
Suriname in what today comprises the nation of Guyana, became places
of intense investment for Clarke in the 1740s and beyond. He purchased
thousands of acres of land to build plantations. To ensure those plantations had enough labor, he began shipping African captives from Barbados. Over time, this evolved into a more general illegal slave trade to the
colonies.[17]

All of these examples demonstrate that Gedney Clarke was an active
slave trader, and his investment in human trafficking only increased over
the course of his career. Beyond solely seeking profits, there were other
reasons why Clarke engaged in this practice. After the passage of the Molasses Act made it difficult to smuggle foreign sugars and molasses through
Barbados, merchants on the island sought other activities to make money.
As Barbados was one of the main ports of disembarkation for British slaving vessels coming from West Africa, there were always captives available
for purchase and sale. Clarke had access to New England ships and contact
with merchants and agents in other colonies such as William Fairfax, Robert Pringle, and Edward Tothill. He could easily facilitate an intercolonial
slave trade by drawing upon all these connections. Outside of crass economic considerations, Clarke had little concern about the impact his actions had on the enslaved people he trafficked. Nevertheless, his attitudes
and business practices shaped their experiences in a profound way. And
in no place was that clearer than on the *Rising Sun*.

* * *

Identifying the enslaved people on board the *Rising Sun* in 1743 is difficult. We do not know anything about the enslaved people sold in Suriname before the *Rising Sun* departed. Even tracing the fifteen people still on board the schooner during the mutiny is no easy task. Nevertheless, much like other parts of the smuggling ring, the connections between various participants offer clues to whom these enslaved people were.

Henry Lascelles, the wealthy London merchant and Gedney Clarke's business partner, patron, and close friend, had an interest in all facets of the West Indian trade, from owning plantations to selling sugar and investing in the African slave trade. In the case of the slave trade, Lascelles was something of an innovator. In 1736, he and a group of other investors devised a scheme to more efficiently and effectively buy captives on the West African coast. They called it the "floating factory."

Although the slave trade had grown dramatically in the decades prior to the *Rising Sun*'s voyage, it was still inefficient. When merchants dispatched ships to the African coast, captains had to venture from port to port to acquire a full cargo of captives. Not only did this require captains to navigate the treacherous waters and politics of West Africa, but it also exposed the captain, crew, and captives to the region's tropical diseases. The "floating factory" offered solutions to these problems. The investors stationed a ship, called a "factory," off the Gold Coast (modern Ghana) port of Anomabu. There, the ship served as a waystation for slaving. Instead of traveling from port to port, captains would just stop at the factory, unload trade goods, load captives, and depart for the Americas, minimizing their time spent in Africa. The merchants used the slave ship *Argyle* to serve as the factory, appointed a man named George Hamilton as its captain and the manager of the trading venture, and purchased two other ships to sail along the West African coast, acquiring captives and conducting diplomacy. The *Argyle* operated as the floating factory from 1737 until early 1743.[18]

Over the factory's six years of existence, Lascelles insisted that all ships that purchased captives from the factory head to Barbados. Waiting to receive those ships would be Henry's brother Edward and Gedney Clarke. While this practice certainly furthered Lascelles's interests, other investors were not as keen on the scheme. Barbados's slave market, despite being large, was not the best in the West Indies and constantly glutted, driving down prices. The recipients of the captives—Edward Lascelles and Clarke—received a 10 percent commission from their sale, cutting into profits. These two issues, along with corruption by Hamilton and the other captains hired, contributed to the scheme's collapse. Nevertheless, while in existence, the factory dispatched thousands of captives to the Americas.[19]

The final cargo departed the factory in early 1743 and contained 330 captives. Some of them probably ended up on the *Rising Sun*. Correspondence from Hamilton notes that this last ship, captained by John Dunning, long an associate of the factory scheme, went to São Tomé, an island in the Gulf of Guinea to the southeast of Anomabu. That, however, would not have been the final destination for Dunning, and he ultimately sailed to Barbados. Although at first it seems odd to sail southeast to São Tomé only to then head west across the Atlantic, this was a common route. São Tomé, despite being Portuguese territory, served as an important waypoint for slave traders of all nations, who purchased provisions and took on water there before crossing the Atlantic. The island was also positioned just north of the South Equatorial Current, which flowed from West Africa, across the Atlantic, up the northeastern coast of South America, and into the eastern Caribbean. The current practically delivered ships from West Africa to Barbados, making it faster than sailing due west across the Atlantic.[20]

Examining the floating factory provides details about the lives of some of the enslaved people on board the *Rising Sun*. Like most captives sold through the *Argyle*, they would have been captured in Anomabu's hinterland. In the four decades prior to the voyage of the *Rising Sun*, Anomabu's leaders transformed the town from a sleepy fishing village into one of the most important slave trading ports in West Africa. Europeans had been trading in this region since the fifteenth century, originally for gold, but over time captives became the primary export.

Anomabu was located in the area of the Gold Coast dominated by the Fante, an Akan-speaking ethnic group. It was the Fante's chief city and an important point for them to access goods from around the world. In the late 1730s and early 1740s, however, Europeans did not have a fort or trade post on land in Anomabu, meaning most trade passed through the floating factory.[21]

Beginning in the late seventeenth century, the Gold Coast was in a near constant state of war as various Akan speakers vied with each other for territorial control. Most importantly, in the 1730s, two states, Akyem, near the coast, and Asante, more inland, emerged as the leading powers, defeating smaller states and amassing ever larger amounts of territory. They waged war by equipping armies with firearms purchased from Europeans. To acquire these guns, they traded captives. Some of those captives came from the near constant state of war in the region, while others came from slave raiding deep into the interior. The cycle of exchanging captives for guns sparked a "military revolution" as Akan-speaking groups began trading for firearms and forming political alliances. The Fante formed a confederacy following an embarrassing defeat at the hands of Akyem in 1738. They used Anomabu, the largest Fante settlement, to access European trade goods by shuttling captives through the town to the floating factory.[22]

There are accounts of captives being trafficked and sold through Anomabu that help to better understand the plight of those on board the *Rising Sun*. Venture Smith, a freed man born deep in the interior of the Gold Coast, captured as a child in 1739, and sold into slavery, provided one narrative. In 1798, Smith sat down with a local schoolteacher in Connecticut to dictate his life story. He was around seventy years old and, over the previous thirty years, had won his freedom and amassed a considerable amount of land and other property. Despite being of African descent, he had become a successful farmer in the early United States. Although elderly, he remembered his early life in Africa in vivid detail, helping to illuminate the experience of the enslaved children on board the *Rising Sun*.

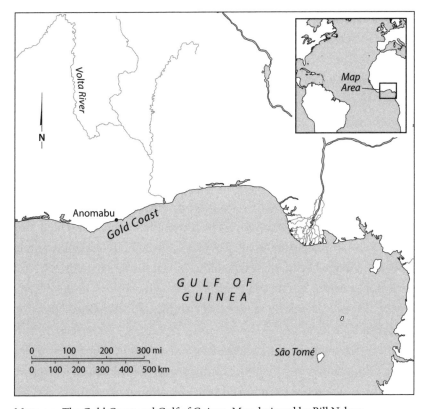

MAP 3.1. The Gold Coast and Gulf of Guinea. Map designed by Bill Nelson.

Born between 1724 and 1729, Venture Smith was the son of a "Prince of the Tribe of Dukandarra," most likely a village headman. Smith's original name was "Broteer," and he was the first son of his father's first wife, making him his father's heir.[23] Even decades later he recalled his life in Africa, including a dispute between his mother and father when Smith was around six years old. His mother left his father for some time and took Smith with her. While on the move, she apprenticed him to a farmer, and there he learned the rudiments of farming and animal husbandry. Although his mother eventually returned to his father, Smith remained with the farmer until his parents resolved their dispute.[24]

Shortly after returning home, the world Venture Smith knew turned upside down. A messenger arrived in his village reporting that a "numerous army, from a nation not far distant" had invaded neighboring territory. According to Smith, the army was "instigated by some white nation who equipped and sent them to subdue and possess the country." Smith's memory failed him here. While the army certainly had been armed by European slave traders, it was most likely an Akyem slaving party in search of captives.[25] Regardless, Smith's father informed the messenger that people from the neighboring lands could settle on his. Soon after refugees began pouring into Smith's homeland.

As the invading army continued marauding and seeking captives, they came to Smith's village. To keep the invaders at bay, his father paid a ransom, but they attacked anyways. Although Smith's family fled, the army eventually captured them. They took special interest in his father, who, as a village headman, was wealthy. When his father refused to tell the raiders where he hid his wealth, they tortured him to death. For Smith, it was a "shocking scene" that "to this day" remained "fresh in [his] mind."[26]

After "destroying" his father, the marauders headed back toward the coast, taking Smith and the other captives with them.[27] Smith witnessed the army attack more villages and procure additional captives on their march. By the time the raiders and their slaves were on the outskirts of Anomabu, their reputation preceded them. Shocked by the "conduct they had persued," the "inhabitants" of the town attacked and captured everyone, soldiers and slaves, and sent them to the "castle [to be] kept for market."[28] Most likely, the Akyem army that captured Smith was itself attacked and taken prisoner by the Fante near Anomabu. While conflict with Akyem had started to subside around the time Smith arrived at the coast in late 1738, the Fante were desperate for trade. Perhaps needing captives, they attacked the party holding Smith. Or another possibility is that the Fante engaged in a practice called "panyarring," where they seized the Akyem soldiers and their property to settle debts they had with Fante merchants.[29]

Regardless of the context of Smith's capture, he was then held in a "castle and kept for market."[30] Anomabu did not have a fort at this time,

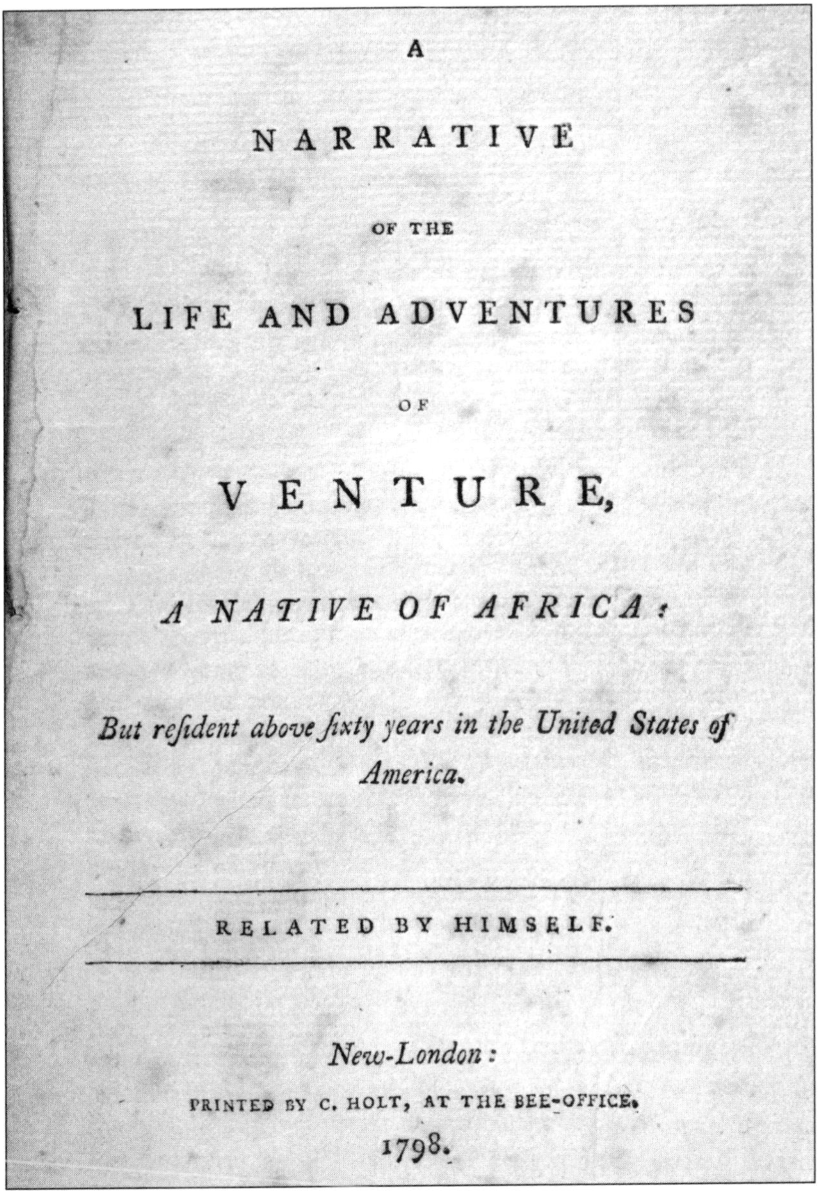

A

NARRATIVE

OF THE

LIFE AND ADVENTURES

OF

VENTURE,

A NATIVE OF AFRICA:

But reſident above ſixty years in the United States of America.

RELATED BY HIMSELF.

New-London:
PRINTED BY C. HOLT, AT THE BEE-OFFICE.
1798.

FIGURE 3.1. The cover page of Venture Smith's autobiography. Courtesy of the American Antiquarian Society.

suggesting that Smith was held either in a private house in the town or at a castle in a neighboring settlement and was then trafficked through Anomabu. It is possible that various merchants and captains arranged his sale (and those of the people captured with him) at the floating factory.[31] Eventually, however, his captors put him in a canoe and rowed out to a Rhode Island slaver, the *Charming Susanna*. Robinson Mumford, the ship's steward, purchased Smith for four gallons of rum and a piece of calico. These goods were Mumford's own property, called a "private venture" in the eighteenth century. "Thus," Smith recalled, "I came by my name."[32]

Soon after his purchase, Smith began his journey across the Atlantic, called the Middle Passage. This was not merely a voyage, however, but something more insidious. Slavers trafficked captives away from their African homeland, subjected them to a perilous passage, and sold them as slaves in the Americas. The Middle Passage, which trafficked more than twelve million people across the Atlantic between the fifteenth and nineteenth centuries, was a process of commodification. Living, breathing human beings became things to be bought and sold.[33] For children like Smith, the voyage was harrowing, but the crew left the children unshackled and allowed them to roam the ship. Nevertheless, they were still crowded on board with hundreds of other people—260 in Smith's case—and subject to the poor diet and even poorer hygiene of slave ships. They were also not immune to the corporal punishment meted out by the crew or the disease that stalked slavers. Indeed, a "great mortality by the smallpox" struck Smith's passage, killing nearly 60 of the captives.[34] The slow, tortuous, and disease-ridden voyage lasted two to three months before Smith and the rest of the captives finally arrived in Barbados.[35] While the crew sold almost all the captives there, Smith "and three more" returned to Rhode Island with the ship.[36]

Specific details of Smith's capture and sale aside, his experience reflected that of the enslaved children on board the *Rising Sun*. They possibly came from the interior of the Gold Coast, captured as pawns in the region's fractious politics. They likewise would have been between the ages of ten and fourteen at the time of their capture and experienced the Middle Passage to Barbados as adolescents. Like Smith's, their experience of captivity was traumatic and not something easily forgotten. Nearly sixty years after his capture, Smith could still recount his father's grisly murder and recalled in detail the hills, forests, and rivers of the Gold Coast. He remembered the name of the ship captain who stole him away from his homeland and knew the number of fellow Africans kidnapped alongside him. The experience of war, murder, and human trafficking, in short, haunted Venture Smith for the rest of his days. And they would haunt the children on the *Rising Sun* too.

When the captives arrived in Barbados, Clarke, Ledain, and Jackson prepared them to board the *Rising Sun*. Outside of the second inventory taken of the ship, however, there are no direct records relating to the captives. As such, it is nearly impossible to determine the number of captives placed aboard the *Rising Sun* or investigate the individual experiences of those captives. Nevertheless, using information about the ship and the stories of other captives trafficked in the inter-American slave trade can help better understand the voyage. All told, Jackson and Ledain trafficked upward of fifty people from Barbados to Suriname.[37] Centering their possible experiences of being placed on board the *Rising Sun*, living aboard the ship on its voyage, and ultimately being sold in Suriname illustrates the illicit trade in human flesh.

In Barbados, Clarke and possibly Edward Lascelles would have placed the captives either in a "pen," a fenced area with shelter, or in some sort of dungeon until loaded on the *Rising Sun*. They would not have had to wait long. Famed abolitionist Olaudah Equiano, whose eighteenth-century autobiography inspired a generation of antislavery activists, was himself trafficked in the inter-American slave trade from Barbados to Virginia. He, much like many of the captives later on board the *Rising Sun*, arrived in Barbados from Africa. A merchant purchased Equiano, placed him in a "yard" or pen, and shipped him to Virginia. Equiano estimated that his time spent in Barbados was "not above a fortnight," or less than two weeks, before being loaded on a sloop for the Chesapeake.[38]

The act of being corralled and loaded on the *Rising Sun* was itself destructive. Being penned and shipped away from Barbados destroyed the community formed during the Middle Passage. As horrific as the Atlantic crossing was, it nevertheless created opportunities to build relationships. Many onboard transatlantic slavers were from the same region of Africa, meaning they could often communicate with one another and find common cause. By separating the cargo and placing some on the *Rising Sun*, Clarke broke those ethnic and linguistic bonds.[39]

Most harrowing, considering the large number of children who remained on board the *Rising Sun* during the mutiny, there is a high likelihood that this voyage ripped families apart. Even if the children were not blood relatives to others, older captives would often look after and adopt children during the Middle Passage, ensuring they had some level of protection. Slavers had little regard for real or fictive familial bonds and instead allowed conditions for trafficking and selling enslaved people to be dictated by market forces. "Relations," as John Newton, a former slave trader turned abolitionist, later described to the House of Commons, "were separated as sheep and lambs are separated by the butcher."[40] Newton's passive voice elided the conscious decisions men like Clarke, Ledain, Jackson, and Tothill made when they destroyed families. For the enslaved children on board the *Rising Sun*, the mutiny was not the only horror they faced, but rather another step in a process of exploitation and alienation.[41]

Destroying family and communal bonds required the physical act of loading the captives on board the *Rising Sun*. The ship itself was a topsail schooner, a type commonly used in the West Indies. While larger than the average American-built schooner, which usually ranged from twenty to forty tons, it would have still been small, probably around sixty or seventy tons.[42] As a point of comparison, the average sailing vessel in the intercolonial slave trade was forty-eight tons, making the *Rising Sun* large by the standards of the trade. Nevertheless, the average ship involved in the transatlantic slave trade was 158 tons.[43] For the captives on board the *Rising Sun*, this meant that the captain and merchants probably purchased a much larger number of captives to traffic than did most intercolonial slavers. They could not, however, force hundreds of people aboard like on the transatlantic trade, especially considering the *Rising Sun* carried other goods.

The captives were the last cargo placed on board the ship. Forced below deck into the hold of the ship, they would have had to find space around barrels of salt fish, bolts of cloth, planks of timber, and naval stores. At most, the hold itself was only nine feet high and sixty-five feet long. There were also cabins for the crew below, and the cargo hold was possibly divided into multiple decks. While avoiding various casks, crates, and boxes, enslaved people also had to crouch down and squeeze into spaces that were no more than three to five feet high.[44] About the only relief for the captives on the *Rising Sun* was that they did not have to share the hold with the horses ubiquitous in the New England–Suriname trade. Even without the presence of equine travelers, however, with so many people and so much cargo on board, the only way to describe the *Rising Sun* as it departed Barbados was cramped. Privacy and comfort were difficult to find. The children, however, were small enough to squeeze into the nooks and crannies of the ship, in the spaces between the barrels and gaps between decking and perhaps find a rare moment for themselves.

Once under sail, the voyage was crowded and, given how low schooners rode in the water, wet, but it was at least fast—by eighteenth-century standards at least. Schooners were among the fastest ships available in the early modern Atlantic and the preferred choice for smugglers. Their speed allowed them to evade authorities and make quick escapes. The *Rising Sun's* voyage from Barbados to Suriname would have taken between four and seven days depending on sailing conditions.[45] Thus, the captives' second voyage was significantly shorter.

Their experience on the *Rising Sun* would have differed from the transatlantic passage in other ways. Most significantly, the voyage was, in Venture Smith's own description of his intercolonial experience, a "comfortable passage."[46] In the slave trade, all things were relative, and

Smith was correct. Compared to the Middle Passage, the trip on the *Rising Sun*, while cramped and crowded, was more "comfortable." Jackson purchased fresh provisions in Barbados that lasted the entire short journey to Suriname. Captives would not have been subjected to the diet of starchy root vegetables and salt provisions that transatlantic slavers fed them. Likewise, on intercolonial passages, captives were not restrained and were free to roam the ship. Such treatment was not because Jackson was somehow more kind than transatlantic slavers. Rather, chains and handcuffs tended to cause sores and bruises. In a four- to seven-day passage, those wounds had plenty of time to develop but little time to heal, making it difficult to sell "damaged" human cargo.[47]

Finally, unlike the Middle Passage, the crew had, in the words of one historian, "less oversight" over the captives. There were only nine crew members working on the *Rising Sun* in addition to Ledain and his clerk. At the very least, the captives outnumbered the crew by about five to one, making it near impossible, even with the size of the ship, for the crew to watch every captive, especially if they were not shackled. Surveillance came second for sailors focused on delivering their cargo safely and efficiently. Such freedom of movement, even in the confined spaces of the *Rising Sun*, allowed the captives to find a bit of autonomy away from the watchful eye of the crew.[48]

After five days or so at sea, the *Rising Sun* entered the mouth of the Suriname River and used the tide to sail into Paramaribo. There, Jackson told his lie about needing wood and water and docked under Fort Zeelandia on the riverfront of Suriname's capital.

How Jackson and Ledain sold the captives remains something of a mystery. Tothill was certainly involved. Most likely, under the cover of darkness, a small boat would have rowed up to the *Rising Sun* and accepted captives and other cargo to be rowed away and trusted to the care of Tothill. Given that the ship lingered for more than a week before departing, this must have been a slow process. Part of it may have been the clandestine nature of the trade, ferrying a few captives away every night while avoiding authorities. Attempts at being secretive seemed to fail as Governor Mauricius ultimately stationed soldiers on the ship. That may have stopped the illicit trading altogether and explain why fifteen enslaved people were still on board when the vessel departed.

Likewise, it seems that the market conditions were not great and there were problems selling the captives, causing Jackson and Ledain to linger too long. In the month before the arrival of the *Rising Sun* to Paramaribo, four slave ships arrived from Africa carrying 940 captives for sale in the colony. One of those, the *Surinaamse Galei*, arrived the day before the *Rising Sun* and offered 208 captives for sale, while the *Gulde Vrijheid* arrived on 8 May offering 246. These were legal Dutch voyages direct from the coast of Africa that glutted the market for enslaved Africans.[49] Suriname's planters had an insatiable demand for slave labor, but there were limits to the number they could purchase. Tothill may have moved the captives off the *Rising Sun*, but he would have struggled to sell them over the course of five days. Such a slowdown almost ensured the crew would be caught and made it difficult to sell all the captives, especially those less desirable.

His cargo arriving to an inundated market demonstrates that Gedney Clarke did not have as good of intelligence regarding Suriname's slave market as he did those in Virginia and South Carolina. In those places, Clarke had trusted confidants like Robert Pringle and William Fairfax, while for Suriname he had George Ledain. Ledain was not resident in the colony and dependent upon the information provided by his "good friend" Edward Tothill. Relying on secondhand information hurt the profitability of the voyage and, had the mutiny not occurred, may have further undermined Clarke's confidence in Ledain.

Nevertheless, it does seem Ledain and Jackson were able to put most of the captives ashore. It was Tothill's responsibility to sell them, and he had to confront the glutted slave market. Unfortunately, there are no records of Tothill's sales of the captives. He most likely held them in his mansion on Watermolenstraat near the fort where the *Rising Sun* moored. Although slave traders still preferred to sell captives at public auction, that was difficult to do with contraband. Instead, Tothill sold them in prearranged consignments or looked for buyers, probably the planters with whom he did business.[50] He also managed a number of plantations for absentee proprietors and could have shifted some of the captives to those properties as part of his caretaking duties. Regardless of the process by which Tothill sold the captives, awaiting them was nothing short of a living nightmare.

After being sold, a few captives may have remained in town to serve in households, but most scattered to one of the colony's more than four hundred plantations.[51] They were forcibly loaded on small boats, rowed across the colony's many rivers, and transported one last time against their will. Regardless of their final destination, they entered a society driven by a collective sadism and sociopathy that placed productivity above all else. It was a world of calculated terror, violence, and horror.

In many ways the enslaved people arrived in what was the perfect location for building a plantation economy in the eighteenth century. Suriname shared a similar climate with the rest of the West Indies, but unlike the Caribbean islands, its location on the South American mainland meant there were huge tracts of land to develop. Plantations could expand production and grow a diversity of crops without worrying about running out of space. Moreover, a system of rivers and creeks all eventually drained into the Suriname River, which itself flowed into the Atlantic. Transportation was relatively easy as plantations abutted the river system.

The most fertile land near the coast, however, was prone to flooding when the rivers and creeks swelled from rain and from the flow of tides. The Dutch, masters of water control, recreated the *polder* system: an intricate system of dykes, dams, sluices, canals, and culverts meant to keep the land dry. Eventually, planters harnessed the tides and used their water control system to power mills and other machinery. Combined with the ease of transportation, the *polder* in Suriname forged one of the most technologically sophisticated, efficient, and productive plantation systems in the Americas.[52]

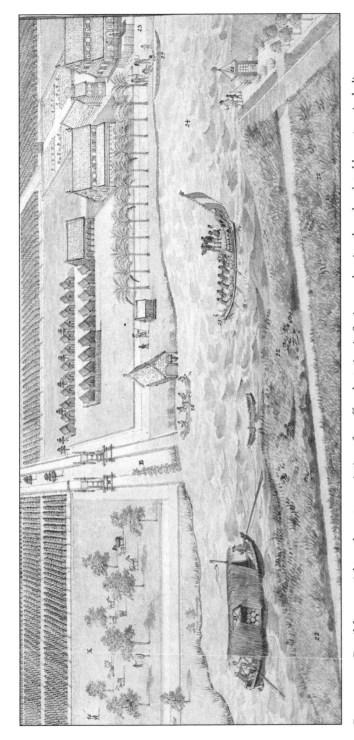

FIGURE 3.2. Detail from an eighteenth-century painting of a coffee plantation in Suriname showing the colony's *polder* system, including canals, dikes, and sluices. Anonymous, *Gezicht op de koffieplantage Leeverpoel in Suriname Plantagie Leeverpoel Geleegen Rievier Cottica* (ca. 1700–1800). Courtesy of the Rijksmuseum, Amsterdam.

FIGURE 3.3. A detailed sketch of a sluice—a gate used for controlling the flow of water—on a plantation in Suriname. Dirk Valkenburg, *Sluis op de Plantage Palmeniribo te Suriname* (1708). Courtesy of the Rijksmuseum, Amsterdam.

Yet ultimately powering these plantations was the labor of thousands of enslaved Africans. As plantation production expanded throughout the eighteenth century, so did the colony's enslaved population. During the same quarter century that the *Rising Sun* arrived in Suriname (1726–1750), the Dutch imported over seventy thousand enslaved Africans to its plantation colonies, most to Suriname.[53] This figure is also probably low as it does not account for the extensive illicit slave trade to the Dutch colonies like the voyage of the *Rising Sun*.

As tens of thousands of captives poured into Suriname, they were put to work on the colony's sophisticated plantations growing sugar, coffee, cotton, cacao, and tobacco. They also outnumbered the white population by a large percentage. By the 1750s, more than forty thousand enslaved people of African descent lived in Suriname, compared to two thousand people of European descent. Yet that number obscures the actual demographic imbalance. There was, for example, a growing population of mixed-raced people of color, the descendants of white planters and overseers and their enslaved concubines who had been freed. Likewise, a significant portion of the colony's white population lived in Paramaribo. In the rural plantation areas, the number of enslaved to free could sometimes exceed one hundred to one.[54]

When the captives arrived on their plantation, they began a period contemporaries called "seasoning." This was the time when recently arrived enslaved people acclimated to their work regimen, disease environment, and climate. The process was arduous and grueling. Historians estimate that between 15 and 20 percent of all recent arrivals died during seasoning, which usually lasted about a year.[55]

For those who survived this period of acclimation, death became a familiar companion. In slave societies like Suriname, deaths far outstripped births, forcing planters to purchase ever more Africans to ensure plantations had enough labor. The colony imported more than 124,000 African captives between 1730 and 1780, but its total slave population in the 1780s was only 50,000.[56]

Disease, brutality, and overwork caused this great mortality. Unlike other plantation regimes, planters, agents, and overseers in Suriname ensured that plantations grew and purchased enough food to support the enslaved population.[57] Even that was not enough, however, to mitigate death. Suriname's equatorial jungle climate created the perfect conditions for mosquito-borne illnesses like malaria and yellow fever to thrive. Other tropical diseases and parasites, such as Guinea worm, plagued the colony. Enslaved people, exposed for long hours in the fields with little protection, died of these diseases.[58] Moreover, planters, overseers, and colonial officials used extreme violence and torture on Suriname's enslaved population. Without the use of wanton violence, whites feared enslaved people would rebel and destroy the very foundations of the economy. And with that destruction, the sugar, molasses, coffee, and cacao Europeans coveted disappeared.

Exacerbating disease and brutality while exacting its own death toll was overwork. Enslaved people, especially those working on sugar plantations, toiled for long hours with little rest day after day, month after month, year after year. Over time, heavy labor took its toll on the body, "gradually and incrementally" destroying enslaved bodies. As one historian describes, this "violence of the mundane" murdered enslaved people and was one of the chief causes, if the not the leading cause, of the high mortality rates on plantations. The average life span for an enslaved person working under these conditions was five to seven years. Thus, even those enslaved people from the *Rising Sun* who survived seasoning still faced shortened, immiserated lives.[59]

Perhaps the only saving grace—if there can be such a thing under miserable slavery—was that the enslaved people arrived in Suriname in a moment of great change. Beginning in the 1730s, Suriname's plantation economy diversified. Instead of focusing solely on growing sugarcane, as they had in the late seventeenth century and early eighteenth, by the 1730s planters began experimenting with coffee, cotton, and, most important for this story, cacao. These commodities were lucrative, especially given the willingness of foreigners to smuggle them, but also significantly less deadly for enslaved laborers than sugar.

With sugar, planting, harvesting, and processing required slaves to perform hard labor for upward of twenty hours a day while working around dangerous machinery and, for boiling the sugarcane juice, open flame. This type of work killed people through exhaustion and accident. Planting the new crops, while requiring menial, tedious, and sometimes difficult labor, was not as grueling. Indeed, studies have shown that enslaved people working on coffee plantations in Suriname had lower mortality and higher birth rates than those on sugar estates.[60] Thus, some of those who arrived on the *Rising Sun* may not have ended up planting sugar. Circumstantial evidence from the mutiny suggests as much. In a cruel and ironic twist of fate, at least a few members the *Rising Sun*'s human cargo ended up working on a plantation that produced cacao—the very commodity that upended their lives in the first place.

Evidence for their sale to a plantation that grew cacao comes from the activities of Edward Tothill. After the death of his second wife, Tothill had an account of his property taken. The inventory also recorded his debts and money owed to the merchant. Many of these creditors and debtors were not people at all but rather the plantations that conducted business with Tothill. Using this inventory and other records reveals that two of these plantations, Fairfield and Mopentibo, grew cacao.[61] In 1740, Mopentibo owed Tothill money. To settle its debts with Tothill, Mopentibo's caretakers serviced debt, in part at least, by providing him with cacao from one of the plantation's 4,800 trees.[62] Meanwhile, Tothill owed money to Fairfield Plantation. Like Mopentibo, Fairfield produced cacao. Perhaps Tothill had the inventory taken at a moment when he had recently purchased cacao from the estate to provide to the smuggling ring. Regardless, following Tothill's business transactions demonstrates that some of the cacao smuggled by Jackson, Ledain, and Clarke came from Mopentibo and Fairfield. In exchange, Tothill may have dispatched some of the enslaved people to these estates.

Of the two plantations, Fairfield was probably more important for the smuggling ring. As its name suggests, there was a New England connection. Fairfield belonged not to a Dutch proprietor but rather to a highland Scot named Henry McIntosh, who founded the estate in the 1670s.[63] McIntosh later relocated to Bristol, Massachusetts (now Rhode Island), and his granddaughters, Elizabeth and Mary, inherited Fairfield upon his death in 1725.[64] Elizabeth and Mary's husbands, Isaac Royall Jr. and Thomas Palmer, respectively, took an interest in Fairfield and requested Dutch authorities take an inventory of the estate shortly after Royall reached his majority in 1740. Even at such a young age, Royall was the largest enslaver in Massachusetts and owned plantations across the Americas. He also was affiliated with Christ Church, suggesting that was the space where he made contact with the smuggling ring.[65]

FIGURE 3.4. Cacao trees (right) growing on a plantation in Suriname. Anonymous, *Gezicht op de Plantage Cornelis Vriendschap in Suriname* (ca. 1700–1800). Courtesy of the Rijksmuseum, Amsterdam.

Located on a tributary of the Commewijne River east of Paramaribo, Fairfield was a large plantation that grew sugar, coffee, and cacao. It spread across 2,415 Dutch acres.[66] Of those, over 800 acres were under cultivation, mostly with sugarcane, and there was an unknown amount of pasture for the estate's cows, sheep, and goats. Nevertheless, even after nearly seventy years of cultivation, there was still extensive amounts of undeveloped land at Fairfield. Much of it was thick jungle that made it easy for the ninety-nine enslaved men, women, and children who lived there to steal away if they desired. In addition to cane fields, pastureland, rice paddies, and jungle, Fairfield dedicated three acres of land to the cultivation of 1,800 cacao trees.[67]

Even if some of the enslaved people ended up at Fairfield, however, it is unlikely that they worked with the cacao full-time. By the time the *Rising Sun* arrived in Suriname, planters had developed an effective system for growing and processing cacao. It was, in many ways, the perfect crop to be grown alongside sugar. For most of the 1740s, cacao prices remained high, making it very profitable. Although finicky and susceptible to disease, cacao was not labor-intensive. "A Great Advantage in Cultivating Cacao," John Gabriel Stedman, an eighteenth-century soldier sent to Suriname, described, was "that *fewer* Slaves are Required than in any other Branch of the Planting Business."[68] A Suriname planter estimated that once cacao trees were mature, one enslaved person with the proper horticultural training could maintain upward of two thousand.[69] Fairfield was home to an enslaved man named Chocolaet, who presumably tended to the estate's trees.[70]

Dedicating land and training men like Chocolaet to cultivate cacao was a smart investment. According to Stedman, cacao trees bore "two Crops Annually" after they matured. Each tree produced between 30 and 300 fruits, or what Stedman called "Pods." When mature, the pods were about eight inches long and three inches in circumference and yellow "like a Large Lemmon, with Ribs like the Melon." Each fruit contained about 30 nuts, called cocoa, and 300 nuts weighed roughly one pound.[71] If Fairfield plantation had 1,800 mature cacao trees and

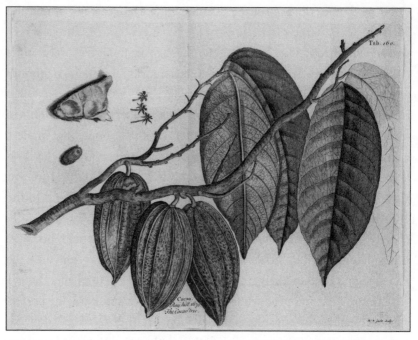

FIGURE 3.5. Eighteenth-century print of a cacao tree branch with pods. From Hans Sloane, *A Voyage to the Islands Madera, Barbados, Nieves, S. Christophers and Jamaica . . .* (London, 1707). Courtesy of the John Carter Brown Library.

we assume those averaged 100 pods per tree, it would produce 18,000 pods per harvest or 36,000 per year. If each pod, in turn, contained 30 nuts, Fairfield produced 1.08 million cocoa nuts weighing 3,600 pounds per year. In the 1740s, cacao sold for 10 stuivers per pound.[72] It took 20 stuivers to compose a guilder, meaning a pound of cacao sold for half a guilder. While the smuggling ring was active, 3,600 pounds of cacao per year would have netted the plantation 1,800 guilders. That was a sizable sum of money for a supplemental crop, especially considering the relatively low cost of maintenance once the trees were mature.

Nevertheless, there were moments when the crop required more work than Chocolaet could provide. At harvest time, it was all hands on deck. The *bassia*, or driver, and overseer at Fairfield rotated enslaved people from their regular duties working in the sugar and coffee fields to harvest cacao. From there, the fruits had to be cut open and the cocoa nuts removed. They would be spread out in a shaded area and left to "Undergo a verry Strong Perspiration."[73] Once dried, the nuts would be packed in barrels to be shipped around the Atlantic. Men like Newark Jackson transformed these cocoa nuts—possibly picked, processed, and packaged by some of the very enslaved people he trafficked over his career—into chocolate.

For the time being, the enslaved children who remained on *Rising Sun* were spared the miserable experience of plantation slavery. Within a day of departing Suriname, however, they faced the new horrors of mutiny and murder. Yet for many of those children the past year or more of their lives had been dictated by factors far outside their control. Wars and geopolitical concerns in their African homeland ripped them away from family and community. European demand for African bodies to labor on New World plantations ensured there would be buyers. They then crossed the Atlantic in a horrific, transformational passage. After landing in Barbados, they were once again forced aboard a ship against their will. Waiting for them at that final destination was the horror show of slavery. While the mutiny may have brought shock, it was just one of many terrors in the macabre spectacle that characterized the children's experience of Atlantic capitalism.

Following the murders, the fate of the enslaved children on the *Rising Sun* was in the hands of the mutineers. The rest of the surviving crew also had to face the dilemma of what to do with the human cargo now that they were no longer in control of the ship. The struggle between the mutineers and the rest of the crew—part of which involved those in the ship's hold—would profoundly shape the future for everyone on board the schooner.

4

The Crew

The enslaved children must have seen John McCoy, George Ledain's clerk, as he pulled himself through the hold of the ship, attempting to hide from the mutineers after having been stabbed nine times.[1] As McCoy bled out in the run of the ship, the violence continued above. Jackson and Ledain lay on the deck grievously injured; one of the mutineers, Joseph Pereira, who had stolen Jackson's cutlass from his cabin, attacked John Shaw, the boatswain on watch, wounding him. Shaw fell to the deck, but before Pereira could finish the job, he was summoned over to help throw the bodies of Jackson and Ledain overboard. Shaw escaped to his cabin below.

After disposing of the captain and merchant, the mutineers turned their attention to John Skinner, the captain's cabin boy. Skinner fled the initial violence, making it up onto the deck unscathed, and to further avoid the attack, he skittered up the shrouds on the *Rising Sun*'s main mast. Thomas Lucas coaxed Skinner down after a couple of minutes, assuring him the mutineers would spare his life. As soon as the boy's feet hit the deck, Ferdinand da Costa charged at Skinner, bludgeoned him to death, and "hove him overboard."[2]

They had not forgotten about John McCoy. All three men went into the hold to hunt for the clerk and, upon finding him nearly dead from loss of blood, dragged him up onto the deck. There, Pereira threw him into the sea.

Watching all of this in horror was the *Rising Sun*'s mate, William Blake. The screams of Jackson and Ledain woke Blake in his cabin below deck. He went to investigate, but as soon as he scaled the ladder onto the deck, one of the mutineers stabbed him in the shoulder. Somehow, he was still cognizant enough to try to stop the mutineers from inflicting any more death. When they went after John Shaw, Blake intervened. By this point the mate understood he was alive only because the mutineers needed him to pilot the ship, a skill that none of the three "Portuguese" men had. Now his job was to convince the mutineers that they needed Shaw too. Blake told the men that Shaw "had been Severall Voyages to Esequeba and that he knew the Land very Well" and would help navigate. They agreed.[3]

The mutineers gathered the surviving crew—Blake, Shaw, and the ship's two "Lads," Josiah Jones and Henry Deveries—and made their demands.[4] They desired to be taken to Orinoco, in the Spanish colony of Venezuela to the west of Suriname. It would be a relatively short journey, and once there the mutineers would dispose of the ship's cargo and begin a new life for themselves. They did not mention their plans for the rest of the crew.

After they made their intentions known, the rest of the voyage became a struggle between the desires of the mutineers and the resistance of the others. This situation was a sea change from the reality of just hours before. The mutiny shattered any sense of solidarity and revealed the divisions between the crew members. Whereas they had all once been under the command of Jackson and Ledain, the attack revealed racial, ethnic, and class divisions. The mixed-race "Portuguese" sailors, Da Costa, Pereira, and Lucas, who had been at the bottom of the social order, were now in charge. Those crew members who held power or were upwardly mobile in the maritime working world—Jackson, Ledain, Blake, Shaw, McCoy, and Skinner—were either dead or wounded. Meanwhile, Deveries and Jones, young sailors who had the most in common with the mutineers, suffered no harm.[5]

Yet the mutiny merely revealed those divisions and competing interests. Conflict, whether between captain and crew, between merchant and crew, or among various crew members, had always been there. Especially in the world of smuggling, but really in any maritime setting, all these groups and individuals had their own agendas. These aspirations were often at odds with the goals of their employers, and unless they themselves were somehow vested in the outcome of the voyage, most of the crew had little incentive to fully comply with their employers' demands. Reconstructing the lives of the crew reveals these tensions and conflicts and demonstrates how the mutiny on the *Rising Sun* was an expression—albeit extreme—of this struggle.

There were eleven crew members on board the *Rising Sun* when it departed Suriname. Two of them, George Ledain and John McCoy, were solely in charge of the ship's cargo and not involved in the day-to-day operation of the ship. While Jackson and Ledain have already been examined in detail, getting to know the other nine provides more detail about who was on board the *Rising Sun*, their place in the smuggling ring, and how they interacted with one another.[6]

The youngest member on board the schooner was John Skinner, described as the "Captns Boy."[7] He was the ship's cabin boy and, like Jackson and Ledain, a New Englander.[8] No more than thirteen years old, he was most likely from a middling family with deep ties to the sea.[9] Perhaps his father, grandfathers, and brothers were also mariners. An adolescent, Skinner was Jackson's apprentice, learning how to command a ship while traveling with Jackson from Boston to Barbados and then to Suriname. He waited on the captain and probably Ledain as well and assisted the cook, Thomas Lucas.[10] Meanwhile, Jackson taught Skinner the basics of provisioning, manning, navigating, and piloting a ship along with how to keep accounts and conduct trade.

Skinner learned all these skills while smuggling. When trying to understand why American colonists were so eager and willing to engage in illicit commerce, Skinner's presence on the *Rising Sun* offers some answers. In short, he was socialized into illegal trade. At the same time he learned how to keep accounts and navigate, Jackson and Ledain also taught him how to conduct illegal trade, the ideological and economic arguments in favor of it, and how to evade authorities. Smuggling was such a common, everyday facet of Skinner's apprenticeship and career that, had he grown older, it would have largely gone unquestioned.

FIGURE 4.1. Detail of a British North American ship in the Suriname River. Small vessels such as this one and the *Rising Sun* were fixtures of the Suriname trade during the eighteenth century. Frederik Jägerschiöld, *Gezicht op de Stad Paramaribo* (1772). Courtesy of the Rijksmuseum, Amsterdam.

Had Skinner survived, he would have become a ship's officer.[11] The mutiny cut those opportunities short. Skinner probably reminded Jackson and Ledain of their own experiences as cabin boys. While the two men would not have hesitated to discipline the boy if he stepped out of line, he nevertheless would have been one of their favorites. Skinner slept in the captain's cabin alongside Jackson. His experience of shipboard life, despite performing some of the most menial of tasks, was nevertheless something hardworking, marginalized workers would have envied. It should be no surprise that the mutineers wanted Skinner dead as his loyalty lay with the captain.

John McCoy, George Ledain's clerk, had also once been a cabin boy, but by the time of the mutiny he had begun to establish himself. And also much like John Skinner, the mutineers had good reason to target and kill McCoy. As Ledain's clerk, the young merchant and mariner's allegiance was to his employer. Surviving evidence demonstrates that McCoy was a direct beneficiary of the smuggling ring, even if only in a supporting role, ensuring McCoy's loyalty. As a clerk, McCoy would have helped Ledain manage the cargo, record business transactions, and keep accounts of credits and debts.

Why Ledain required a clerk on the *Rising Sun* is unclear. Since he was not responsible for piloting or navigating, Ledain's entire job was managing the cargo. He could have easily completed that task himself. Perhaps it was out of prestige and to signal to everyone, but especially Jackson, Clarke, and Tothill, that he was an established merchant with a clerk. There is also the possibility that McCoy was not really needed at all. Jackson and Ledain arrived in Barbados separately and then boarded the *Rising Sun* for their trip to Suriname and Cayenne. Outside of the documents related to the mutiny, all other records of McCoy described him as a "mariner," suggesting that he was some sort of ship's officer, perhaps Ledain's mate on his voyage to Barbados.[12] Jackson or someone else, however, opted to hire a different mate, William Blake, for this journey. Ledain kept McCoy on board to learn more about the operations of the smuggling ring, personally introduce him to Clarke and Tothill, and possibly cultivate him as a captain for future trading ventures.

Unlike Skinner and the other crew members, McCoy's family did not have deep New England roots. As his surname suggests, McCoy or his parents were born in Scotland or Northern Ireland.[13] He was in his mid- to late twenties at the time of his murder, old enough to be married and established enough for authorities in Boston to create an inventory of his property. Much like Jackson and Ledain, by 1743 McCoy was "of Boston," despite probably not having been born there. A 1741 marriage record from Boston's First Presbyterian Church—the religious denomination of most Scots migrants—does not note that McCoy or his wife, Jean, were from elsewhere, suggesting McCoy had lived in Boston long enough to be a legal resident.[14]

McCoy was deeply involved in the operations of the smuggling ring. Court authorities found little property when they inventoried his estate. The list of property he did own, however, reads like a manifest of the goods traded to and from Suriname. Some of the most valuable items were large pieces and rolls of calicoes, chintzes, and seersucker, cloth that New England merchants illegally traded in Suriname and Cayenne. He owned six "Looking Glasses," a popular product with planters and merchants in Paramaribo. And of course he had cacao worth more than forty-three pounds.[15] There is a possibility that all these products, especially the cacao, had been remitted to Jean McCoy following the mutiny in compensation for John's death. Either way, the fact that these goods composed such a conspicuous and significant part of his estate demonstrates McCoy's commitment to the smuggling ring. If the mutineers were looking to win over the crew after they attacked, McCoy would have been unwilling.

Much like Skinner and McCoy, there is little information about the two "Lads," Henry Deveries and Josiah Jones, who survived. The only post-mutiny record of the two men is Deveries's marriage at Boston's King's Chapel in 1746. Deveries and his wife are both listed as "of Boston."[16] Deveries's marriage suggests that he and Jones were most likely New Englanders and, like the cabin boy, traveled to the Caribbean with Jackson. They were nevertheless different than Skinner. Whereas the cabin boy came from an established family and could look forward to a career as a ship's officer, that avenue was closed to the two lads, from working-class or poor families in New England. They took to the sea out of necessity. Since their families were not wealthy or connected enough to set these youth up for success, they had to find their own path forward. Shipboard work offered one possibility. Wages were relatively high, and working for a few years at sea, especially when young and their bodies could handle the hard labor of maritime life, was one way of achieving financial independence.[17]

Young men like Deveries and Jones were the sailors who kept New England's maritime economy afloat. Called "ordinary seamen" in maritime parlance, they may have had only the most basic of sailing skills—thus the rest of the crew calling them lads—but captains and merchants were desperate for workers. Boston never had enough sailors to fill all its shipping needs, requiring captains to look far and wide and lower their standards.[18] To recruit them, Jackson drew on religious connections—Deveries was Anglican after all—and the word-of-mouth networks that stretched from Boston across coastal New England. Striving to create their own competencies, Jones and Deveries answered Jackson's call. Once hired, they were dependent on Jackson's patronage and did not question his trading activities. They may have turned a blind eye to smuggling, but never could they have predicted that they would be witness to murder.

The mutineers spared the lives of Deveries and Jones, who escaped the attack unscathed. Since there is such little record of their presence on the *Rising Sun*, speculation is necessary. Jackson broke the crew into two teams or "watches" who were on duty at different times of the day. He led the "captain's watch," while the mate, William Blake, was in charge of the "mate's watch." The attack occurred during the captain's watch, and Jackson's team included Pereira, Shaw, and himself, who, as captain, had the privilege of going to bed before the watch was over. Deveries and Jones were on the mate's watch and thus fast asleep when mutineers struck shortly before midnight. They would have been easy targets.[19]

Obviously, Deveries and Jones were not high on the list of people to kill when seizing control of the ship. Nevertheless, the mutineers wounded William Blake, whom they wanted to keep alive to help them pilot the *Rising Sun* to Orinoco, and they sought to murder John Shaw until Blake intervened. Yet Deveries and Jones were unharmed. Perhaps the mutineers did not see the young men, provincial New Englanders plucked from their homes and now in a foreign and alien place, as a threat. It is possible that this voyage was their first outside of North American coastal waters. Now, with Jackson and Ledain dead and Blake and Shaw neutralized, they were rudderless. That made them easier for the mutineers to intimidate and control. Likewise, Jones and Deveries, as regular sailors, shared the most in common with the mutineers. They may have been spared out of a sense of solidarity or a belief by the mutineers that they were too naïve to fully comprehend what had transpired. As the ship ventured to Orinoco, perhaps the mutineers could win the young sailors over.[20]

There was a clear pattern to the violence deployed by the mutineers. Those murdered were in command or their servants, while those spared were the least powerful and most similar to the mutineers. With the two officers on board the *Rising Sun*, the mate William Blake and boatswain John Shaw, however, the mutineers found themselves in a bind. Despite spending their lives at sea, the mutineers had little idea of how to pilot a ship. They required the expertise of the mate and boatswain. Yet keeping those two men alive was dangerous. Were they loyal to their fellow sailors, to Jackson and Ledain, to someone else, or to their own agenda?

Through his testimony and the publication of his journal, mate William Blake provided much of the information about the mutiny, but, ironically, his background remains an enigma. Blake is a common English surname, and it is unclear where he was from, making him nearly impossible to track in the records. And there is next to no discussion of Blake in the aftermath of the mutiny. One possibility is that Blake succumbed to his wounds. He likewise may have shipped out from Suriname, found new work as a mate, and slipped into the anonymity of the maritime world. Nevertheless, the documents do demonstrate that Blake was competent and the one officer the mutineers wished to keep alive.[21]

Mates, like captains, kept logs of their journeys, recording the weather, the ship's course, and interactions with the crew.[22] Following the mutiny, Blake's log documented the experience of being on board an illegally seized vessel. It was later used as evidence at trial and somehow ended up in the hands of Edward Tothill. Tothill and others copied parts of the journal, which were printed and distributed and served as a basis for the narrative of the mutiny read across the English-speaking world.[23]

As second in command, Blake had other duties. He was the ship's pilot and navigator. Navigation required a tremendous amount of learning on the job, including spending time in an apprenticeship or as a cabin boy and reading the innumerable texts available on the subject. Engaging in this high degree of learning transformed ships' navigators into a "self-made elite" in the maritime world, receiving higher compensation and prestige for their expertise.[24] Certainly Blake had mastered the skills necessary to succeed. Likewise, although Blake did not have to worry about the cargo with Ledain and McCoy on board, he was in charge of the day-to-day management of the ship and kept his own watch. He was also, in the event of Jackson's death, expected to take command of the vessel. Blake took that responsibility seriously.

There is a possibility that this voyage was Blake's first involvement in the smuggling ring. When Blake recorded the *Rising Sun*'s departure from Suriname in his logbook, he mistook the Commewijne River, which flows into the Suriname River, for the Cottica River, which flows into the Commewijne farther to the east. This mistake suggests someone just learning the geography of the region.[25] Moreover, after the mutineers attacked, he saved John Shaw's life by claiming Shaw had expertise of the Wild Coast, implying that while Blake knew how to pilot a ship, he was not familiar with the region itself. Perhaps and possibly like McCoy, this voyage was meant to introduce Blake to the world of cacao smuggling and some of its key figures, cultivating him as a future captain.

There is much more information available about John Shaw, the boatswain—pronounced "bosun"—who was in charge of the ship's rigging, sails, small boats, and anchors. He maintained the equipment that kept the vessel moving and doubled as the ship's chief safety officer, ensuring the sails and rope were fit to use, properly installed, and secure. The boatswain also acted as the foreman for the sailors, calling them to work, setting them to task, and ensuring they performed their duties properly. It was a skilled job that required years of shipboard service to master but was nevertheless open to common sailors.[26] Through his work with the smuggling ring, John Shaw found that opportunity.[27]

Shaw had been affiliated with the smuggling ring since at least 1740, but probably earlier. Like Blake, he has a common English surname that makes it difficult to track him in the records. Nevertheless, he was most likely born in New England but became a full-time sailor who spent little time there after reaching adulthood. He first appears in the records as a common seaman in the 1740 Wingfield expedition. It was an inauspicious beginning. In Ledain's lawsuit against Wingfield, the court called Thomas Wilson, the *Charming Rebecca's* mate, to testify. Not only did Wilson acknowledge all of Wingfield's backroom dealing, but he also took the time to mention "John Shaw a Sailer on board."

According to Wilson, Shaw openly disobeyed his and Wingfield's commands. When the ship reached Barbados from Cayenne, Wingfield ordered the cargo hold locked and the hatches battened down. Nobody was to remove any of the cacao aboard the *Charming Rebecca*, even if it was part of their personal venture, until the captain had spoken to Gedney Clarke. The future boatswain, however, had other plans. In the middle of the night, Shaw "carry'd a Shore" an unknown quantity of cacao.[28]

Such underhanded behavior did not hurt Shaw's reputation. He continued working on ships smuggling cacao out of Suriname. As William Blake later told the mutineers in an attempt to save the boatswain's life, Shaw had been on "Severall Voyages to Esequeba," "knew all the Land very Well," and spoke "pretty good Dutch."[29] As this testimony suggests, Shaw had spent a considerable amount of time in Dutch colonies and had become a trusted employee, eventually serving as boatswain on the *Rising Sun.*

There is evidence to suggest that Shaw's promotion was not entirely due to his abilities as a seaman. He seemed particularly loyal to Gedney Clarke. In the aftermath of the mutiny, Clarke, in a letter to the Lascelles that no longer exists, described the mutiny and mentioned Shaw by name. In the Lascelles' response, they seemed familiar with Shaw and called him "honest."[30] Later events gave reason for the Lascelles' high praise of Shaw, but their familiarity with him and his reputation implies a long-standing connection. Likewise, according to Ferdinand da Costa, Shaw attempted to proclaim that he was the new captain after Jackson's murder. Of course the mutineer may have been attempting to cast doubt on Shaw or distract from his own actions, but if it happened, it was a peculiar move. In the line of succession, the mate, William Blake, should have become commander. Yet Shaw aspired to the position. Perhaps he sought control of the ship to salvage the voyage and protect Clarke's interests.[31] Such loyalty to Clarke and, by extension, the Lascelles can also cause us to reinterpret Shaw's actions on the *Charming Rebecca*. Maybe he did not abscond at night merely for personal gain but also to warn Clarke of Wingfield's double dealing. Shaw's relationship with Clarke may have also helped him obtain the position of boatswain on the *Rising Sun*.

With this affiliation in mind, it is reasonable to assume Shaw and perhaps William Blake had been assigned to the *Rising Sun* by Gedney Clarke. While captains tended to have control in choosing their ship's crew, merchants often became involved in that process and mandated captains hire particular people, usually as officers.[32] Clarke also had significantly more leverage to dictate these matters in the case of the *Rising Sun*. He owned the ship and had only recently hired Jackson. It is entirely possible that Clarke imposed the two ship's officers on Jackson and Ledain. For Clarke, this was a smart business move as neither Shaw nor Blake had particularly large private ventures and were entirely dependent on Clarke's beneficence for employment opportunities and wages. That, in turn, ensured a certain degree of loyalty from the ship's crew. As the Wingfield case demonstrated, captains and perhaps even business partners looked out for their own interests first. Having his own loyalists on board ensured Clarke at least a watchful eye if not an effective deterrent to behavior against his interests.

Regardless, the mutineers required the officers' skills to sail and navigate the *Rising Sun*. It was only a few days journey to Orinoco—and before anybody in a position of authority could ask questions. Perhaps they thought Blake and Shaw could be bought off in the meantime. If not, two wounded men would be easy enough to dispatch. The mutineers, however, misunderstood just how dependent they were on the ship's officers to carry out their plan.

While certainly part of the *Rising Sun*'s crew, the three men who mutinied and murdered Jackson, Ledain, Skinner, and McCoy and wounded Blake and Shaw stood out. Their names were Ferdinand da Costa, Joseph Pereira, and Thomas Lucas, and unlike the others, they were unconnected to the smuggling ring. They were sailors who lacked the formal training and connections to rise through the ranks of the maritime world. And most significantly they were not Anglophones, and two of them were not white. All of these factors played a role in the events that transpired on the *Rising Sun*. Luckily for modern observers, two of the mutineers, Da Costa and Lucas, later offered testimony, providing us insight about who they were and helping us make sense of the mutiny.

One of the most conspicuous details in various accounts of the mutineers was their race. Printed accounts described them as "Portuguese Negroes" or "Portuguese Negro Sailors," while Dutch authorities called them "mulattoes," a term to describe those of mixed European and African ancestry.[33] They were also all free men, although at least one of them had been born a slave. It is difficult, however, to discern their actual racial backgrounds. The court seemed adamant in finding out. When reviewing the criminal complaint, the court's clerk inserted—using an editing caret (^) in the manuscript—the phrase "both being Negroes" to refer to Pereira and Lucas.[34] Ferdinand da Costa, however, openly denied being Black. When asked by Dutch authorities if he was a "white man," the mutineer responded "Yes."[35] There was little reason for Da Costa to lie about his background. He was already on trial for the mutiny and was most likely going to be executed. At the very least, Da Costa's interrogation offered him the opportunity to clear the record about his race.

As their names suggest, Da Costa and Pereira were from Portugal or the Portuguese Empire. In his testimony, Da Costa said he was from Moita, a small fishing village across the Tagus River from Lisbon.[36] Since

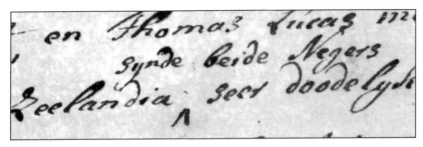

FIGURE 4.2. The clerk's editing caret noting that Pereira and Lucas were of African descent. From "Criminal Complaint against Ferdinandus Da Costa and Thomas Lucas," 3 August 1743, Oud Archief Suriname: Raad van Politie, 1.05.10.02 (Processtukken betreffende criminele zaken), inv.nr. 796 (1743), NA Netherlands. Courtesy of the Nationaal Archief, the Netherlands.

Pereira, whose surname Dutch officials spelled "Pareijra," did not testify, it is unclear where he was from. Although Lisbon had a large Black population dating back to Portugal's early involvement in the slave trade, it is possible that Pereira was Brazilian or even West African.[37] Portuguese and Brazilian ships employed large numbers of sailors of African descent, especially in the slave trade. These sailors of color were both free and enslaved and often found opportunities on board ships that were not possible in employment on land.[38]

Thomas Lucas, however, was not Portuguese. Lucas, according to his testimony, was born in a village outside of the Italian city-state of Venice.[39] While Venice was not on any of the major Atlantic slave trading routes, sub-Saharan Africans began arriving in the city as slaves in the fifteenth century. Wealthy Venetians came to value enslaved Africans, especially women, as maids and household servants.[40] Indeed, Lucas's mother was one such domestic. And like many Venetian patricians, Lucas's enslaver freed him and his mother on his deathbed.[41] Although the Italian states did not have any colonies in the Americas, Italian sailors manned ships for many different nations, especially the Iberian kingdoms.[42] Having probably served alongside Iberian sailors, Lucas learned Portuguese. He was so well versed that the British crew and, until his examination, Dutch officials mistook him as a Lusophone.

There are a number of reasons why three multiracial, non-English sailors found themselves on board the *Rising Sun*. First and foremost, Da Costa, Pereira, and Lucas were men of the sea. In both their testimonies, Lucas and Da Costa, despite being relatively young, reported long careers aboard ships. Lucas told the court that he was thirty-five or thirty-six years old and had been at sea since he was a child. Lucas spent long periods working and had not returned home to Venice in nearly a decade.[43] Da Costa was younger than Lucas, twenty-six or twenty-seven years old, but had likewise spent many years at sea.[44] By the standards of their profession, the men were seasoned veterans. Despite their youth, collectively they had decades of sailing experience. Moreover, they worked a physically taxing job that took its toll, breaking the bodies of seamen by the time they were in their early to mid-thirties. Lucas would have been considered an "old salt," an older sailor about to age out of the profession.[45] Whereas Deveries and Jones were the ship's ordinary seamen, the three mutineers were the ship's "able seamen," or those with experience.

Likewise, despite being foreigners and of African descent, the three men would have made good wages. While there was certainly some pay discrimination, wages from sailing were far better for free men of color and more comparable to those of white workers than in most other occupations.[46] Jackson offered Pereira and Da Costa fifty-five Barbadian shillings and Lucas fifty shillings a month, good wages that speak to the sailors' skills and experience.[47] There was also, given the life-and-death dynamic of shipboard life, more social harmony between white and black workers than in other occupations.[48]

Finding a crew in Barbados would have been difficult under normal circumstances, which may have pushed Jackson to hire the three men. While there was a small free seafaring population in Barbados, they would have almost all been employed in the island's own shipping industry.[49] Jackson could have used enslaved sailors, but that meant haggling with enslavers over wages and assuming the risk of caring for another's property. Oftentimes there were transient sailors looking for work in places like Barbados, but they would have been difficult to find in 1743. Britain was at war, meaning able seamen would have been in high demand and easily found employment—or been impressed by the Royal Navy. These factors not only pushed Jackson to employ foreign sailors but also ensured higher wages.[50]

That said, Jackson may have enthusiastically hired the three men for an illegal slaving voyage. Jackson, Clarke, and Ledain would have preferred crewmembers with experience in the slave trade, and Da Costa, Pereira, and Lucas were most likely veterans of that nefarious commerce. There are a number of clues to suggest as much. During this period, British ships tended to have multiracial and multiethnic crews, and slave ships were especially diverse. Often desperate for sailors, slaving captains employed any capable seaman regardless of background.[51] Lusophone sailors, especially those of African descent, were also renowned for their expertise in handling enslaved people and working onboard slave ships.[52] Having spent time in Portugal, Jackson may have been aware of this reputation.

Other evidence suggests a connection to the slave trade as well. In his testimony, Da Costa mentioned he knew Pereira from London and that they had traveled to Barbados together. Many of the slave ships dispatched to the floating factory left from London. Da Costa and Lucas could have been hired from the large pool of sailors looking for work in the imperial capital. Moreover, slave ship captains, looking to increase profits, were notorious for discharging crew members in the West Indies before returning home. Captains drove sailors especially hard toward the end of the Middle Passage, hoping they would desert once they arrived in port, while others simply left those sailors too sick to carry on behind. If seamen deserted or were left behind, captains and shipowners would not have to pay their wages. Such tactics cut labor costs and increased profitability. For the sailors, it left them stranded to find new work or die if they were too sick. Foreign and nonwhite crew members were especially vulnerable to this practice and Barbados, a major destination for slave ships, became a dumping ground for men like Da Costa, Pereira, and Lucas.[53]

FIGURE 4.3. John Singleton Copley's *Watson and the Shark* depicts a multiracial, multiclass, and multigenerational New England ship's crew similar to that of the *Rising Sun*. John Singleton Copley, *Watson and the Shark* (1778). Courtesy of the National Gallery of Art.

What is clear is that until hired by Jackson, Da Costa and Pereira did not know Lucas before reaching Barbados—Da Costa later mentioned he thought Lucas was Genoese and not Venetian. Nevertheless, as foreign and Catholic sailors in a British colony, they could have easily found common cause.[54] And when a random New England ship captain offered a good wage to sail on the *Rising Sun*, they took him up on the opportunity. Da Costa and Pereira would serve as able seamen, while Lucas doubled as a sailor and cook. The three men did not know the captain, the supercargo, or the man who sponsored the voyage, but that was not unusual.[55]

Yet when the *Rising Sun* departed in May 1743 certain tensions and desires probably simmered in the minds of the sailors. Having most likely been discharged from a slave ship without good cause proved their vulnerability. They were also beginning to age out of their profession. The fact that the oldest and most experienced sailor, Thomas Lucas, agreed to be a cook, often considered one of the lowest positions in the shipboard hierarchy, and was paid less than Pereira and Da Costa suggests as much. And where were these men, at least two of them not white and all three of them used to working on foreign ships, supposed to turn if they retired from the sea? Surely they would face discrimination if not outright deportation if they remained in the British Empire. And even if they could remain, their wages would never be comparable to what they made at sea. Could they even find work? What about returning to their homelands? If so, were there even opportunities there?

Those questions help explain why the mutiny occurred. When looking for the motive behind the mutiny, it is hard not to craft elaborate conspiracy theories. Part of that has to do with a total lack of evidence about the motive. When Dutch officials interrogated Da Costa and Lucas, like most legal proceedings of the time, they were concerned more with establishing guilt than with motive. The crime had already occurred, so now justice and punishment, not explanation, were the court's imperative. Likewise, there were so many conflicting agendas on board the *Rising Sun* and within the smuggling ring that it is easy to think the murders were less than random. Nevertheless, that was not the case. The mutiny was the result of a confluence of events and decisions made by Da Costa, Pereira, and Lucas.

The mutineers' plan was to commandeer the ship and take it to Orinoco. Once there, they agreed to sell the ship and its cargo of cacao, sugar, molasses, cloth, and African captives. They would then divide the money. It is unclear if the mutineers planned to recruit the other crewmembers on their voyage or murder them before arriving in Orinoco.

This scheme leads to two questions: why mutiny in the first place, and why Orinoco? After departing Suriname, the *Rising Sun*'s hold was full of valuable cacao, sugar, and coffee, various types of cloth, and the fifteen African captives. Also present was a sizeable amount of gold and silver coinage. Why, however, is not entirely clear. Specie was always in short supply in the colonies, generally remitted to the mother country for manufactured goods and infrequently used in intercolonial trade. Tothill, however, may have been charging planters and estate managers hard currency for enslaved people. Although slaves were often purchased with bills of exchange or tropical commodities in Suriname, some cash transactions also occurred.[56] Illicit trade, especially, may have been conducted in cash because bills of exchange and other financial instruments created a paper trail. A sense of the amount of gold and silver aboard comes from Newark Jackson's estate. His widow Amey received eight gold pesos and twenty-six ounces of silver "from Suranam" worth more than 120 pounds Massachusetts currency.[57] Jackson's estate was only one recipient of the coinage, suggesting a significantly larger amount on board the ship.[58] Finally, the ship itself was worth money and readily salable. If the mutineers were able to successfully take control of the *Rising Sun*, pilfer the gold and silver, and sell the ship and its cargo, they would have—even if divided three or more ways—made off with a massive financial windfall.

Enticing as the ship's riches were, profit for profit's sake was probably not the motivating factor. The promise of a life free of the rigors and draconian discipline of the maritime world had to be tempting. Shipowners pinched pennies, while captains relished the opportunity to mete out violent punishments. Sailors resisted such treatment, and open rebellion always simmered beneath the surface.[59] Evidence of the desire for independence comes from an exchange between Shaw and Da Costa. On the night of the mutiny, despite being wounded, Shaw, according to Da Costa, announced that since Jackson was dead, he was the new captain. Da Costa simply replied "they were all captains" now.[60] Da Costa had not committed murder merely to submit to a new captain. Rather, he helped seize control of the *Rising Sun* to escape the difficulties of life as a sailor and to reject the hierarchy of the maritime world. It was not just that the *Rising Sun* and its cargo were valuable, but the sale of the ship and the goods on board offered Da Costa, Pereira, and Lucas the chance of autonomy and independence. Whether they planned to remain in Orinoco, go elsewhere, or move home, the proceeds of sale offered opportunities.

Much like there was a logic behind the mutiny, there was also one to their choice of Orinoco as a destination. This region, to the west of Suriname, was underdeveloped and contested. The Spanish colonized the area, which was part of the province of Venezuela, in the sixteenth century.[61] Once the Dutch began settling in Essequibo in the mid-seventeenth century, however, conflict raged over the border between the two colonies. To bolster their claim in the early eighteenth century, the Spanish subsidized missions to convert the region's Indigenous population and promoted tobacco production. These led to a bit of development, but the region still struggled to attract settlers and commerce. Moreover, in 1704, the province enacted a policy that welcomed runaway slaves, both African and Amerindian, and deserting soldiers and sailors provided they pledged their loyalty to Spain and became Catholic. Over the next few decades, hundreds of slaves, sailors, and soldiers succeeded in fleeing to Orinoco.[62] Marginal and welcoming of outsiders, Orinoco made sense as a destination for the mutineers. Their desire to trade, despite being technically illegal, offered locals access to goods and would have allowed the mutineers to make inroads in the Spanish colony—provided they could make it there in the first place.[63]

Yet how did Da Costa, Pereira, and Lucas decide on Orinoco as a destination? The *Rising Sun* had resupplied in Paramaribo and probably could have gone anywhere in the Caribbean. They nevertheless chose a very specific, marginal place. The mutineers were experienced sailors and may have learned of opportunities offered by Spanish colonies from their many travels. Nevertheless, there is a tantalizing clue. During the interrogation of Da Costa and Lucas, Dutch authorities asked the men about a "Spaniard" who had been on the *Rising Sun* and with whom they

FIGURE 4.4. Detail of an eighteenth-century French map of the Guianas with the Orinoco River delta on the left and Cayenne, the intended destination of the *Rising Sun*, toward the right. From Jacques Nicolas Bellin, *Description Geographique de la Guiane* (Paris, 1763). Courtesy of the John Carter Brown Library.

had many conversations. They offered authorities few details except the man's name, which was "Gousinh." Jackson, according to the mutineers, "set him ashore," in Paramaribo before departing.[64] Da Costa and Lucas both told the court that Gousinh had first proposed murdering the captain and taking control of the ship.

It is important to remember, however, that the testimony of Da Costa and Lucas is not the most trustworthy. Court officials caught the men, especially Lucas, lying multiple times. They may have invented the Spaniard to try to deflect blame and perhaps save their lives. Likewise, in all the surviving documents related to the *Rising Sun*, the surviving crew never mentioned him.[65] Nevertheless, there is a possibility that there was a mysterious "Spaniard" aboard. He could have been the person who told the mutineers about the Spanish colonies and their policy of welcoming runaways and deserters. Gousinh, if he existed, may have implanted the idea of mutiny and the possibility of an independent life free of drudgery in the minds of Ferdinand Da Costa, Joseph Pereira, and Thomas Lucas.

Who could this mysterious Spaniard have been? One of the contexts for understanding events on the *Rising Sun*—and, by extension, the Spaniard Gousinh—is that they occurred in the midst of a war. In 1739, Britain declared war on Spain, a conflict a long time coming. After the end of a previous war, the War of Spanish Succession, in 1713, Britain received extensive trade concessions, including the *asiento*, the monopoly on trading slaves, in Spain's American colonies. Over the next twenty-five years, however, Spain became alarmed by the sheer volume of British trade, legal and illegal, in their colonies and began more carefully regulating commerce. Most significantly, the Spanish allowed local governments in the Americas to commission *guardacostas*, or coast guard ships meant to protect colonies from smuggling and piracy. These ships often overstepped their boundaries, harassing British shipping more generally under the guise of stopping illicit trade. The 1739 war received its name—the War of Jenkins' Ear—from the abuse a British ship captain, Robert Jenkins, received at the hands of a guardacosta when the Spanish crew cut off his ear for allegedly smuggling.[66]

In effect, the War of Jenkins' Ear started as a trade war between Britain and Spain. Early on, the Caribbean was the main theater of the conflict. Britain committed extensive naval resources to the fight, wrestling control of Portobello, in modern Panama. Within a year, however, the war bogged down and Britain's early victories turned into a series of stinging defeats, culminating in the failure to capture Cartagena in 1741. After that, combat operations shifted from the Caribbean to Europe.[67]

Nevertheless, the British government still sought to thwart the guardacosta and undermine Spanish shipping more generally. As they drew down naval forces in the West Indies after 1741, British officials turned to private subjects and remaining Royal Navy vessels to continue the fight. The administration in London empowered colonial governors to issue letters of marque or documents that allowed private ships to commit acts of piracy against the Spanish. These privateering voyages became moneymaking opportunities for American merchants, who invested in ships and crews. Moreover, the Admiralty granted the Royal Navy free rein to capture Spanish privateers and other vessels, allowing their captains and crews to claim them as prizes. Merchants would likewise invest in naval prize cargoes, effectively speculating on the potential of the Royal Navy to capture lucrative trade goods. And one colonial merchant, Gedney Clarke, participated in these activities.

From the onset of conflict in 1739, Clarke invested in privateering and naval prize cargoes. While he sometimes acted on his own, he often joined with Edward Lascelles and Royal Navy admiral Peter Warren. Warren was especially active in capturing Spanish prizes. He arrived in the West Indies in late summer 1739 and remained there for nearly five years. Although assigned to larger squadrons, Warren was often independent of them and tasked with hunting guardacosta. He profited immensely from this enterprise, and one historian estimates Warren netted more than twenty thousand pounds sterling from captured Spanish vessels.[68] Clarke enjoyed some of those profits and served as an agent selling the cargoes that Warren captured.[69]

Clarke's investment in prize cargoes during the War of Jenkins' Ear explains the presence of the Spaniard Gousinh on board the *Rising Sun*. If Gousinh was real, he would have belonged to a group of people whom contemporaries called "Spanish Negroes." During the eighteenth century, crews of Spanish sailing ships tended to be multiethnic and multiracial. Vessels that patrolled American waters, such as guardacosta, were especially diverse and crewed by large numbers of men of color both enslaved and free. When British privateers or naval vessels captured these ships, however, they did not bother to investigate the status of the sailors aboard. Instead, prize courts and colonial officials often condemned, based on skin color alone, Spanish sailors of color to be sold as part of the cargo. These "Spanish Negroes" were then trafficked as slaves across the British colonies.[70]

Just months before the *Rising Sun* departed for Suriname, Warren captured numerous Spanish vessels and claimed them as prizes. On a trip from the British island of Antigua to New York in March 1743, Warren captured three ships. Gousinh was possibly a sailor on one of these vessels, condemned to be sold and then transferred to the care of Gedney Clarke or Edward Lascelles. They then added him to the cargo consigned to the *Rising Sun*. If—a big if—Gousinh existed, by encouraging mutiny, the Spaniard enacted his revenge.

The Spaniard, real or invented, was gone by the time Da Costa, Pereira, and Lucas decided to murder the crew and take control of the ship. Even if the mutiny was not their idea, their actions brought death and mayhem to the *Rising Sun*. Now in control of the ship, all they had to do was make it to Orinoco, sell the schooner and its cargo, and retire to a good life. William Blake and John Shaw had other plans.

5

Endings

The morning after the mutiny, an oddly normal event occurred. Da Costa, Pereira, and Lucas went on deck and, like most days, began cleaning. It was not the dust and grime of the previous day they scrubbed, however, but blood and gore. Quickly, though, the mutineers reminded the crew how abnormal their new situation was. The three men began destroying evidence of their crime, throwing bloody clothes and the ship's papers overboard. Having disposed of anything incriminating, they asserted their control over the rest of the crew. They ordered Deveries and Jones to help Shaw and Blake dress their wounds. Although the mutineers committed to democratic rule, Da Costa, the white mutineer, posed, in the words of William Blake, as the "pretended Captain" of the *Rising Sun*.[1] Now appearing to be on an otherwise typical voyage, the ship sailed west toward Orinoco.

Yet this situation would not last. Unbeknownst to the mutineers, Blake and Shaw, as the only two who knew how to navigate, had the upper hand. Almost immediately, the men seemed to have deliberately slowed the schooner while still assuaging the mutineers' demands to head for Orinoco. Having no idea of how long it took to reach the Spanish colony, the mutineers unwittingly allowed Blake and Shaw to stall, formulate a plan to stop the mutiny, and bring its perpetrators to justice.

The ship lumbered slowly westward over the next three days. To pass the time, Da Costa, Pereira, and Lucas began inspecting the cargo they planned to sell. As they broke open the casks and pillaged the cabins, they found the gold and silver. Da Costa would later describe that he and the others found thirty-five pieces of gold and an unknown quantity of silver. He also claimed to have divided the coins evenly among the entire crew and not just the mutineers. John Shaw, Da Costa later asserted, helped locate the silver and knew its true value.[2] It is unclear if Shaw was actually involved in divvying up the cargo. Most likely, Shaw helped break open the casks and count the silver to distract the mutineers while he and Blake plotted against them.

In addition to the gold and silver, the mutineers found other commodities. It is difficult to piece together the entire cargo, but there was a considerable amount of cloth on board the ship. Some of that was probably from Britain or British colonies that the crew planned to sell in Cayenne. Other pieces may have been purchased in Paramaribo for sale in Barbados and New England.[3] There was likewise an untold amount of sugar, coffee, and, of course, cacao.[4]

Finally, there were the fifteen enslaved Africans in the hold. Despite at least one of the mutineers being a former slave, two of them being mixed race, and all three of them coming from marginal backgrounds, there is no evidence of solidarity between them and the captives. They did not mutiny to free the captives and probably disdained them. Much like Jackson, Ledain, and the others, Pereira, Da Costa, and Lucas understood that the sale and ownership of enslaved people was a way to wealth in the Americas. Not only would they have had a keen understanding of the monetary value of enslaved people, but they also probably saw themselves as better than the captives. The mutineers were experienced seamen versed in the rhythms of Atlantic commerce and the languages of multiple empires. As sailors, they had shared a rough equality with Europeans while at sea for their entire careers and probably identified more with their fellow brethren of the sea than those in the *Rising Sun*'s hold.[5] After all, despite their lowly status and, for Lucas and Pereira, African ancestry, they were still free, skilled, and self-possessed. Whereas the enslaved were property subject to the whims of others, they were, in that moment at least, agents of their own destiny. In other words, they were the opposite of slaves. Instead, they stood to profit from slavery.[6] Rather than being liberators, the mutineers probably sought to secure and prepare the enslaved children for sale.

These goods were worth a lot of money. Without creditors, owners, and investors to reimburse, the cargo would bring a considerable profit once sold in Orinoco. In their interrogations, Da Costa and Lucas did not describe how they felt about this potential windfall. Nevertheless, as it had already enticed them to mutiny, breaking open the casks and inspecting the cargo probably reassured them of their decision. When the ship came across the mouth of a large river on 5 June, four days after the murders, the mutineers were especially heartened and thought they had finally reached the Orinoco.[7]

Dense jungle enveloped the river, and the *Rising Sun* proceeded against the current using the incoming high tide. One mile turned into two, which turned into thirty as the ship creeped around islands and the river narrowed, becoming increasingly shallow. When they had still not encountered any habitation after traversing so far inland, Da Costa became worried. Blake reassured the sailor, telling Da Costa that if they were not in Orinoco, the mutineers could "cut off his head."[8] Finally, nearly twenty leagues (about sixty miles) upriver, the crew saw a house and Blake told the mutineers that it was a "Spanish House."[9] Da Costa ordered the crew to stop the ship and throw the anchor overboard.

Blake encouraged Da Costa to form a delegation to go meet with the people at the house. Da Costa, the "pretended captain," donned Ledain's silk clothes, wig, and "Lac'd" hat to play the part.[10] The rest of the crew, save Shaw, who remained on the ship, would join Da Costa for the parlay. At this point, Da Costa had to be thinking he could pull the ruse off. He only had to fabricate a story about the ship's voyage and destination, perhaps even trying the old smuggler's trick of claiming to need repairs. With a plan in mind, Da Costa, the other two mutineers, Blake, Deveries, and Jones boarded the *Rising Sun*'s boat and rowed ashore.

Out of the house came a group of white men. They greeted the *Rising Sun*'s party . . . in Dutch.

In the days after the mutiny, Blake and Shaw deliberately delayed the voyage to Orinoco.[11] They do not discuss the fact in their testimony, but

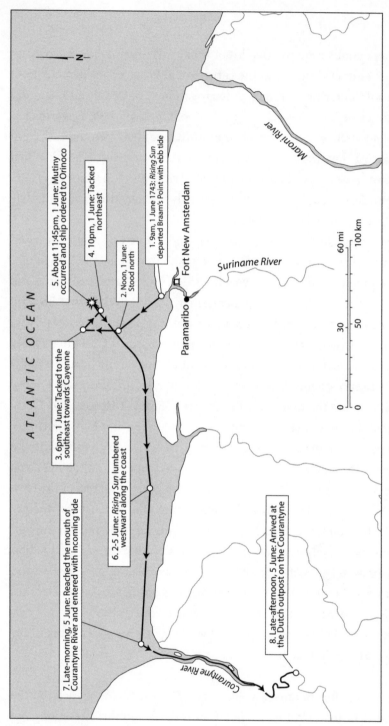

MAP 5.1. Voyage of the *Rising Sun*, 1–5 June 1743. Map created by Bill Nelson.

Text labels within the map:

5. About 11:45pm, 1 June: Mutiny occurred and ship ordered to Orinoco

4. 10pm, 1 June: Tacked northeast

2. Noon, 1 June: Stood north

1. 9am, 1 June 1743: *Rising Sun* departed Braam's Point with ebb tide

3. 6pm, 1 June: Tacked to the southeast towards Cayenne

6. 2–5 June: *Rising Sun* lumbered westward along the coast

7. Late-morning, 5 June: Reached the mouth of Courantyne River and entered with incoming tide

8. Late-afternoon, 5 June: Arrived at the Dutch outpost on the Courantyne

ATLANTIC OCEAN

N

Maroni River

Suriname River

Fort New Amsterdam

Paramaribo

Courantyne River

0   30   60 mi

0   50   100 km

sailing westward to Orinoco should have been a quick trip, taking no more than a couple days. All they would have had to do was sail northward into the Equatorial Current, turn west, and then drop south once they reached the Orinoco River. Yet the ship lumbered along the coast, moving very slowly. So slow, in fact, that four days after the mutiny, on 5 June, the ship was still off the coast of Suriname. The *Rising Sun* entered not the Orinoco but rather the Courantyne, a river that constitutes Suriname's western border. In his log, Blake noted arriving in the Courantyne, meaning he or, more likely, John Shaw knew exactly where the ship was.[12] Keeping Shaw alive for his knowledge of the Wild Coast was indeed a great move—just not for the mutineers.

Shaw was probably also familiar with how remote this area was for Europeans. The Dutch had not developed the Courantyne, focusing their energies instead on the Suriname and Berbice river sheds. On both banks of the river was dense, near impenetrable jungle. About the only Dutch presence in the area was the house and some outbuildings, surrounded by a short defensive wall. It was home to a *posthouder* or postholder, Corporal Jan Heijse, one of the men who greeted the *Rising Sun*'s crew.[13]

Heijse's job was to conduct diplomacy and facilitate trade with the local Indigenous peoples, the Kali'na or Carib and Arawak.[14] Both the Kali'na and Arawak had long been allies of the Dutch, helping them contest the border with the Spanish, capture runaway slaves and soldiers, and conduct a brisk trade in food, timber, annatto, hammocks, and Amerindian slaves. To facilitate all these activities, the Dutch armed their Indigenous allies with guns.[15] Postholders also controlled the movement of people and goods in the region. This was a long list of responsibilities, and the Dutch preferred "respected soldiers" when filling the position.[16] Heijse fit the bill. When the beleaguered ship arrived, a handful of Amerindians, some other soldiers, and a few assistants (called *bijleggers* in Dutch) lived at the post with Heijse.[17]

The postholder was probably not surprised by the arrival of the *Rising Sun* but was nevertheless perplexed. Very few ships visited the post, al-

FIGURE 5.1. Detail from a nineteenth-century artistic rendition of a rural outpost in Suriname. The Courantyne post would have looked similar. Jacob Marius Adriaan Martini van Geffen, *Post Victoria Gezien Vanaf de Suriname Rivier* (1850). Courtesy of the Rijksmuseum, Amsterdam.

most all of them small coasting craft from Paramaribo or Berbice. Only on rare occasions did foreign vessels appear, and they were usually lost. To be approached by a foreign ship's crew was a strange occurrence at the isolated outpost. Nevertheless, the Kali'na or Arawak had probably warned Heijse of the ship's approach, and he could prepare accordingly.

Taking advantage of Da Costa's confusion, Blake maintained the ruse. He asked Heijse—it is unclear how or in what language—if they were in Orinoco and the Dutch officer replied they were still a long way away from the Spanish colony. It gave Blake the excuse he needed to return to the *Rising Sun* and gather his navigational charts and instruments to plot the course to Orinoco.[18] Joining Blake on his return was Shaw. Shaw, who "talk'd pretty good Dutch," started speaking at length with Heijse. He explained the mutiny and everything that had transpired, even explaining why he and Blake wore so many bandages. Heijse told Shaw that he needed until morning to gather a force to arrest the mutineers. Until then, the Dutch officer extended his hospitality and the crew stayed at the post long into the evening.[19]

By the time they returned to the *Rising Sun*, the mutineers suspected something was amiss. They knew Shaw had told the truth about the situation. Furious at Shaw, Pereira and Lucas decided to throw the boatswain overboard, hoping he would drown. Da Costa, however, intervened, telling them that it was more important to start moving first, then they could murder the mate and boatswain. The three men started to raise the ship's anchor. As they heaved, Shaw saw an opportunity. Tied and floating beside the schooner was the landing boat. Although wounded, Shaw jumped into the boat, got free of the *Rising Sun*, and rowed ashore to the postholder's house.

Panic ensued after Shaw's escape. The mutineers could not pursue Shaw because he took the ship's boat. In haste, Pereira cut the anchor rope. Doing so allowed for a quick escape. It was ebb tide and the river was flowing out to sea rapidly.[20] The problem, however, was that it was dusk and the Courantyne was shallow that far inland. Now, with the ship moving quickly in the dark, maintaining control was near impossible. A few miles upriver, the *Rising Sun* ran aground. Since it was low tide, she was stuck until the tide came back in. The ship floated the next morning but ran aground again just a few miles upriver, stranding the schooner, mutineers, and remaining crew for another night.[21]

When they awoke on 7 June, Da Costa, Pereira, and Lucas hoped to float and be free again. Looking south to the horizon, however, they saw three boats approaching them. Leading the way in the *Rising Sun*'s boat was John Shaw with Heijse and three Dutch soldiers.[22] Flanking them were two canoes full of Amerindian warriors.[23] Pereira wanted to fight, loading the *Rising Sun*'s cannons. But the ship had only one bottle of gunpower, and Pereira was a novice gunner.[24] There was little chance of hitting his target and even less of one at being able to sustain fire long enough to drive the three boats off.

Da Costa realized they could not win a fight or escape. With the schooner run aground, they were a sitting target. Pereira went to fire the cannons, but Da Costa stopped his fellow mutineer, knowing it would do little good.[25] As Pereira and Da Costa argued, Jones and Deveries saw an opportunity and jumped overboard into the Courantyne River, risking the piranha-infested waters to reach the rescue party.[26] When the three boats were within firing range, they scooped up the two young sailors and started to surround the *Rising Sun*. Da Costa and Lucas willingly surrendered. Pereira, however, did not want to place his fate in the hands of Dutch authorities. He dove off the deck of the ship into the river and swam ashore, fleeing into the jungle. Meanwhile, Heijse and Shaw boarded the ship and placed Da Costa and Lucas in chains.[27] After nearly a week, the mutiny on the *Rising Sun* was over.

What happened over the next two and a half weeks is a bit of a mystery. Between the apprehension of the mutineers on 7 June and their arrival in Paramaribo on 26 June 1743 (7 July NS), there is little record of what transpired.[28] Almost immediately after arresting them, Heijse searched Da Costa and Lucas, finding a significant quantity of gold and silver on their persons, including a "Silver Watch ty'd about" Da Costa's "Private Parts."[29] The postholder then organized a search party for Pereira, which the crew readily joined. The fact that Blake, Shaw, Deveries, and Jones, wounded and exhausted from the mutiny, aided in searching for the escaped mutineer shows they wanted revenge. When the party failed to find Pereira, the surviving crew sailed the *Rising Sun*, now damaged from being run aground twice, back to the postholder's house.[30] Heijse then secured the prisoners at the post, created an inventory of the cargo on board the *Rising Sun*, and carefully counted the gold and silver, detailing everything in a report to Governor Mauricius.[31]

These events probably transpired over several days, and when a small trading vessel departed the post for Paramaribo, Heijse placed Da Costa and Lucas on board, along with Blake and Shaw to seek medical attention. To ensure that the two mutineers would not conspire again, Heijse assigned two canoes full of Amerindian warriors to trail the ship. That would have significantly slowed the trip to Suriname's capital, and it may have taken over a week to arrive. Once the mutineers, Blake, and Shaw reached Paramaribo, it was time to seek justice.

Almost immediately upon their arrival in Paramaribo, Governor Mauricius had the mutineers placed in Fort Zeelandia's dungeon under constant guard. He and Jacobus van Halewijn, Suriname's *Raad Fiscaal* or attorney general, then had to determine the best course of action for prosecuting them. According to a letter written by Tothill and later published, "Dutch Authority seem'd at a loss what Punishment to inflict on these Villains, suitable to their Barbarity."[32] They had time to ponder and debate, however, as they did not want to go to trial until Blake and Shaw had convalesced, the rest of the crew and ship arrived from Courantyne, and Heijse captured Pereira.

Deep in the jungle of western Suriname, Pereira was on the run. The mutineer spent days living in the bush. The tropical jungle of Suriname is dense and nearly impenetrable. Unless someone had deep familiarity with the terrain, it was easy to get lost, turned around, and frustrated. Making matters even worse, the forest was home to caimans, anacondas, and jungle cats hunting for their next meal, and of course insects. Within hours of his escape, Pereira would have been covered in mosquito bites and possibly bitten by fire ants.[33] It was also June when, in the words of one eighteenth-century naturalist, the "rains became incessant."[34] Within hours of escaping from the *Rising Sun*, Pereira was probably trudging through the swampy morass that was the jungle during the rainy season, harassed by its flora and fauna.

Heijse had already enacted a plan to catch the fugitive. After returning the *Rising Sun* to the post, the corporal hired a posse of Amerindian warriors, offering them a bounty for capturing Pereira dead or alive. This party searched the forests near where the schooner had run aground. Records do not indicate how long the hunt took, but soon the warriors were on the mutineer's trail. They eventually found him.

FIGURE 5.2. A Kali'na or Carib warrior with his family. From John Gabriel Stedman, *Narrative, of a Five Years' Expedition, Against the Revolted Negroes of Surinam . . .* (London, 1796). Courtesy of the John Carter Brown Library.

When he spotted the search party, Pereira drew his knife, ready for a showdown. As the warriors surrounded him and closed in, the fugitive raised the blade. He did not fight, instead stabbing himself. The warriors, realizing Pereira was too "obstinate" to be taken alive, surrounded Pereira, restrained him, and ended the "Business" by "severing his Head from his Body."[35]

Between the initial apprehension of Da Costa and Lucas, their escort to Paramaribo, and the hunt for Pereira, Heijse had hired fifty Amerindians in his quest to capture and secure the mutineers. It cost him a small fortune, almost 440 guilders, to ensure the Kali'nas' and Arawaks' loyalty. While the Dutch generally maintained good relationships with the Indigenous people of the Wild Coast, hiring them posed certain risks. Heijse later sought compensation for himself, his soldiers, and his Indigenous allies from Suriname's authorities. He certainly exaggerated the danger of apprehending the mutineers, but his petition did express a very real concern. In hiring Amerindian warriors to assist him, Heijse placed his allies' lives in danger. Had one of them been harmed, it could blow back on the posthouder, not only hurting relations but perhaps even bringing conflict between the Dutch and their Amerindian allies. Heijse expressed this worry, using eighteenth-century racist stereotypes, that if one of the warriors had been hurt, the "beastly creatures" may have ended up attacking or harming Heijse and his men. Luckily for the corporal, this ended up not being the case.[36]

About the same time the search party returned to Heijse with Pereira's head, a crew dispatched by Governor Mauricius to sail the *Rising Sun* to Paramaribo arrived. Heijse joined the voyage and the ship journeyed to Suriname's capital, Pereira's head in hand, on 10 July (21 July NS).[37] Once the *Rising Sun* arrived along with confirmation of Pereira's death, Da Costa's and Lucas's trial could begin.

There was no doubt about the mutineers' guilt. During this time there was no presumption of "equality before the law" in the Dutch judicial system, and those accused of crimes were "tried and punished in accordance with their social status."[38] As lowly, foreign sailors who murdered a ship captain and wealthy merchant, the mutineers could not expect a fair hearing. They had no right to a lawyer and remained imprisoned in Fort Zeelandia's dungeon for the duration of the trial.[39] Rather, the entire process aimed to extract confessions and determine the appropriate punishment.

As such, the trial moved quickly, lasting only ten days, 13 to 23 July (OS). When the Court of Policy and Criminal Justice, Suriname's highest court that tried capital offenses, convened, jurists immediately interrogated Da Costa and Lucas and, after receiving their confessions, called on the rest of the *Rising Sun*'s surviving crew to testify. Despite the presumption of guilt, there was nevertheless a commitment to the judicial process. The court hired Moses Bassano, most likely one of the many Portuguese Jews living in Suriname, to translate during the mutineers' interrogation.[40] For the English crew, the court also hired a translator but also included the written English deposition in the case file. The court's clerk likewise recognized them as British subjects, allowing them to swear their oaths to tell the truth as they would in British courts.[41]

Da Costa's interrogation was first, on 13 July (OS). He answered all seventy-seven questions court officials asked him. At first the examiners asked Da Costa about his background, but the queries quickly turned to the case at hand. Almost none of these questions concerned motive but rather were aimed at figuring out which of the three mutineers devised the plan, who attacked whom, and their actions following the mutiny. He was also shown Pereira's head to confirm his identity. Knowing a similar punishment awaited him, the Portuguese man willingly confessed his crime and resigned himself to his fate. When asked if he thought he deserved to be executed for his crimes, Da Costa replied simply that regardless of his answer, the court was going to sentence him to death.[42]

Lucas's interrogation was the day after Da Costa's. Examiners asked him a similar set of questions, and this was when Lucas described being born a slave in Venice. When it came to answering who plotted the mutiny and how they murdered the other crew members, however, Lucas resisted and refused to answer questions or confess. Insisting that Pereira and Da Costa murdered the other crew members, he never implicated himself in the plot and eventually stopped answering questions. Indeed, of the seventy-five questions the judges drafted to ask the mutineer, Lucas answered only thirty-four. Court officials found Lucas's testimony frustrating and misleading. Following his interrogation, they sat him in the same room with Da Costa, forcing the former allies to confront one another and get the story straight. To further corroborate the joint interrogation, they used the initial testimony of Shaw and Blake as guidelines. It seems that after facing the overwhelming weight of evidence from his co-conspirator and two of the victims, Lucas did eventually confess.[43]

After the interrogations, there was a lull in the trial between 15 and 21 July (1 August NS). Perhaps the court had other business or was gathering the formal statements of Blake, Shaw, Deveries, and Jones. Although they had already offered oral depositions, they submitted their written testimony to the court on 21 July. It was an amalgamation, opening with Shaw's observations while he was on watch, ending with Blake saving Shaw's life, and signed by all four men. Like the interrogations of the mutineers, the testimony does not delve into the motive or even the aftermath of the mutiny. Rather, it provides a short account of the act itself, cataloging terror and violent death.

The crew's testimony was the final piece needed to obtain a guilty verdict. On 23 July 1743 (3 August NS), the court condemned the mutineers to death. Yet the men could not simply be executed. Pereira, Da Costa, and Lucas had challenged, subverted, and perverted what Dutch authorities—and European observers everywhere—believed to be the natural hierarchy of maritime life. Sailors, especially those who were not white, were at the bottom of the social order, and the actions of the mutineers threatened to overturn it. Their actions constituted a direct threat to shipboard life and, by extension, commerce itself. As such, they had "to be punished most rigorously for the protection of seafaring vessels."[44] It was imperative that the mutineers received an execution fit for their crimes.

After nearly a month of rumination, Governor Mauricius and Raad Fiscaal Jacobus van Halewijn decided on a method of execution. Authorities in Suriname wanted to not only execute Da Costa and Lucas but also make an example of them for all sailors. The execution would be as much about performance as about justice. It began on the very day that the Court of Policy and Criminal Justice handed down its sentence, 23 July (OS).

First, the governor ordered the *Rising Sun* to moor near Fort Zeelandia at the heart of Paramaribo's bustling town center. All ships in the river had been told to gather and their crews encouraged to watch the forthcoming spectacle. Next, the executioners, always Black and usually enslaved men in slave societies like Suriname, hung a yard—a wooden beam—on the main mast of the *Rising Sun*.[45] The two offenders, Da Costa and Lucas, were then brought up from the fort's dungeon, placed on the ship, "slung by the Armpits," and "hoisted up" onto the yard. After suspending the mutineers for a few hours in that position, the executioners approached the two men with "red-hot Pinchers" and began pulling off pieces of skin. They targeted the areas of the prisoners' bodies where they had stabbed Jackson, Ledain, McCoy, Skinner, Blake, and Shaw.

From there, the men were brought down from the yard and displayed on the deck to all those watching. The executioners then jammed a giant iron hook through each of the mutineers' rib cages. This was a common method of execution used in the Dutch colonies against enslaved people and other offenders. Attaching a rope to the end of the hook, the executioners hoisted Lucas and Da Costa up the yard again. There they would hang for an entire day. The pain was so excruciating that one of the two men, it is unclear who, died while suspended. On 25 July (OS), after nearly two days of torture, it was time for the formal execution. The executioners lowered the two men from the mast of the *Rising Sun*, took them into the town square, and beheaded them. They then burned the bodies and displayed the mutineers' heads as a warning to any sailor contemplating mutiny.[46]

FIGURE 5.3. Detail of Fort Zeelandia, the place where Dutch officials detained and interrogated Da Costa and Lucas and where the *Rising Sun* moored for the execution. From Frederik Jägerschiöld, *Gezicht op de Stad Paramaribo en het Fort Zeelandia* (1772). Courtesy of the Rijksmuseum, Amsterdam.

This account of the execution is not to reinscribe the terror and violence inflicted upon Da Costa and Lucas but is indicative of the logic of racial capitalism. Their suffering allowed them to become examples and to terrorize other sailors into compliance. Government officials, leading merchants, and ship captains believed such grotesque acts were necessary for commerce to properly function.[47]

Even before the executions, word of the mutiny began to spread. By early August, British American newspapers had picked up the story. From there, it spread to the corners of the English-speaking world. One of the chief storytellers was, unsurprisingly, Edward Tothill.[48] Tothill sent letters to merchant friends and probably the newly widowed Mary Ledain, Amey Jackson, and Jean McCoy in Boston. Instead of writing out the details himself, Tothill made a copy of William Blake's log that he attached to his correspondence.

Tothill wrote the letter he sent to Boston on 13 July (NS). Although the newspapers that published his letter did not reveal the author, To-thill gave himself away by describing George Ledain as "our good friend." The letter also contained a postscript discussing how Dutch authorities were at a loss of how to punish the mutineers, insider information that Tothill had.[49] Moreover, the merchant had direct access to Blake's journal. Tothill helped the mate and Shaw prepare their initial testimony and may also have translated parts of Blake's log for the court. Considering the sheer number of North American ships coming and going from Suriname, his letter probably departed shortly after he composed it and arrived in Boston at the end of July (OS).

The first two newspapers to print Tothill's letter were the *Boston Evening Post* and the *Boston Gazette*, on 1 August and 2 August (OS), respectively. They were the exact same article, extracted from Tothill's letter and Blake's log. The letter reported all the known details of the mutiny to that point, meaning, for readers in Boston, Pereira was still on the run and Da Costa and Lucas had not gone to trial. The story itself got basic facts wrong, calling George Ledain "Charles." The *Boston Gazette*, printed the day after the *Evening Post*, lifted the latter's article word for word. Mistaking Ledain's first name and plagiarism suggest an article hastily typeset. Tothill's letter probably arrived only a couple of days before the newspapers went to print, explaining the rush. Meanwhile, the *Boston News-Letter* printed a verbatim piece of Tothill's letter and most of Blake's journal on 4 August. The couple extra days gave the printer, John Draper, the time needed to print the longer version.[50]

Over the next two months, news of the mutiny trickled into Boston. Reports of Pereira's death came in the middle of August. The *Boston News-Letter* ran the story on 11 August (OS), while the *Boston Post-Boy*, which had not previously published anything on the mutiny, ran the exact same story on 15 August (OS).[51] At the end of September (OS), the *News-Letter* published the final article in the Boston press about the mutiny. It recounted the gruesome execution of the mutineers.[52] Whether Tothill supplied this information is unclear, but the continual appearance of articles in the Boston press suggests townspeople were following the story.

Meanwhile the articles published in Boston began to appear across the British Empire. The first newspapers to reprint stories of the mutiny were in Philadelphia on 11 August (OS), and they carried the story through the death of Pereira.[53] There seemed to be some interest in the story in Philadelphia, despite the victims not having connections to there. On the same day the *Pennsylvania Gazette* ran the story of Pereira's arrest, it also copied the version of Blake's journal from the *Boston News-Letter*.[54] Those same stories also crossed the Atlantic and appeared in the London newspapers beginning in late September and early October (OS). They were copies of the original article, with reference to George Ledain as "Charles" and all.[55]

As the Boston stories circulated, however, a second narrative emerged. First published in New York City's *New-York Weekly Journal* on 15 August 1743 (OS), like the initial article in Boston, it arrived in the form of a letter containing a copy of Blake's journal. Described as a "Letter from a Gentleman in Surenham to his Friend in New York," the document contains a much more detailed version of the log. Instead of just an "extract," the New York letter allegedly contains a "Melancholly Journal taken from a True Copy of the Mate's."[56] Yet at the end of the document, the names "William Blake, Mate" and "John Shaw, Boatswain" appeared.[57] The enclosed document in the merchant's letter was not Blake's journal but rather a copy of Blake and Shaw's initial testimony. It was most likely the document used against the mutineers during their interrogations.[58]

The document printed in New York differed from the news delivered in Boston. It is unclear whom the author of the letter was. Certainly, Tothill could have written the letter. He was from New York and maintained contacts in the city. Nevertheless, unlike the Boston letter, the author left no clue about having insider information. Tothill may have handled the testimony, but there were other British merchants working with colonial officials on the case who would have likewise had the opportunity to make a copy.

There was another difference that would have a lasting impact on interpretations of the case for the reading public. In all the articles printed in Boston and reprinted in Philadelphia and London, the mutineers were referred to as "three Portuguese Fellows" or "3 Portugueze Sailors" when discussing them collectively, while Pereira was described as the "Portugeze Villain" and Da Costa and Lucas as the "Two Portuguese who were guilty of the barbarous Murder."[59] The testimony reprinted in the *New-York Weekly Journal*, however, describes them simply as "three Portuguese Negro Sailors." Before this news article, the only references to the race of the mutineers were in the Dutch records. With the publication of this article, their alleged race appeared in print and in English for the first time.

Although this letter was the only account of the mutiny to appear in the New York press, it quickly circulated around the Atlantic. It was published in full in newspapers across England beginning in early November (OS).[60] That account, complete with its racial categorization, appeared shortly before the story of the execution, which British publications copied exactly from Boston newspapers.[61] Soon, however, the two stories blended. The *Gentleman's Magazine*, one of the earliest monthly news magazines, printed an account of the mutiny and execution in its November 1743 issue. In it, Da Costa, Lucas, and Pereira were the "Portuguese Negro Sailors" subjected to horrific violence. "Indians" beheaded Pereira, while Da Costa and Lucas faced gruesome torture and execution.[62]

Articles like the one that appeared in the *Gentleman's Magazine* did not just mash up facts. Rather, they served a cathartic purpose. Transforming the mutineers into "Negro Sailors" had great explanatory power. It helped British and British American readers, many of them merchants and ship captains, make sense of a seemingly senseless event. Instead of introspection about the ways in which Atlantic commerce consumed the bodies of slaves, sailors, and other working people, it explained away the mutineers' criminality by linking it to their Blackness. And the unimaginably grotesque, gratuitous "justice" served on Black bodies restored the "natural" order of the world—of government over subjects, captains over sailors, and white over Black.

These stories of the mutiny moved the voyage of the *Rising Sun* away from the reality of a routine smuggling voyage gone awry and into a story of inexplicable violence, brutal yet proper justice, and racial triumph. In doing so, the press obfuscated key questions about what actually happened. Jackson and Ledain were no longer part of an international slave and cacao smuggling ring that subverted trade laws and defied imperial authority. Instead, they became victims of a solitary voyage struck by horror and catastrophe. The press recast smugglers and slavers, who actually perpetrated racial violence, into victims. Meanwhile, fifteen enslaved people, who were never mentioned in the press, languished in the hold of a cursed ship, three men had been tortured to death, and four people, including a child, had been murdered. This was the true human toll of smuggling.

6

Aftermaths

Edward Tothill was probably annoyed by the execution. Certainly, he wanted to see justice served and may have even enjoyed watching the men who murdered his "good friend" George Ledain receive their comeuppance. Nevertheless, Governor Mauricius's insistence on spectacle impeded Tothill's ability to deal with the mutiny's fallout. It was up to him to salvage the schooner and its cargo, notify Gedney Clarke, the widows, and other business partners, and help resolve any questions and disputes over property. To ensure that happened, Tothill had to work within Suriname's legal structure, using the personal relationships he had cultivated with planters and local officials, while also drawing on his New England contacts. It was a delicate balancing act.

As Tothill helped spread word across the Atlantic, the survivors and family and friends of the victims had to deal with the aftermath of the mutiny. It is hard to fathom how the mutiny affected the individual lives and psyches of those involved. Legal records, account books, and business correspondence—the archive of this study—rarely convey emotion. Yet it is also difficult to reckon with the sheer tragedy of it all. The mutiny shattered families and communities, destroyed relationships, jeopardized livelihoods, and threw lives and futures into chaos.

Paramaribo was a small town, and Tothill was well connected. As soon as Blake and Shaw arrived on 26 June 1743 (7 July NS), he learned of the mutiny. The news of Ledain's death must have shocked Tothill. Heartbroken, the merchant felt duty bound not only to his friend but also to the newly widowed Mary Ledain. Since Ledain was part owner of the *Rising Sun*, he immediately requested the governor send a crew to recover the schooner.[1] In doing so, Tothill established himself as the go-to person for Dutch officials in regard to the case and the caretaker and executor of Ledain's interests in Suriname.

Tothill's desires, however, were more easily requested than achieved. Almost immediately, Governor Mauricius encountered problems with recovering the ship and its cargo. On 27 June (OS), the day after Blake and Shaw arrived with the mutineers, the governor complained about his inability to find a crew to go to Courantyne and retrieve the *Rising Sun*. Ship captains in Paramaribo were resistant, complaining that it would take upward of two months to complete the task. Even offering money and other incentives, including part of the ship's lucrative cargo, could not change their minds. Eventually, the governor found a captain willing to lend his ship and gathered individual sailors and others to man the vessel. Mauricius asked Tothill to select a British merchant to accompany the voyage. Although this merchant's name is never given, Mauricius wanted the ship and its cargo assessed according to British custom. By this point, the governor had to know that enslaved people were part of the cargo, either from Heijse's report or from his encounter with the *Rising Sun* the previous month. The governor did not promulgate any specific instructions about the captives but nevertheless prepared for the arrival of a ship full of contraband.[2]

When the *Rising Sun* arrived in Paramaribo eleven days later, an argument ensued between the governor and Jacobus van Halewijn, the Raad Fiscaal. Mauricius had gathered a small group that included himself, Halewijn, and two judges to determine the fate of the ship and its cargo. Halewijn believed that the ship should be seized by the government as a prize and sold for the benefit of the colony. According to Mauricius's account of Halewijn's arguments, the latter's position rested on two beliefs. First, since the mutineers destroyed the ship's papers and were not British subjects, authorities could not confirm the *Rising Sun* was actually a British ship. As such, they could legally seize the schooner without regard to commercial treaties between Great Britain and the Netherlands.[3]

FIGURE 6.1. Jan Jacob Mauricius, governor of Suriname. Cornelius Troost, *Portret van Joan Jacob Mauricius, Gouverneur-generaal van Suriname* (1741). Courtesy of the Rijksmuseum, Amsterdam.

Second, and more obliquely, Halewijn asserted that the *Rising Sun* was full of contraband and thus liable for seizure. In his own account of the discussions over the fate of the schooner, Governor Mauricius asserted he had "no doubt" that the ship was British and the cargo belonged to "British subjects."[4] Halewijn thought differently. The goods on board the *Rising Sun* were contraband, whether it was the cacao illegally exported from Suriname or the enslaved children, who were not allowed to be sold in Suriname from foreign ships. Now in the hands of the government, the contraband could be seized.

Technically speaking, Halewijn was right. Everyone in that council meeting knew that the *Rising Sun* had been illegally trading in Suriname before the mutiny. Indeed, Mauricius's argument that the ship was British rested on the fact that everyone knew Jackson and Ledain from their many voyages to Suriname.[5] Yet Mauricius chose where to look at the greater context of the case and where to follow the letter of the law. When it came to countering Halewijn's first argument, the ship was British because everyone knew the captain and supercargo, who were British subjects. As for the cargo, however, that belonged to British subjects and its legal status mattered only at the time of the mutiny, not at the time of purchase. It also meant that when it came time to sell the cargo, Dutch and British merchants could participate in the sale.[6] The other two council members warmed to the governor's argument and the *Rising Sun* was not claimed as a prize.

Halewijn did receive one concession, however. The Raad Fiscaal would be placed in charge of the ship and its cargo. To that end, an official inventory, overseen by Halewijn and other magistrates, was made. This inventory was the final word on the ship and its cargo and superseded the one created by Posthouder Heijse. Nevertheless, once again following his belief that the goods belonged to British subjects, Mauricius ordered three British subjects, two merchants and a ship captain, to assist Halewijn in taking the inventory. One of those merchants was Edward Tothill.[7]

It took three days to make the full, official inventory of the *Rising Sun* and its cargo. Halewijn exercised his powers over the cargo, seizing the gold and silver on board for safe keeping.[8] The government used it to pay the expenses of the case, including almost 940 guilders to Heijse and his men for hiring the Amerindian warriors, arresting the mutineers, and maintaining the ship at the Courantyne post.[9] This may have also been the moment when the decision was made, by whom and under what pressure is unclear, to enumerate the enslaved children as part of the ship's inventory. It was possibly a legal maneuver by Halewijn to disallow selling the enslaved children in Suriname (again). By the time the inventory was complete, Halewijn warmed to Mauricius's perspective on the matter and requested the governor lay out his arguments in a formal declaration. It is unclear what happened in the course of taking the inventory, but the Raad Fiscaal's acquiescence allowed the government to begin selling the ship's cargo.[10]

In the course of their debates and taking the inventory, Mauricius and Halewijn revealed many of the problems that officials confronted when dealing with illegal trade. If the men followed the colony's trade laws, Halewijn's argument about seizing the *Rising Sun* was correct. Yet in the course of taking the inventory, even he became convinced that the ship was not a prize and that Mauricius's course of action was best. There were a few factors at play. It cannot be ruled out that the men were on the take. There's a possibility that Mauricius turned a blind eye, perhaps bribed to do so, to the *Rising Sun*'s initial foray in Suriname, which made it imperative to continue doing so. Meanwhile, Halewijn spent days taking the inventory with Edward Tothill, who may have offered the Raad Fiscaal a cut of the proceeds from sale.

Even discounting malfeasance, it paid to ignore illegal trade. Had Suriname officials seized the ship, it would have had a chilling effect on commerce. Foreign trade, legal and illegal, was the lifeblood of Suriname's economy. To ensure a constant supply of foodstuffs, livestock, and other products, it behooved the government to allow smuggling. While this fact was true of any place where contraband trade was important to the local economy, the specific location mattered. Suriname was disease ridden and dangerous for Europeans and North Americans. In a place where British captains and crews regularly died of disease, seizing the *Rising Sun* established a bad precedent. Any time a captain died and there was any hint of contraband on board his ship, it was liable for seizure. Such a standard would have actively driven commerce away.

Although Halewijn did relinquish his prize claim, he nevertheless exercised considerable control over the sale of the cargo. For one, the enslaved children were not for sale. Moreover, while Mauricius allowed British merchants and ship captains to buy the goods, the Raad Fiscaal seems to have forced them to follow the colony's export laws. That meant certain commodities, such as sugar, coffee, and cacao, could not be legally exported outside of the Dutch realm. All three were on the *Rising Sun*, and British North American merchants bought them as part of the sale, presumably to take home.[11]

Edward Tothill, unsurprisingly, found a way to circumvent Halewijn. On 2 August (OS), Tothill reported to a local magistrate that he had loaded a ferry with seventeen barrels of sugar, nine barrels of cacao, and a barrel of coffee. Samuel Dowse, a New England ship captain, purchased them from the *Rising Sun*'s cargo. Tothill was merely a middleman in the transaction, in charge of moving the goods out of the custody of the Raad Fiscaal and to Martin Moulder, a Dutch ship captain in Suriname at the time. Moulder would then produce his papers to show Halewijn, transport the goods out of the colony, and sell them at his destination, presumably Amsterdam. If Tothill or Moulder were caught either transporting or selling the sugar, cacao, and coffee outside of the conditions imposed by colonial officials, the goods or proceeds from sale would be seized.[12]

In theory, it is completely possible that New Englander Samuel Dowse entrusted a Dutch ship captain, whom he may or may not have known, to sell commodities for him in Amsterdam.[13] More likely, it was a trick used by Edward Tothill to illicitly traffic the *Rising Sun*'s cargo

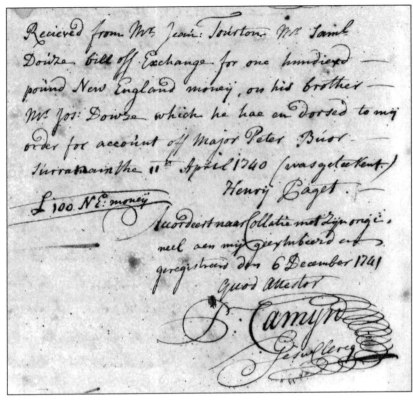

FIGURE 6.2. Copy, in English, of a 1741 bill of exchange drafted by Samuel Dowse for money taken from his brother Joseph's account with Providence, Rhode Island, merchant Henry Paget. Paget, who owed Joseph Dowse money, gave his permission for Samuel Dowse to draw 100 pounds "New England money" to cover the costs of goods in Suriname. Bills such as this one were common financial instruments and demonstrate how deeply interconnected the economies of Suriname and New England were. See 6 December 1741, Notarissen Suriname tot 1828, 1.05.11.14, inv. nr. 759, f. 87, NA Netherlands. Courtesy of the Nationaal Archief, the Netherlands.

out of Suriname. It is unlikely that after Halewijn inspected Moulder's paperwork anyone pursued the issue further. If they insisted on snooping, it was easy enough for Moulder to leave Paramaribo with the goods, rendezvous with Dowse at some prearranged location, and offload the cargo onto Dowse's ship. Halewijn may have created a few extra steps for contraband trading, but his enforcement mechanisms were largely toothless.

After nearly a month of selling the *Rising Sun*'s cargo, it was time to dispose of the schooner itself. There was never an attempt to sell the ship, although Dutch authorities did impound the vessel until almost all the cargo was gone. Of course, it was also the centerpiece in Governor Mauricius's theatrical execution of the mutineers. In early August, Tothill petitioned to obtain custody of the ship and hire a captain to return it to Barbados. Colonial officials believed returning the schooner was in the best interests of its owners, Gedney Clarke, Henry Lascelles, and Mary Ledain, and granted Tothill's petition.[14]

Although they agreed with Tothill, Dutch authorities placed stipulations on him obtaining custody of the ship. Most importantly, he had to have an inventory taken, which was conducted the following week.[15] Tothill's thoughts on having to take yet another inventory are unclear, although it did document the state of the ship, its estimated value, and the number of enslaved people on board.[16] Shortly after having the inventory taken, Tothill hired Boston captain John Tufton Mason to pilot the ship to Barbados. On 19 August (OS), Mauricius granted Mason permission to leave and the *Rising Sun* departed for Barbados.[17] Shaw, Jones, Deveries, and Blake, if he was still alive, left with the vessel.

Throughout the entire process, the enslaved children were still aboard the *Rising Sun*. There is next to no evidence of their experience, but it must have been harrowing. More likely than not, they would have been forced to remain in the hold of the *Rising Sun* after the mutiny and while the ship moored at the post on the Courantyne. They spent weeks in the hot, stuffy schooner, perhaps occasionally being allowed up on deck or onshore to breathe fresh air and exercise. Deveries and Jones would have cared for them while awaiting passage to Paramaribo, but provisions would have been in short supply. Jackson prepared for a three-week voyage, and even with a reduced crew, food and water would have run low. The postholder provided some victuals, but he was dependent on faraway supply lines and trade with Amerindians.[18]

Uncomfortable, already in poor health, and now on limited rations, the captives aboard the *Rising Sun* suffered. A few may have perished in the squalid conditions, leaving the possibility that there were more enslaved people aboard than were later inventoried. They were then taken to Paramaribo, subjected yet again to more time at sea. Once they arrived in the capital, they remained detained in the belly of the cursed vessel. The Raad Fiscaal feared the captives would be sold as contraband, and Mauricius sent soldiers to secure the vessel and its human cargo.[19] By the time of the execution, however, they had probably been moved on land, perhaps in the custody of Halewijn or held, under supervision, on one of Tothill's properties. The captives were entirely at the mercy of colonial officials and Tothill. Once the merchant sorted everything out, he had the terrified captives assessed, inventoried, and sent back to Barbados. Their ordeal continued.

When the *Rising Sun* departed Suriname in mid-August 1743, there were eighteen or nineteen survivors on board. It is unclear if William Blake was still alive. The last time he appeared in the records was when he signed the written testimony offered by the crew on 21 July. Had he lived, he, along with John Shaw, would have assisted John Tufton Mason. From there, he probably finished healing and looked for work as a ship's officer. The two "Lads," Josiah Jones and Henry Deveries, likewise disappeared, although Deveries married in Boston in 1746.[20] They probably returned to New England and, now with a bit of cash in their pockets, began building their futures. Young men like them often returned to the sea for at least a few more years. Now experienced and hardened seamen, they earned better wages. The mutiny, however, may have proven to be a bit too much adventure, and they could have retired to land, using their wages to establish themselves in a trade. It is easy to imagine the mutiny and the violence they witnessed haunting them for the rest of their lives.

Unlike the other surviving crew members, there is more documentation about John Shaw. Once the *Rising Sun* reached Barbados, Gedney Clarke wrote a letter to the Lascelles, which no longer survives, explaining what happened. Shaw probably supplied most of the information to Clarke. In their response, the Lascelles heaped praise on the boatswain, agreeing with Clarke "that honest John Shaw ought to be rewarded." They promised to "recommend him to the utmost of our power to be considered for what he has done." In the minds of Clarke and the Lascelles, Shaw was the hero, saving the *Rising Sun* and its cargo from certain theft and possible destruction. He proved his loyalty.[21]

After the discussion of his service, however, Shaw disappeared from the records for nearly two decades. Then, in January 1763, a curious entry appeared in the land grants for the Dutch colony of Essequibo. A "John Shaw" conveyed all but one acre of the land he owned on Vlaggen Island to William Vernon.[22] John Shaw was a landowner in the colony where he "had been Severall Voyages."[23] Most likely, Shaw's reward for his loyal service to Clarke was to become one of the merchant's agents on the Wild Coast. As Clarke's investments in the region grew, he could use someone like Shaw, who had knowledge of Essequibo, spoke Dutch, and could be trusted. The position paid well, offering the opportunity for Shaw to purchase land and enslaved Africans of his own.[24] Why he sold the land in 1763 is unclear, although land prices in Essequibo increased dramatically in the 1760s and Shaw may have been looking to retire.[25]

The remaining survivors on board the schooner were the captives: thirteen children and two young adult men. Once they arrived in Barbados, most of them were probably sold without being given time to convalesce.[26] At this point, the captives were probably in poor health. In the crass logic of slavery, they were a depreciating asset. If Clarke spent money on doctors, provisions, and lodging while they recovered, they may have been a little more valuable. Nevertheless, there was a serious chance of death after being crammed in a ship's hold for over three months. Clarke had to sell them as fast as possible.

Of the fifteen enslaved people aboard the *Rising Sun*, there are clues about their possible fate following the mutiny. Two pieces of evidence suggest a situation where Clarke attempted to offload the enslaved people onto others far away. The first is the presence of an enslaved man named Frank in Jackson's probate account and whom Amey Jackson sold to settle Newark's debts. Amey and Thomas Greenough, Jackson's other executor, recorded the sale of Frank, a "Negro man rec'd from Barbadous."

Most likely, Frank was one of the young adult men aboard the *Rising Sun*. Clarke possibly sent Frank to Amey Jackson to help settle his account with Jackson. After all, Clarke owed Amey Jackson her husband's wages plus whatever was in his private venture. Sending Frank was a nod toward the money owed. Amey was able to quickly sell Frank in September 1743 for 115 pounds of Massachusetts currency, or, given how depreciated that currency was, about 21 pounds sterling.[27]

The other piece of potential evidence concerns one of the enslaved girls from the *Rising Sun*, whose name is unknown. Clarke sent this girl to Robert Hooper, a merchant in Marblehead, Massachusetts.[28] In March 1743, Hooper wrote Clarke asking the Barbadian to send him a "negro Girle 11 or 12 Years Old," preferably direct from Africa, to work in his household.[29] Clarke seems to have ignored Hooper's request for a few months, but the merchant continued asking.[30] Finally, sometime in September or October, Hooper received an enslaved girl from Clarke. But she "dy'd in 16 hours after she came to my house." Hooper attributed her death to a lack of "propper Care on board" the ship that delivered her.[31] Perhaps Hooper was right. The child could have died due to neglect on the voyage from Barbados to Salem. Nevertheless, the timeline suggests an alternative possibility. Clarke, having been nagged for months by Hooper, saw an opportunity to offload one of the children from the *Rising Sun*. After noting the girl's death, however, Hooper never mentioned her again. Instead, he requested another enslaved girl for his household in early 1744.[32]

As Clarke dispersed property and decided what to do with the enslaved children, the widows, Jean McCoy, Amey Jackson, and Mary Ledain, began picking up the pieces of their shattered lives. Little is known about the fate of Jean McCoy, but there is considerably more information about Amey Jackson and Mary Ledain. Both of their husbands had been men of standing, providing comfortable lives for Mary, Amey, and their children. They lived in nice homes furnished with fine mahogany and walnut furniture, dressed in the latest London fashions, and consumed exotic goods like coffee and chocolate.[33] The children could expect a comfortable upbringing with access to good careers for the boys and good marriages for the girls. Now, all of that was in danger.

Being a widow was not that unusual in eighteenth-century Boston. Large numbers of Massachusetts men perished in shipping disasters, like that which befell Jackson and Ledain, and imperial conflict, leaving hundreds of women husbandless. By the early 1740s, nearly 15 percent of the women residing in Boston were widows.[34] Widows were often left destitute, and it is possible Jean McCoy was. For women like Amey Jackson and Mary Ledain, whose husbands were moderately prosperous, however, widowhood offered opportunities. Once widowed, women were free from the laws of coverture, which, among other things, prohibited them from owning, buying, or selling property without their husband's permission. If a husband and wife had prepared for the man's premature death, the newfound freedom would allow the woman to use her husband's estate to become an independent entrepreneur or attract a new husband.

Newark and Amey Jackson did not prepare. Although Jackson wrote a will before departing on a voyage in 1738, it was five years out of date by the time of the mutiny.[35] In that space of time, he and Amey had two more children, overextended themselves in business, and sank deeply into debt. Amey had to sell almost all the family's property to cover Newark's debts. It took nearly two years to pay off Jackson's creditors.

About the only valuable property left to Amey and children was some of the real estate Jackson purchased in Boston's North End, which was still in the family in the early 1770s.[36] Left without assets, Amey seems to have struggled financially for most of the 1740s, eventually letting the lease on the family's pew at Christ Church expire—along with the status that pew ownership brought.[37]

After selling the family pew, the Jackson family tried to move on. Amey was able to protect the family real estate and settle Newark's debts, but it is unclear if she kept making and selling chocolate. In December 1753, she remarried, this time to a David Gardner, most likely a merchant in Boston.[38] As for the children, Amey Jr. possibly married in 1758, while Newark Jr. never appeared again after his baptism, suggesting he may have died young.[39] Elizabeth Jackson, Newark and Amey's oldest daughter born in 1738, relocated to Newburyport, Massachusetts, and married once she reached adulthood. Her husband was a local merchant, Isaac Walker. In January 1769, the couple welcomed a little boy to the world, Newark Jackson Walker.[40] Outside of legal documents dealing with the estate, the boy's birth was the first mention of his grandfather since the mutiny in 1743, suggesting that, more than twenty-five years later, the memory of Jackson lived on.

Mary Ledain fared better in the short term. The Ledains were wealthier than the Jacksons and had money on hand, allowing Mary to navigate the legal system. George Ledain died intestate, meaning he did not leave a will. Often, the court appointed widows to manage an intestate husband's estate.[41] Along with shipwright Benjamin Hallowell and blacksmith Samuel Jackson (no relation to Newark), Mary posted bond and the court recognized her as an administrator. She now had control of important decisions regarding her murdered husband's affairs.[42] And unlike Amey Jackson, those decisions were less influenced by nagging creditors and more in the best interests of her family. Mary Ledain had to take out an advertisement in the newspaper for the exact opposite reason as Amey Jackson. She posted notice for all the people indebted to her husband.[43]

Although she wanted to collect from her husband's debtors, the most immediate issue was the fate of the *Rising Sun*. Since Ledain was an owner of the schooner, part of the ship and a significant portion of its cargo now belonged to Mary Ledain. Had George Ledain's relationship with Gedney Clarke been strained, the widow would have surely known about it. Obviously, Mary Ledain sided with her husband and did everything in her power to claim what was rightfully hers.

At the very least, Mary Ledain distrusted (and disliked) Gedney Clarke. After the mutiny, Clarke entrusted Boston merchant Edward Bromfield to help settle his accounts with Ledain. After months of jostling with Mary Ledain through Bromfield, Clarke was still "not Satisfied" with the state of their affairs. For serving as Clarke's messenger, however, Bromfield became a target for Mary's vitriol. In response to Clarke's complaints about how long the settlement was taking, Bromfield announced he had chosen "not to have any thing [more] to do in the Settlement of Mrs. Ledain's acct." "I am so old," the merchant continued, "I scarce know how to deal with a Woman especially one of so much Spirit."[44] Bromfield was forty-eight.

Not only was Mary Ledain obstinate in dealing with Clarke, she had Edward Tothill's assistance. From the moment he heard about the mutiny on the *Rising Sun*, Tothill "implored commiseration for [Ledain's] widow."[45] In all of his petitions and discussions of the *Rising Sun* and its cargo, he never referenced Clarke until asking to release the ship to its owner in Barbados in early August 1743, over two months after the mutiny.[46] By that point, Tothill had already notified Mary Ledain. It seems at the same time Tothill sent his letter to Boston that was later published, he also sent separate correspondence (or perhaps the same letter) to Ledain's widow. She received the news the last week of July 1743 (OS). On 4 August (OS), she posted bond and the probate court recognized her as administrator of her husband's estate. The following day, she signed over her power of attorney to Edward Tothill. Whether Tothill requested this in correspondence or Mary did it of her own volition is unclear. Nevertheless, she explicitly instructed Tothill to deal with the "Schooner . . . and Cargo and all Papers and writings relating thereto and acquittances . . . for Me."[47]

Although Tothill had already dispatched the *Rising Sun* to Barbados by the time he received Ledain's power of attorney, he acted in the deceased supercargo's interest from the beginning. Doing so brought him into conflict with Clarke. It is unclear if Tothill and Clarke had a preexisting relationship or if they knew each other only through George Ledain. Nevertheless, after the mutiny, Tothill placed the interests of his "good friend" and that friend's widow ahead of his acquaintance.

Much of the jostling between Clarke and Tothill centered on two related issues. The first concerned the insurance that Clarke, along with the Lascelles, purchased for the *Rising Sun* and its cargo. Henry Lascelles secured 1,500 pounds worth of insurance. Lascelles personally put in 500 pounds and found nine other underwriters, including Andrew Pringle, brother of Clarke's South Carolina business partner Robert Pringle.[48] When he learned of the fate of the ship and the cargo, Clarke wanted to file a claim. There were a number of problems, however. Clarke sold the *Rising Sun*, making it difficult to prove any damages it sustained. Likewise, the ship and its cargo were partially intact, requiring clear documentation of what had been lost and saved. Had it been lost entirely, it would have been easier to receive a payout.[49]

At first, the insurers refused to pay anything. Andrew Pringle in particular claimed that Clarke knew the risks and still had something—the schooner and the remaining captives—to show for the voyage. Likewise, the insurers contended the ship could not have been in that poor of condition if Clarke sold it.[50] Henry Lascelles had to get lawyers, including the attorney general of Great Britain, involved. They did little to help resolve the case but did cause the insurers to relent a bit, however, and they instead demanded evidence of the condition of the *Rising Sun*, desired specific details about how much of its cargo had been lost, damaged, or sold, and wanted to wait until any of the unsold "Effects are got away from Surinam."[51] It could take years to resolve the claim.

The second issue concerned the proceeds of the sale of the cargo. Not only would the insurers count the money made from the sale against the claim, but many of the goods Ledain purchased in Suriname had been consigned to the Lascelles in London. The mutiny, although certainly cutting into the proceeds, did not necessarily preclude the voyage from being profitable. Once they factored in an insurance payout, the mutiny may not have cost Clarke and Lascelles that much at all.

Of course, the only person positioned to provide evidence to the underwriters, deliver the proceeds of sale, and consign any unsold cargo was Edward Tothill. To make matters even more complicated, the insurers, including Henry Lascelles, appointed Jan Couderc, a merchant in Amsterdam, to work with Tothill. Tothill would send the paperwork and goods to Couderc, who would then dispatch them to Lascelles in London.[52] At first it seemed Tothill cooperated with Clarke and Lascelles. In December 1743, Lascelles reported to Clarke that he had received some "Dutch Papers" to present to the insurers.[53] After that, however, despite Lascelles constantly hounding Couderc, Tothill rarely sent documents and never any "Effects." It ground any attempt to profit from the voyage and make an insurance claim to a halt.

Between December 1743 and June 1745, Edward Tothill did little to assist Lascelles and Clarke. Reading between the lines of the Lascelles' correspondence, however, Tothill was still active in resolving the case of the *Rising Sun*—just not for Clarke. It seems that once Tothill received power of attorney from Mary Ledain, he began working in her favor. He continued assisting the Raad Fiscaal in the sale of cargo, while remitting money to Mary Ledain and probably keeping some for himself too. Only in June 1745 did Tothill finally write to the Lascelles (through Couderc). It was more promises of accounts, official documents, and bills of exchange for goods sold.[54] When the paperwork arrived a few months later, they were "such villanous accounts as no Man ever made up but himself." All told, Tothill promised to send over 2,400 pounds sterling, all from selling the *Rising Sun*'s cargo. Nevertheless, he only sent 880 pounds, in the form of bills of exchange, leaving over 1,500 pounds un-

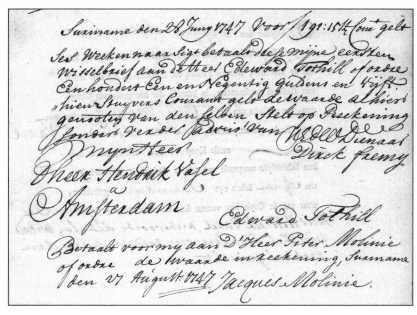

FIGURE 6.3. Notarial copy of a 1747 bill of exchange signed by Edward Tothill. The bill he sent to the Lascelles—through Jan Couderc—would have been similar. Notariële archieven, archiefnummer 5075, inventarisnummer 11311B, aktenummer 452046, Gemeente Amsterdam Stadsarchief, Amsterdam, the Netherlands. Courtesy of Gemeente Amsterdam Stadsarchief.

accounted for. Even with the amount he did send, however, Tothill gave "no orders" to Couderc to pay the Lascelles.[55]

More likely than not, much of that missing 1,500 pounds went to Mary Ledain. While Mary continued battling directly with Clarke over the fate of the *Rising Sun* and her husband's account more generally, including having a cask of "Worm Eaten Cocoa" foisted on her, Tothill helped her salvage her husband's portion (and probably more).[56] From the Lascelles' perspective, however, Tothill's actions were unconscionable. They believed he swindled them and Clarke out of the proceeds of the voyage. In their final correspondence with Clarke about the *Rising Sun*, the Lascelles were angry but powerless to do anything. Tothill, in their estimation, was "as much a Pyrate as the dogs who murdered the People and run away with the Scooner."[57]

In the end, Edward Tothill chose Mary Ledain over Gedney Clarke. He openly disregarded instructions to the advantage of Ledain's widow. It may have cost Tothill future business with Clarke, but by the mid-1740s Tothill had firmly established himself as a leading merchant and agent in Suriname. Ensuring Mary Ledain received what Tothill believed was rightfully hers was worth the cost of losing Clarke as a trading partner. It was the least he could do for his good friend.

Clarke, however, did not see it this way. Jostling with Tothill over the *Rising Sun* was just one of many commercial disputes Clarke had with New Englanders—his own "countrymen"—in the mid-1740s. Indeed, at the same moment Edward Bromfield was trying to settle Ledain's account for Clarke, he and the Barbadian were in an argument over a hundred-pound bill of exchange drawn on a London merchant firm. Bromfield won the dispute.[58] Meanwhile, some of Clarke's oldest business partners in Essex County, Joseph Swett and Robert Hooper, refused to sell rum Clarke consigned to them at his desired price.[59]

A decade after moving to Barbados, Clarke faced a stark choice. Although his family and business connections in New England presented opportunities, these were increasingly a liability. It was clear that the men he traded with put the interests of New England above those of Barbadian merchants and London investors. As the Lascelles began pouring thousands of pounds into Clarke's ventures and he forged relationships with leading planters and merchants in Barbados, Jamaica, Virginia, South Carolina, and the French and Dutch colonies, he questioned how worthwhile it was to maintain his relationship with New England. Certainly, he would help his family in Salem and maintain friendships.[60] His commercial interests, however, lay elsewhere.

When trying to balance the interests of his North American business partners and his West Indian and metropolitan connections, as was the case with the *Rising Sun*, Gedney Clarke ultimately favored the latter. He found himself caught in the middle of what would three decades later become a nasty imperial separation.[61] After Tothill outmaneuvered him,

Clarke never again engaged in ventures that required balancing the interests of New England and the West Indies. He still did business with New Englanders, just unilaterally. His decision to ultimately embrace Caribbean and London business partners was monetary. They had far more capital to invest in his enterprises.

And invest they did. In the years following the affairs of the *Rising Sun*, the Lascelles loaned Clarke thousands of pounds sterling. He used that money and his own wealth to begin purchasing land in Demerara and Essequibo. If he could not conduct business in Suriname without dealing with men like Edward Tothill, he could buy property in the neighboring colonies and build his own plantations. He already had built the trade infrastructure to traffic the enslaved Africans he needed to work the land. The best part was that doing so was not entirely illegal. The Dutch welcomed foreign, especially British, investors in these underdeveloped colonies. Much like the Suriname trade, once part of the venture was legal, the floodgates opened to all sorts of illicit commerce. By 1755, Clarke owned over eighty thousand pounds sterling worth of property in Demerara and Essequibo. Using his metropolitan connections and his access to land in Dutch colonies, Gedney Clarke became a "super merchant" and was one of the wealthiest men in the British Empire at the time of his death in 1764.[62]

Meanwhile, the illicit cacao trade continued. In many ways, the growing rift between the West Indian and North American colonies proved to be a boon to the chocolate market. While most of Gedney Clarke's and other British investors' plantations in Demerara and Essequibo grew sugar and cotton, they also produced cacao.[63] With cacao now being produced on land owned by British subjects, merchants could more easily circumvent the Navigation Acts and supply the British market. North American colonists, meanwhile, continued smuggling, purchasing contraband cacao in the Spanish, Dutch, and French colonies to ship home and sell abroad. Consumption across the British Empire, but especially in North America, increased dramatically in the decades before the American Revolution.[64] The mutiny on the *Rising Sun* was a minor glitch in the otherwise effective ability of illegal trade—and the immiseration and exploitation of others—to satiate the British Empire's sweet tooth.

The aftermath of the mutiny on the *Rising Sun* was largely about property relations. It was a question of who got what from the ship and its cargo. Much like other parts of this story, however, the rifts that emerged between the parties involved ultimately reveal the relentless rise of racial capitalism. Regardless of the individual fallout, the chocolate trade continued to grow and develop. Business squabbles did not disrupt the trade's core logic. The production, dissemination, and sale of chocolate not only was built upon ever-shifting networks and partnerships but also relied upon the exploitation of Black and Brown bodies. Certainly, that was apparent on the brutal plantations of the Wild Coast where thousands of enslaved Africans toiled in deadly conditions. Yet it was apparent in subtler ways as well: hiring Amerindian warriors to capture runaway slaves or mutineers, recruiting free men of color to work on board ships. And when those sailors resisted, the state violently suppressed and gratuitously executed them. The violence at the heart of racial capitalism ensured a steady supply of chocolate and the ability to deliver it to market. Disputes between the *Rising Sun*'s various stakeholders—owners, investors, and ship's officers—then, were ultimately battles over the spoils of an exploitative system.

Epilogue

Reckoning

In spring 2013, a new and curious historical attraction appeared on Boston's famed Freedom Trail. Called Captain Jackson's Historic Chocolate Shop, the site, located in the eighteenth-century Clough House behind the Old North Church in Boston's North End, offered visitors the opportunity to learn about the history of chocolate in early America. It was part of a larger mission of the Mars Wrigley Confections Company, especially the late Forest E. Mars Jr., to tell the history of chocolate. With Mars's backing, the Old North Foundation, which interprets the Old North Church's history for the public, embarked on opening the shop and developing a program exploring the history of chocolate. The site became an important piece of the foundation's mission to interpret Boston's colonial history.

In addition to operating Captain Jackson's, the Old North Foundation tells the history of the Old North Church, known as Christ Church in the eighteenth century and where Newark Jackson, George Ledain, Edward Tothill, and William Wingfield were parishioners. Central to the foundation's mission are the themes of "freedom, liberty, and civic engagement."[1] Interpreting those themes largely centered around the church itself, which was made famous on 18 April 1775 during Paul Revere's Midnight Ride. Lanterns were hung in the window of the church's steeple to signal to Revere and his associates the way British soldiers would be moving out of Boston the following morning—one lantern if soldiers were going over land and two if by sea. The first shots of the American War of Independence were fired the next morning, 19 April 1775. Old North played an important role in the events leading to that

Figure e.1. Sign for Captain Jackson's Historic Chocolate Shop. Courtesy of Getty Images.

moment and has been understood—and interpreted—as a shrine of American liberty ever since. All the while, it is still a functioning Episcopal Church—the American successor to the Anglican church—with an active congregation.

Expanding into the chocolate business strained the Old North Foundation's interpretative themes somewhat, but the shop still offered the opportunity to explore Boston's history for the millions of tourists who travel to the city every year. But what to name the shop? The foundation, looking to connect the chocolate program with the larger historic site, browsed their records to see which, if any, eighteenth-century parishioners had been chocolatiers. There they came across the name Newark Jackson. Certainly there were other members of Old North who made chocolate, but something about Jackson's name rolled off the tongue.[2] And Jackson's occupation as a ship captain offered a title to add some heft—and more than a little schmaltz—to the shop's name.

The Old North Foundation did their due diligence in researching Jackson, hiring a professional genealogical firm to research the captain and his life. All told, they confirmed that Jackson was a mariner and had sold chocolate. They also found details about his family life and an—at least at the time—alleged story about him being murdered in a mutiny off the coast of Suriname in 1743. Satisfied with the research, the foundation proceeded to open the shop and even placed an educational plaque on the pew (number 13) inside the church that Jackson owned in the early 1740s.

Fast-forward three years. By 2016, Captain Jackson's was a popular attraction on the Freedom Trail. But new details began to surface as the foundation, especially the educational and interpretive staff, became more curious about the namesake of their historic chocolate shop. Despite their initial work unearthing Jackson's will, researchers did not examine the inventory or accounts taken of Jackson's estate following his death. Those records revealed that Jackson owned slaves.

One of the burning questions about Jackson since the shop opened was where he acquired the cacao to make chocolate. This is where I entered the picture. Inadvertently, my first book, *Unfreedom: Slavery and Dependence in Eighteenth-Century Boston*, uses Jackson as an example of a slaveholder. When the foundation invited me to give a talk in September 2016, they asked me about Jackson and the enslaved people he owned. My response was "who?" I had forgotten that I used Jackson's probate inventory in my book, seemingly picking it at random among the more than 650 inventories of slave owners I had cataloged.

Nevertheless, the question opened a conversation about Jackson as an enslaver and merchant. Had Jackson been murdered off the coast of Suriname in 1743, that would point to the possible source of his cacao. I sent an email to Karwan Fatah-Black, a historian at Leiden University in the Netherlands and specialist in the history of Suriname. Almost immediately, Professor Fatah-Black, whose first book examined the intertwined history of smuggling and slavery in Suriname, found records of Jackson smuggling to and from the Dutch colony. We then knew where the cacao came from.

A few days after my initial correspondence with Professor Fatah-Black, I received a follow-up email with the subject "Murder!" I had mentioned the alleged mutiny, and he found evidence in the journal of Governor Jan Jacob Mauricius that it had indeed occurred. He later discovered that the mutineers had been put on trial, creating a record of the crime and its aftermath.

The recovery of the trial records suggested that there was much more to the story of Newark Jackson and the mutiny on board the *Rising Sun*. The Old North Foundation secured a second Forrest E. Mars Jr. Chocolate History Research Grant from Mars Wrigley Confectionery and a smaller one from the U.S. National Park Service to further this research. I was the principal investigator on the grants and hired a multinational team of researchers to dig into archives in New England, the Netherlands, Barbados, Great Britain, and Suriname. Tracing the people involved in the trial, we unearthed a smuggling ring that illegally trafficked cacao out of Suriname. The research also increasingly decentered

Newark Jackson, moving him from the middle of the story to the role of a hired captain at the whims of his employers, the ring's organizers, George Ledain and Gedney Clarke.

Yet the biggest surprise came in fall 2018. Ramona Negrón, the project's researcher in the Netherlands, found the inventory taken of the *Rising Sun* following the mutiny as Edward Tothill prepared to send it back to Barbados. In that inventory were the fifteen enslaved people, mostly children. The discovery was a game changer. This smuggling ring not only traded illegally but also bought and sold people. Captain Jackson was no longer a quaint chocolatier. He was a human trafficker.

Jackson's ownership of enslaved people posed some problems for a foundation whose central mission was interpreting the history of American liberty, but slave trading was an order of magnitude worse. From the beginning of the research into Jackson, the Old North Foundation had been open, honest, and willing to show Jackson's entanglement with slavery. Staff updated signage in the shop to recognize Jackson owned enslaved people, including printing their names, while acknowledging his role as a smuggler. It worked well, allowing the site to use the history of chocolate to open up a larger conversation about slavery and illegal trade in colonial America. But to have a site named after a man who trafficked children?

The answer was no. After extensive soul-searching and discussion with various stakeholders at Old North—the Foundation, current parishioners, and the community, among others—including public forums and numerous board meetings, the Old North Foundation decided to act. In fall 2019, the Foundation removed the plaque from pew 13. Then, on 13 November 2019, the board voted to remove Jackson's name from the chocolate shop entirely.[3] Yet in renaming and reformulating the historic chocolate shop, they decided to center the history of slavery and smuggling found in the records generated by Jackson's death. As Catherine Matthews, the Old North Foundation's education director, described at the time, "It's our responsibility to tell the story—all of the story—that relates to our site and history."[4]

In the middle of wider conversations about race, justice, and the legacy of slavery in the United States today, the Old North Church and Foundation are reckoning with their own history. As the nation wrestles with a more complicated yet complete understanding of its past, sites like Old North will be at the forefront of interpreting that history for the public. While historical documents, such as those created by the mutiny on the *Rising Sun*, open doors and create possibilities to confront the past, the way those histories are told and how they are presented is a conversation for the present. Simplistic stories about "freedom" and mythical conceptions of "liberty" cannot withstand the burden of historical reality. Slavery, slave trading, and illegal commerce are just as much part of Old North's history as that fateful night in April 1775.

Nevertheless, uncovering that historical reality is not always easy. We know so much about Newark Jackson and the *Rising Sun* because of a blip. A fluke. A contingency. Had three men not committed murder, this journey, like so many other smuggling runs, would have been largely unrecorded. Maybe there would be a few account book entries when Jackson, Ledain, or Clarke sold the cacao. Clarke might have sent a letter or two to the Lascelles about a successfully completed voyage. A customs official, himself possibly on the take, may have recorded the arrival of the ship in Barbados. Those documents, however, would not reveal the enslaved people. The sailors were an afterthought. Even Blake and Shaw might have gone unnoticed. Entire human lives erased by the dictates and rhythms of routine, albeit illegal, Atlantic commerce. But this voyage was not routine.

Significantly, the mutiny created records that show how important smuggling was to not only the economy but also the society, politics, and culture of early America. The mutiny occurred on one of thousands of voyages in a world of illicit trade. Whether in Boston, Barbados, or Suriname, entire lives revolved around the trade in contraband. And sometimes part of those lives meant *being* contraband. Because if smuggling is key to understanding the American colonies, slavery was equally, if not more, significant. The case of the *Rising Sun* shows how these two early American institutions intersected. Without slavery, many of the commodities that incentivized illegal trade would have been unavailable in the quantities that made smuggling profitable. Slavery also contributed to the dynamism of contraband trading, facilitating the trade in new products and helping transform what had been luxury goods into everyday consumer products. That was certainly the case with chocolate, one of the main products traded by Ledain and Clarke's smuggling ring. In that sense, smuggling literally had the ability to define and refine tastes.

At its most basic, however, the case of the *Rising Sun* shows how smuggling and slavery positioned early Americans in the wider world. Whether it was investors, slave traders, planters, or consumers, the smuggling ring, despite revealing rifts and intraimperial conflict, also had a binding effect on the British Empire. It provided cacao and other products to consumers, while ensuring markets for African captives and salt cod. What is most fascinating, however, is that it reveals the deep entanglement with places beyond Britain, the British West Indies, and the future United States.[5] For a case that had repercussions in the Anglophone world, Dutch authorities in Suriname created those consequences. Cascading out from Fort Zeelandia, in the heart of a colony where British subjects were largely forbidden, were a series of decisions that affected lives in Boston, Barbados, and London.

And what of those lives? When Ferdinand da Costa, Joseph Pereira, and Thomas Lucas seized control of the *Rising Sun* and William Blake and John Shaw fought back, their actions opened a window on a world that contemporaries deliberately and emphatically shut. That open window allows us to reconstruct a smuggling ring and examine the people who, willingly or unwillingly, participated in it. There was a captain seeking his fortune and stability, a merchant facing the Herculean task of managing and maintaining an illicit trade network, young men at sea for the first time, and seasoned sailors, marginalized as racial and ethnic others and hardened to the terrors of seafaring life. And there were fifteen young captives, stolen from their homeland, largely erased from the records, and pawns in everyone else's game. Nearly three centuries later, the case of the *Rising Sun* reveals not only illegal commerce, but also a deeply human history. It is a story of ambition, greed, coercion, desire, and, ultimately, tragedy.

ACKNOWLEDGMENTS

All works of history are collaborative endeavors, but that is especially true of this book. Without the patient assistance of so many different people from so many walks of life, this book would not have been possible. Scholars, public historians, librarians, archivists, and business professionals from three different continents contributed to making this book a reality. Nevertheless, all errors and mistakes remain mine alone.

My foray into this project, detailed in the epilogue, was unusual. Historians tend to start projects with intriguing questions about historiography or an amazing gem discovered in a dusty archive. This book, however, started with a public talk I gave at the Old North Church. While there, I learned about the Old North Foundation's work on Newark Jackson and the history of chocolate. The staff's questions about Jackson's life and world became something of a fascination for me, and their invitation to work with them on answering those questions has been a highlight of my career. Special thanks to retired vicar and former executive director Steve Ayres, former director of education Erin Wederbrook Yuskaitis, director of education Catherine Matthews, director of operations Pamela Bennett, and executive director Nikki Stewart. All of Old North's staff deserve praise for their willingness to confront, interpret, and ultimately tell the history, warts and all, of Old North's connections to smuggling, slavery, and the slave trade.

Making much of this research possible were generous grants from the National Park Service and Mars Wrigley Confectionery. Mars, especially, provided timely assistance, in the form of a Forrest E. Mars Jr. Chocolate History Research Grant to the Old North Foundation. These funds allowed me to hire a multinational team of researchers to gather documents, translate them, and build an archive for Old North's use. At Mars, Dave Borghesani, Kelly Lynch, and Gail Broadright deserve acknowledgment for their support of this project and, along with Valerie Donati of Building Brands Communications, an invitation to present some of this research at American Heritage Chocolate's 2019 annual conference. Dave, especially, has proven to be a steadfast booster of all things related to the *Rising Sun*, and for that I cannot thank him enough.

One of the most rewarding parts of writing this book has been the opportunity to work with gifted young historians who served as the project's research assistants. In Boston, Michael Bailey read and reread (and sometimes read for a third time) thousands of manuscript pages at multiple repositories looking for evidence of the *Rising Sun*. He found incredible material that was vital for piecing together much of the story presented here. Michael is a gifted researcher with an astute mind, and his detective work across such a fragmented archive made for a more complete story. In addition, Susannah Deily-Swearingen conducted research for the project at the Phillips Library and uncovered more about Gedney Clarke's connections to Essex County, Massachusetts. Annie Avila came to the project a bit later and helped edit and compile the manuscript, especially appendix II.

It would be criminally negligent not to acknowledge Ramona Negrón, my research assistant in the Netherlands. To call Ramona a research assistant, however, dramatically undersells the support she provided. At every stage of this project, from gathering documents across the Netherlands to hunting down random eighteenth-century merchants and planters to translating often-arcane eighteenth-century Dutch to helping gather images for the book, Ramona did it all—and more. Her vast knowledge of the Dutch Atlantic and its archives, creativity, keen intellect, and intellectual curiosity have made a lasting impact. Most significantly, Ramona found the inventory listing the enslaved children and, with that discovery, changed the course of the project entirely. Because of her, I was able to write this book. With my deepest gratitude, thank you Ramona.

Many scholars helped me navigate the complicated and disparate subjects covered in this book, answered my often obtuse and obnoxious queries, provided welcome conversation around the project, and served as sounding boards for my ideas. Cátia Antunes, Richard Bailey, Tad Baker, Jerry Bannister, Aviva Ben-Ur, Richard Boles, Lissa Bollettino, Randy Browne, Trevor Burnard, John Collins, Jesse Cromwell, Sara Damiano, Natalie Zemon Davis, Mary Draper, Hannah Farber, Craig Gallagher, Alison Games, Lige Gould, Michiel van Groesen, Deborah Hamer, Stephen Hay, Mary Ellen Hicks, Erin Holmes, Bram Hoonhout, Richard Johnson, Marjoleine Kars, Wim Klooster, Lynn Lyerly, Allison Madar, Dennis Maika, Nicole Maskiell, Joanne Pope Melish, Margot Minardi, Tessa Murphy, Paul Otto, Mark Peterson, Justin Roberts, Alan Rogers, the late Bill Rorabaugh, Annie Ruderman, Brett Rushforth, Rebecca Shumway, Sandy Slater, S. D. Smith, Randy Sparks, Jennifer Spear, Robert Waters, Amani Whitfield, and Gloria McCahon Whiting all deserve acknowledgment. Karwan Fatah-Black deserves special thanks. Not only did he introduce me to Ramona, but we also collaborated early in the project. Much of what I know about smuggling and slavery in Suriname is thanks to Karwan. Lige Gould and Julia Mansfield invited me and Karwan to present on Newark Jackson and smuggling at the McNeil Center's "Entangled Histories" conference in 2018. They offered a great venue for testing some of this book's key arguments. Johann Neem first offered the important insight that this story intersects with the rise of racial capitalism. Finally, Andrea Mosterman, Hunter Price, and Owen Stanwood need to be profusely thanked. Not only are all three "good friends," but they also read the full manuscript. Their excellent feedback made for a much better book even if I could not include a recommended *Law & Order*–style preface.

Knowingly or unknowingly, librarians, archivists, and museum specialists across the Atlantic world aided with this project. I would like to thank the dedicated staffs at the American Antiquarian Society; Baker Library at the Harvard Business School; Barbados Department of Archives; Barbados Museum & Historical Society; Borthwick Institute for

Archives at the University of York; Boston Athenaeum; Boston Public Library; British Library; George Washington's Mt. Vernon; Houghton Library at Harvard University; John Carter Brown Library; Library of Congress; Lincoln's Inn Library & Archives, London; Massachusetts Historical Society; Massachusetts State Archives; National Archives, UK; National Gallery of Art, Washington, DC; Netherlands Nationaal Archief; New England Historical Genealogical Society; New Netherland Institute; New-York Historical Society; O'Neill Library at Boston College; Phillips Library at the Peabody Essex Museum; Rhode Island Historical Society; Rijksmuseum, Amsterdam; Saint Louis Art Museum; Stadsarchief Amsterdam; Suriname Nationaal Archief; West Yorkshire Archive Service, Leeds; and Western Libraries.

Thanks to my colleagues at Western Washington University. Dean Paqui Paredes Méndez and Provost Brent Carbajal have created an environment for the humanities to thrive. In the History Department, all my colleagues and especially Emi Foulk Bushelle, Chris Friday, Steven Garfinkle, Johann Neem, Hunter Price, and Sarah Zimmerman have been supportive of this project and all the work I do. In my humble opinion, I work in one of the most dynamic history departments in the world and am blessed to call such a place my intellectual home.

This book has found a great home at New York University Press. Clara Platter is an editor par excellence. She saw potential in this project and helped shepherd it from a vague story about smuggling into something more significant. Everyone at NYU Press deserves recognition for crafting such beautiful and timely books. Likewise, the two anonymous readers of the manuscript provided constructive, thoughtful comments that helped clarify the importance of the mutiny on the *Rising Sun* for scholars and lay readers alike. Finally, Melissa Johnson deserves credit and profound thanks for compiling the index and helping to proof the book one last time.

I would be remiss to not thank my family for their support and interest in this project. The "chocolate book" is finally finished. My father, Robert Hardesty, and mother, Beth Ervin Hardesty, have always encouraged my academic endeavors. The same can be said of my in-laws, Don and Michelle Weigel. The book is dedicated to my grandparents, Robert and Janice Hardesty and George and Wanda Ervin. The stories they told are what caused me to fall in love with the past and imparted a desire to uncover more stories of those who came before.

Finally, there's Dana. From Boston to Bellingham, from college to COVID, she's been my rock, the love of my life, and my dearest friend. I count myself lucky to have found such a wonderful partner and wife. Seriously, she's the best.

APPENDIX I

On Circumstantial Evidence

Mutiny on the Rising Sun argues that the schooner's voyage from Barbados to Suriname was a clandestine slave trading voyage. There is no direct evidence that this was the case. Never once do the records mention that the ship carried a sizeable number of enslaved people to Suriname and that those captives who returned to Barbados were remainders. Nevertheless, circumstantial evidence demonstrates that Jackson, Ledain, Clarke, and Tothill indeed meant to sell African captives, along with other goods, in Suriname and Cayenne. Although I make this argument throughout the text, here are six exhibits of circumstantial evidence distilled and presented together:

1. In general, it was common to traffic captives from areas where there was extensive slave trading (like Barbados) to plantation areas that were underserved by the trade even if the law banned slave trading across imperial boundaries (which it did in both the British and Dutch cases). While Dutch authorities in Suriname liberalized slave trading, allowing for non–Dutch West India Company ships to provide captives, in 1738 and there was a small glut in the market at the time of the *Rising Sun*'s arrival, there were still issues with the supply of captives to Suriname. Indeed, the total number of arrivals declined in the 1740s compared to the previous decade.[1] Moreover, since the early eighteenth century, Barbados had economic problems stemming from soil exhaustion and lower crop yields, while the plantation economy of Suriname was rapidly expanding.[2] Merchants in Barbados, a center of the transatlantic

slave trade, could make good profits transshipping captives from there to elsewhere.

2. Gedney Clarke's commercial activities provide important context. From the 1730s through the 1760s, he was active in the inter-American slave trade. Within the British Empire, he sold enslaved people from Barbados to New York, Virginia, and South Carolina.[3] Later, Clarke purchased large plots of land in the Dutch Guianas. Using Barbados's position as a major slave trade hub, he illegally transshipped Africans to his plantations.[4] Illicitly trafficking captives to Suriname in the late 1730s and early 1740s was another iteration of these commercial endeavors.

3. There is a plausible counterargument that Jackson, Ledain, and Tothill purchased the enslaved children in Suriname to sell in Cayenne, Barbados, or New England. Nevertheless, earlier voyages undertaken by the smuggling ring suggest that was not the case. In the venture that William Wingfield undertook to Suriname and Cayenne, for example, Gedney Clarke and George Ledain both consigned enslaved people to be sold by the captain.[5] That does not include the general cargo of the voyage, which could have possibly included more enslaved people.

4. There was an insurance policy underwritten in London for the *Rising Sun*'s voyage from Barbados to Suriname. Slave trade voyages were highly risky and thus more likely to be insured than other types of ventures by the middle decades of the eighteenth century.[6] Nevertheless, the only details we have of the insurance policy come from the letters of Lascelles and Maxwell to Gedney Clarke. The Lascelles helped acquire and underwrite the insurance policy.[7] Like most marine insurance of the time, the policy was arcane, and it is difficult to glean information about what exactly the insurance covered or how the coverage worked.

One detail about the policy does stand out, however. Upon first learning of the mutiny and damage to the *Rising Sun*, the Lascelles wrote to Clarke with confidence that the insurers would pay the amount underwritten "after a deduction of the value in your hands on the sales of the Scooner & Negroes."[8] This quote suggests that the Lascelles believed the policy secured and recognized the value of the schooner and its cargo on board when it departed Barbados. It did not, then, cover future proceeds or goods purchased in Suriname. Called a "valued policy," this was a common type of insurance used in the slave trade and operated as a "kind of futures contract reflecting the expected sale price of enslaved people."[9] If it was a "valued policy," the reference to "Negroes" in the letter demonstrates that the initial cargo was composed, in part at least, of enslaved Africans, the remainders of whom would be sold and deducted from the payout.

5. The ship itself, while described as a schooner in most English documents, was described as a "barquetine or schooner" in the Dutch sources.[10] This confusion suggests that the *Rising Sun* was a "topsail schooner," which had two masts like most schooners, but square topsails like a barquentine. These helped the schooner handle better and move faster, especially when facing winds and currents.[11] Topsail schooners also tended to be larger than most other schooners, usually between 50 and 90 tons, and were staples of the West Indian trade (although probably built in New England).[12] Both bigger and faster than other ships, topsail schooners like the *Rising Sun* could carry large, diverse cargoes, including sizable contingents of African captives.

6. Two of the mutineers, Ferdinand da Costa and Joseph Pereira, were Lusophone (Portuguese-speaking) sailors. The third, Thomas Lucas, was from Italy, but spent most of his life at sea on Iberian, most likely Portuguese, ships. Even in the British Empire, these sailors were believed to have a special expertise in operating and maintaining order on slave trading vessels.[13] It is entirely possible the three men were veterans of the slave trade. British transatlantic slaving vessels had diverse, polyglot crews that included non-Anglophone sailors like Da Costa, Pereira, and Lucas.[14] Moreover,

Jackson hired them in Barbados, where it was common for slave ship captains to discharge sailors.[15] Jackson certainly needed crew members to help sail the *Rising Sun*. The fact he employed these three men, however, suggests that the *Rising Sun* had a payload of African captives and he required sailors with expertise in the slave trade.

APPENDIX II

Accounts of the Mutiny

Below are the several newspaper and magazine accounts of the mutiny on the *Rising Sun*, the testimony of William Blake, John Shaw, Josiah Jones, and Henry Deveries made during the trial, and the interrogations of Ferdinand da Costa and Thomas Lucas. The print accounts are arranged by the articles first printed in Boston,[1] followed by the long 15 August 1743 (OS) account—mostly a copy of the initial testimony offered by William Blake and John Shaw—in the *New-York Weekly Journal*, and ending with the story of the execution printed in the *Gentlemen's Magazine*. The *Gentlemen's Magazine* blends the 29 September (OS) *Boston Weekly-Newsletter* story of the execution with details from the *New-York Weekly Journal*.

Boston Evening Post, 1 August 1743 (OS)

By a Letter from Surinam, dated the 13th of *July* past, to a Gentleman here, we have the following very melancholy Account of the Murder of Capt. *Charles Ledain* and Capt. *Newark Jackson* of this Town, with two other Persons, on board a Schooner whereof Capt. *Jackson* was then Commander, and Capt. Ledain Merchant, about two Months ago. They took on board the Schooner at *Barbados*, three Portuguese Fellows as Seamen, and were bound from thence Cayan, but not many Leagues from *Surinam*, the *Portuguese* Villains rose in the Night, while most of the People were at Rest, and kill'd the Captains *Jackson* and *Ledain*, the Book-keeper, and Capt. *Jackson's* Boy, and wounded the Mate (*William Blake*) and the Boastwain, but spared their Lives with two Boys, to navigate the Vessel, which they ordered the Mate to steer for *Oronoque* River, there being Spaniards;

but these new Commanders not understanding Navigation, Mr. *Blake* went to Currentine, a *Dutch* Place, a little to Leward of Surinam, where two of the Murderers were secur'd and carried Prisoners to Surinam, but the other made his Escape on Shore, and was not taken when the Vessel came away by whom we have this Account.

Boston News-Letter, 4 August 1743 (OS)

Exact of a Letter dated, Paramaribo, (in Surranam) July 13th 1743.

> *L A S T Sunday, being the 7th Instant arrived here one of our Indian Men of War from* Currantine, *with two Murderers, the third daily expected; our good Friend* George Ledain *and* Newark Jackson, *with the Bookeeper makes the dismal Catastrophe; as appears by the Journal of the Mate Mr.* William Blake, *who came here with the Prisoners—*

Extract of the said Journal is as follows:

> *Thursday, May 31st 1743.* W E sail'd from the Fort of Surranam, being call'd Paramaribo. *June* 1st wooded near Bramspoint; then stood to the North-ward till 6 at Night (bound to Cayan) then tack'd and stood to the South-ward till 10 at Night; then tack'd and stood to the Northward; and at 11 o'Clock, as I lay in my Cabin asleep, I heard a great Noise, *Murder! Murder!* several Times:—The 3 Portugueze Sailors we had on Board (ship'd at Barbadoes,) having rose upon the Captain and Merchant, and stab'd them in their Cabins, as also the Merchant's Clerk: Whereupon I went upon Deck, and as I was going up the Ladder I was stab'd in the Shoulder. When I came upon Deck, I saw the Merchant Mr. Ledain lying in his Gore of Blood, and the Captain (Jackson) abast, crying, *I am dead! I am dead!* whereupon the Villains shove the Captain over-board: The Villains then went in search for the Merchant's Clerk, who was all the Time hid after they had stab'd him, and they found him in the Run of the Ves-

sel, whereupon they drag'd him up, and hove him overboard. They stab'd our Boatswain also in several Places, but did not quite kill him: They having sav'd alive two Lads we had on board, sent the Boatswain and my self down to their Cabins to dress our Wounds; After which, order'd us to steer for Oronoque, a Spanish Place that was to the Leeward of us.—Next Day they wash'd and scrap'd away every Place that had Blood, and threw all the bloody Cloathes over board, and still kept down along Shore.—*June 5th*, by God's Providence we carry'd them safe into Currantine, a Dutch Place just to the Leeward of Surranam, which we told them was Oronoque; we went 20 Leagues up the River, where we saw a House, at which they were all very glad; but when we went ashore, they found it was a Dutch House; whereupon our Boatswain, talking pretty good Dutch, told them our Condition; and we show'd them our Wounds; whereupon they said, that in the Morning they would secure them: But the Villians understanding that the Boatswain had told the Dutchmen of the Affair, when they return'd aboard with us again, were for heaving the Boatswain over board, but tho't best in the first Place to get up the Anchor; while they were doing which, the Boatswain (John Shaw) jump'd into the Boat and scul'd ashore; they having no Boat to go after him, cut their Cable and let her go, and so drove down with the Ebb.—About 3 leagues from the House they got Ground and lay there that Night.—Next Day got a Float and stood down, but soon got aground again, and lay there all that Night—Next Morning came the Boatswain, with Three Crafts, *viz* Two Canoes and our Boat to retake them, which accordingly they did.—Upon which, one Portugueze Negro jump'd over board & swam ashore; the other two were taken Prisoners and bound.—So we being delivered, Thanks be to God for our fate Deliverance out of the Hands of our Enemies!—The pretended Captain Ferdinando Coasta, who had assumed the Command of the Vessel, upon his being thus taken Prisoner was search'd, and a Bag of Gold and a Silver Watch found upon him; the other being also search'd, 7 Pieces of Gold were found in his Pocket.—We then sent to search after the Negro that was ashore but could not take him.—We then carried the Vessel up near the Dutch Man's House and came to Anchor, and then put the Prisoners under his Care; and he being bound to Surranam, the Boatswain and I went along with the Prisoners and delivered them to the Governour, &c.—The pretended Captain dressed himself (when he went ashore) with the Silk Cloaths, Wig and lac'd Hat of our unfortunate Merchant.–

The Gentleman that sent the above sorrowful Account, indicates in his Letter, that the Dutch Authority seem'd at a loss what Punishment to inflict on these Villains, suitable to their Barbarity.

Boston News-Letter, 11 August 1743 (OS)

Since our last we have Advice from Surranam, That the Portugueze Villain, concern'd in the barbarous Murder of Capt. Ledain, Capt. Jackson, &c. who swam ashore and made his Escape, as mention'd in our last, was discover'd by some Indians in the Woods; and upon their going to seize him, he was so desperate as to pull out his Knife, and by stabbing himself endeavour'd to put an End to his own Life: The Indians seeing him so obstinate, did the Business for him effectually by severing his Head from his Body. The Tryal of the other two was not come on.

Boston News-Letter, 29 September 1743 (OS)

From Surranam we hear, That the two Portugueze who were guilty of the barbarous Murder of Capt. George LeDain and Capt. Newark Jackson, as lately mentioned in this Paper, were condemned to die in the following manner, which was accordingly executed, *viz.* The Vessel in which the Fact was committed was ordered to be brought near the Town, and a Yard to be flung across her Mast, and as many Vessels as could conveniently come round about her to be brought with all their Crews; which being done, the Criminals were brought on board, and each of them being flung by the Arm-Pits, were hoisted up to each Yard-Arm; where, after having hung some Time, the Executioners, with red-hot Pinchers or Tongs, pull'd off Pieces of their Flesh; then they were unhung, and an Iron Hook put into each of their Sides, by which they were hung up again for Twenty-four Hours; at the Expiration of which Time, their Heads were cut off and their Bodies being buried, the Heads were put up at a publick Place, for a Terror to others: It is said one of them was alive when they came to cut off his Head.

New-York Weekly Journal, 15 August 1743 (OS)

Exact of a Letter from a Gentleman in Surenham, *to his Friend in* New York.

SIR,
You have here a Melancholly Journal taken from a true Copy of the Mate's, which happened to the Scooner Rising Sun, Newark Jackson, *Commander; Super Cargo, Capt.* George Ledain; *from Barbados, bound to the Island of* Cyanna; *but fell to the Leeward and arrived at* Surenham, *they refitted here, and proceeded on their intended Voyage, viz.*

WE Sail'd from *Surenham,* called *Paramarebo,* and put the five Soldiers on Shore, which were put on Board of us (not to land any of our Cargo) below at the New Fort at the River called *Cottica,* and the Fort *Amsterdam,* we expected to get no further that Tide, but the Wind sprung up, and Capt. *Ledain* said it would be better for us to proceed down from *Bram Point* to cut some Wood that we might go away that Night, but continued till next Morning, when we get some Wood on board, this was on the 1st of *June;* by 9 o'clock the Tide of Flood being done we weighed and drove out with the Ebb; at 12 o'Clock *Bram Point* bore S. by E. distance about 6 Leagues, we then stood to the North till 6 at Night, when we tacked and stood to the South till 10, then tacked again to the North, and at 11 o'clock as I lay in my Cabin a Sleep, I heard a great Cry; O Murder! Murder! several Times, I still being in a Dose; but awaking, to my great surprise, found that the three Portuguise

Negro Sailors that we had on board had risen upon the Captain and Merchant, and stabbed them in a most inhuman manner in their Cabins, as also the Merchants Clerk, whereupon I was coming upon Deck, and ascending the Ladder I was stabbed in the Shoulder; when I came upon Deck I saw the Merchant weltring in his Blood upon Deck, and the Capt abast crying, I am Dead, I am Dead, whereupon the Villains hove him overboard first, and then the Merchant; the Apprentice Boy being affrighted went up the Shrouds but they soon ordered him down, and as he was coming down they dashed out his Brains, and hove him overboard also.

They then went to search for the Merchants Clerk who was all this Time hid after they had stabbed him, and found him in the run of the Vessel; whereupon they dragged him out and have him overboard; they also stabbed the Boatswain in several Places but did not quite kill him, they saved him and the two Lads that were on board; after which they sent the Boatswain and myself down into the Cabin, and there dressed our Wounds, then they ordered us to steer away for *Oronoque* a *Spanish* Place to Leeward of us; the next Day they wash'd and scrap'd very Place that was Bloody upon Deck, and have the bloody Cloaths over board, we still kept along Shore, and the 5th of June by God's Providence we carried them safe into *Currenteen*, a *Dutch* Place just to Leeward of *Surenham*, which we told them was *Oronoque*, we went about 20 Leagues up the River, when we saw a House, which we told them was a *Spanish* House, at which they seemed very glad, but when we went ashore we found that it was a *Dutch* House, whereupon our Boatswain (who talk'd pretty good Dutch) told them our Condition and shew'd them his Wounds, whereupon they answered, that next Morning they would secure them, but the Villains understanding that the Boatswain had told the People of it, when we came on board they were throwing him overboard, but they said let us heave the Anchor up first, and then we will throw him overboard, in the mean Time while they were heaving the Anchor up, the Boatswain jump'd into the Boat and

got ashore, they having no Boat to go after him they were obliged
to cut the Cable and let the Anchor go and so drove down with the
Ebb Tide, about three Leagues from the House we got aground and
lay there that Night, next Day we got a float again, and stood down
along, and got but little way before we got aground again, and lay
their all that Night; Next Morning came the Boatswain with three
Crafts, viz two Canoes and our Boat to take us, which they did accordingly but one of our *Portuguise* Villains jumped overboard and
swam ashore, but the other two were made Prisoners and bound,
and we relieved (thanks be to God) for our safe deliverance from
the Hands of our Enemies; by the pretended Capt. *Ferdinando Coast*,
when he was taken Prisoner, was found a Bag of Gold containing
l. 42. and a Silver Watch ty'd about his Private Parts, the other being
search'd was found with 7 Pieces of Gold in his Pocket; we then sent
a search for the Negro that jumped overboard but could not find
him, we then brought up the Vessel, and came to Anchor near the
Gentleman's House, soon after we got a Passage up to *Surenham*
and delivered our two Prisoners to the care of the Governour, who
ordered them to be well secured; we since hear that the Negro that
made his Escape is taken by the Indians and expect him daily. We
are dressed duly every day at the Hospital, and our Wounds Cure
bravely, so that in a short Time we hope to be at *Barbados* again, to
acquaint our Owners of this mellancholly Affair.
William Blake, Mate,
John Shaw, Boatswain.

"Extract of a Letter from Surinam, dated Aug. 15, 1743" (OS),
Gentleman's Magazine and Historical Chronicle 13 (November
1743): 609

> THREE *Portugueze* Negro Sailors on board the *Rising Sun*
> Schooner, bound from *Barbadoes* to the Island *Cyanna*, rose in
> the Night and murdered Captain *Newark Jackson*, Commander,

Capt. *George Ledain*, Supercargo, an Apprentice Boy, and the Merchant's Clerk and wounded the Mate and Boatswain, leaving them and 2 Lads alive, whom they ordered to carry [the] Ship to *Oronoque*; but they made for *Curranteen*, a *Dutch* Settlement, when two of the Villains were secured by the Governor and the third swam ashore, who being discovered by some *Indians* in the Woods, endeavoured by stabbing himself with a Knife to put an End to his Life, upon which the *Indians* seeing his Obstinacy severed his Head from his Body. The other two were afterwards executed as follows, the Vessel in which the Fact was committed being brought near the Town, and a Yard flung across her Mast, and as many Vessels, as could conveniently, coming round her with all their Crews, the Criminals were brought on Board and each flung by the Arm-pits were hoisted up to each Yard-arm; where after hanging some Time, the Executioners with red-hot Pinchers pull'd off Pieces of their Flesh; then they were un-hung, and an Iron hook put into each of their Sides, by which they were hung up again for 24 Hours, and afterwards their Heads were cut off (their Bodies being buried) and stuck up in a publick Place. One was alive when they come to cut off his Head.

"Testimony of William Blake, John Shaw, Josiah Jones, and Henry Deveries," 1 August 1743 (NS), Oud Archief Suriname: Raad van Politie, 1.05.10.02 (Processtukken betreffende criminele zaken), inv.nr. 796 (1743), NA Netherlands.

June 1st 1743 Came out of Surrinam River in the Schooner Rising Sun Newark Jackson, Commander Bound for Cyan, with Captain Ledain, the Merchant on board, and at 10 o'Clock at Night, I being in the Captain Watch and at helm and he just Gone Down to Sleep, The three Portuguese, Viz Ferdinando, Joseph, and Thomas, Joseph being in our Watch, as I was at the helm, he came to me and ask'd me Severall Questions about the Compass when Such and Such Points went to, whereupon I told him any thing that Came uppermost and among the Rest of the Points thinking no harm I told him that went to Oronoque whereupon I ask'd him for a Dram, knowing that he had Rum aboard, he then went Down into the Storage and in about 10 Minutes time he came upon again, without the Dram and ask'd me again about the Compass the Same Question, and I gave him the Same answers, whereupon he went Down again, and in about a Quarter of an hour I heard a Great Noise, Murder, Murder, Severall times for the three Portuguese had arose upon us, two of them Viz Fernando and Joseph went into the Cabbin one to the Captain and the other to the Merchant, as they were asleep and Stab'd them as they told us afterwards, and Thomas was at the Merchants Clerk at the same time, and stab'd him 9 times as he told us afterwards, he likewise told us that as the Captain was coming up the Companion Ladder upon Deck that he Caught hold of him with one hand, and stab'd him with the other 8 times, and Likewise the Merchant five times, they then Came upon Deck, one Crying I am Dead, and the other Crying I am Dead, Which Encouraged the Rouges that they soon followed them, and Ferdinando fell upon the Captain with his ax, and Soon Destroy'd him, and Joseph upon the Boatswain with the Merchants Cutlash [*sic*] which they Stole while the Captain was upon Deck and wounded the Boatswain with it in Severall Places, but Did not Quick kill them, the Cap^tns Boy John Skinner Being affrigh'd went up the Main Shrouds, they then ordered him down and as he was Coming Down I heard this Thomas Say, Over with him in English. Whereupon Ferdinando Directly Push'd him over board, they then went to Look for the Merchants Clerk who was all the time hid, and found him in the Run of the Vessell, Bleeding allmost to Death. Joseph then Drag'd him upon Deck, and I Saw him heave him overboard, When they had Done all this, and the Boatswain being Gone Down to his Cabbin, this Thomas told me Severall times, that he would kill the Boatswain, but I Persuaded him very much to the Contrary, by telling him that the Boatswain had been Severall Voyages to Esequeba, and that he knew all the Land very Well and Would Carry the Vessell into Oronoque as they had Ordered us, Next day they Wash'd and scraped the Decks [and]² all Places that was Bloody and hove all the Bloody Cloathes Overboard, and Drest the Mate and Boatswain Wounds they Being Both Wounded Very Much.

William Blake

John Shaw

Josiah Jones

Henry Deveries

"Examination of Ferdinandus [Ferdinand] da Costa," 24 July 1743 (NS), Oud Archief Suriname: Raad van Politie, 1.05.10.02 (Processtukken betreffende criminele zaken), inv.nr. 796 (1743), NA Netherlands.

Translated by Ramona Negrón

1. What is your name?
   Ferdinandus [Ferdinand] da Costa.

2. How old are you?
   About 26 or 27 years old.

3. What is your place of birth?
   Born in a village called Moijta, located three miles from Lisbon.

4. How long has it been since you were in Portugal?
   About two years ago.

5. Don't you know an English captain called Jackson?
   Says that he doesn't know him by name.

6. Where have you been employed to the barque that has sailed under that captain?
   Says on the island of Barbados.

7. Who hired you?
   Says the aforementioned captain and merchant.

8. How long have you been in Barbados?
   About two weeks.

9. What is your religion?
   Roman Catholic.

10. Are you born as a white man?
    Yes.

11. For which function were you hired on the barque?
    As sailor.

12. Were you the only one who has been hired?
    Says that he was hired along with two others.

13. What are the names of the two persons that were hired simultaneously?
    The one is called Joseph Pareijra [Pereira] and the other Thomas.

14. Were they of Portuguese origin?
    The one is a Genoese and the other Portuguese.

15. Were they of white origin or Negros?
    Both of them are Negros.

16. Where did you become acquainted with one another?
    Says that he has known Pareijra from London, and the other in Barbados.

17. Have you been to other places with Pareijra as well?
    Says that he arrived in a vessel in Barbados with four.

18. How much did you earn on the barque [per month]?
    Says 55 Barbadian shillings, and the Negros Pareijra and Thomas as well.

19. Have you been maltreated by the captain?
    Says that he has been wanting more salt, although he received salted meat.

20. Have you ever been in a fight with the captain?
    Says no.

21. When did you discuss to attack the captain?
    Says at night at eleven o'clock.

22. Didn't you already discuss to kill the captain at the moment that you crossed the river for the first time?
    Says that, at that time, a Spaniard was on board who made a conspiracy to kill the captain.

23. How did you know that the Spaniard was making a conspiracy?
    Says that the Spaniard treated him to a dram and said that the captain was wise to set him ashore as he had decided to kill the captain.

24. Didn't you tell ~~Thomas~~ the Negro Thomas about the conspiracy?
    Says no, but that the Negro has told him about the conspiracy as well.

25. Didn't the Negro request that you commit the murder?
    Says that the Negro has not told him anything about this.

26. Why didn't you warn the captain about the conspiracy?
    Says that he believed that the Negro wouldn't execute the plan.

27. When the Negro woke you up to commit the murder, why didn't you shout or make any noise?
    Says that he didn't dare to shout out of fear, as the Negro was carrying a machete, and feared that the Negro would kill him.

28. Where were you when the attack and murder was committed?
    Says somewhere beyond the river Suriname, on a corner he doesn't know by name.

29. At what time did the murder happen?
    Says the first night around eleven o'clock once they had sailed out of this river.

30. Weren't the captain and merchant and the clerk sleeping in their cabin?
    Says that the captain and merchant were sleeping in the cabin, as well as the clerk and coxswain [e.g., the mate William Blake] in their berths in front of the door, and that the boatswain was on the watch.

31. Who was the first to enter the cabin to commit the murder?

    Says the Negro Pareijra, then the Negro Thomas, and after which he, the interrogated, followed with an axe in his hand, that the two Negros had hurt the captain and merchant, and that he, although he wanted to chop his axe, threw it away out of fright.

32. How did the captain and merchant left the cabin?

    Says that they came upstairs independently, after they had been stabbed and hurt.

33. After they came upstairs, who killed them?

    Says that the Negro Thomas then shouted "beat them to death," after which he detainee and the two Negros started chopping.

34. What kind of [weapon] did you have at that moment?

    Says that when the captain came upstairs wounded, he hold the axe that he, the interrogated, had thrown away out of fear earlier, and that he snatched the axe out of the captain's hand and chopped him thrice with it.

35. Who has thrown the merchant overboard?

    Says the Negro Pareijra.

36. Who has thrown the captain overboard?

    Says he, the interrogated, and the Negro Pareijra.

37. Were they already dead when they were thrown overboard?

    Says that the merchant was already dead, but supposes that the captain was still alive.

38. When the captain was thrown overboard, wasn't he still shouting?

    Says yes.

39. Where was the writer when the captain and merchant were killed?

    Says that he was downstairs in his berth.

40. At what place was the clerk killed?

    Says that the Negro Thomas was downstairs and that he doesn't know how the clerk has been killed.

41. Who hunted down the clerk and dragged him up the ladder?
    Says the Negros Pareijra and Thomas.

42. Who threw the clerk into the sea?
    Says that he doesn't know better than that it would have been Pareijra.

43. Was the clerk already dead as well or wasn't he shouting?
    Says that he has heard from the Englishmen that he wasn't dead, and that he was still shouting, but that he, the interrogated, had been standing at the bowsprit.

44. Who has hurt the coxswain?
    Says the Negro Pareijra.

45. Who has stabbed the boatswain?
    Says the Negro Pareijra.

46. Where was he stabbed?
    Says in his abdomen.

47. Did the stab wound release any fat or intestines?
    Says he saw a little bit of fat.

48. Didn't someone cut away some of the fat?
    Says that the Negro Pareijra wanted to push the fat back again, but without success; he cut it away.

49. Why did you try to save the cox and boatswain, instead of killing them too?
    Says he spared their lives, in order to navigate.

50. Isn't it true that one of the English boys fled into the mast?
    Says yes.

51. Didn't one tried to lure the boy to the deck again (while promising him not to harm him)?
    Says he doesn't know anything about such promise.

52. Isn't it true that the boy has also been hurt or stabbed?
Says he hasn't seen anything like that.

53. Who has thrown the boy overboard?
*Says that the two Negros climbed into one of the sides of the rigging each,
and that the negro Pareijra has thrown the boy overboard.*

54. When all of those persons had been killed, what have you been doing all
together?
*Says that the boatswain has said, that he boatswain, succeeded as captain,
and that he, the interrogated, replied that they were all captains.*

55. After that, where did you go to?
*Says that the two Negros told to the coxswain, that they wanted to go to a
Spanish harbor, or to the Orronoque.*

56. What did you people want to do in Orronocque, once you would arrive
over there?
Says once arrived over yonder, [he/they] *wanted to sell the goods and
divide the yield among one another.*

57. At what time did you break the casks and goods open?
*Says three to four days after the murder, and that they broke them open
all together.*

58. Didn't you find any money among those goods?
Says yes.

59. Was it gold or silver?
Says gold and silver.

60. Didn't you know how many golden pieces were there?
*Says that there were thirty-five pieces of gold, which have been divided
among one another and that the Negro Pareijra has stowed away the rest
of it. The boatswain can give the best confirmation about the fact that
they have divided the found silver equally by weight among one another.*

61. Where did you leave your portion of gold?
    Says that he has given it to the boatswain.

62. Didn't you bind it to your body first?
    Says yes, out of convenience.

63. When you left for open sea, did you know that there was money in the barque?
    Says not to have known that there was money on board until after the murder, and that Pareijra then told him about it.

64. Weren't there any papers found among the goods?
    Says that the coxswain and boatswain have told that Pareijra had thrown the papers overboard through the windows of the cabin.

65. When you arrived at a river, didn't you believe that it was the Orronocque river?
    Says yes.

66. Didn't the coxswain tell you that you were in Orronocque?
    Says yes that the coxswain has told them that they were in the river, and could go ashore and that in case that they weren't in the Orronocque, that they were free to chop off his head.

67. With whom did you go ashore, and didn't you wear a red skirt and velvet trousers, and [didn't you] pass yourself off as captain?
    Says he received a shot ~~punch~~ while sailing on the river, and that he consequently dropped the anchor, and that the coxswain told him to dress up and go ashore as captain, after which he went ashore, with the coxswain, the two Negros and the two English boys.

68. Who did receive you ashore?
    Says that the white men who were living there received them, that the coxswain told them (while pointing at him, the interrogated) here is the captain, that the white men asked them where they wanted to go to,

whereupon the coxswain asked to the white men aren't we here in the Or-
ronocque, that the white men replied that it's still miles away from here.
That the coxswain subsequently asked for his maps and instruments on
board, and that then the ~~coxswain~~ *boatswain came ashore as well, that*
he, the interrogated, and the others were warmly welcomed by the white
men and stayed over there until the evening, and then went aboard again
all at once.

69. When you came aboard, didn't you ~~say~~ want to raise the anchor?
    Says yes.

70. Didn't you tell to the two Negros, the coxswain and boatswain have
    betrayed us, we need to throw them overboard?
    Says no, but he has heard that the Negros told that the coxswain and
    boatswain have betrayed us.

71. Didn't the boatswain untie the longboat and fled?
    Says yes and that subsequently the Negro Pareijra cut off the anchor rope.

72. Weren't the [swivel guns] and cannons loaded?
    Says no, but that the Negro Pareijra had loaded them when he saw a
    pirogue with white men and Indians coming.

73. Wasn't there any gunpowder on board?
    Says yes, but one bottle, that was given by the coxswain to Pareijra, four
    days before they came in to the aforementioned river, and that the same
    day that the Indians arrived, the coxswain also gave him bullet.

74. When the white men and Indians arrived, what did you tell them?
    Says, that although he was aware that they were too weak to defend them-
    selves, the Negro Pareijra still wanted to shoot, but that he, the interro-
    gated, has prevented such; That he went with a canoe (by order of the
    white man who was aboard of the Indian vessel) and once arrived there
    he was also enchained [illegible] and that Pareijra has jumped into the
    water, and has fled.

75. Didn't the two English boys (after shouts from the aforementioned white men) jump into the water and swam toward them, before you were in the canoe?

    Says yes.

76. Didn't one show you the head of the Negro Pareijra and isn't he familiar to you?

    Says yes.

77. Aren't you, in your state of mind, convinced that all the violence and murder perpetrated by you, is a heinous act, and [that you] also have deserved the death?

    Replies, whether I say yes or no, [judgment] *will come to happen in such way that the gentlemen will approve.*

"Examination of Thomas Lucas," 25 July 1743 (NS), Oud Archief Suriname: Raad van Politie, 1.05.10.02 (Processtukken betreffende criminele zaken), inv.nr. 796 (1743), NA Netherlands.

Translated by Ramona Negrón

Art. 1. What is your name?

    Thomas Lucas.

2. How old are you?

    35 to 36 years old.

3. What is your place of birth?

    Born 12 miles away from the city of Venice.

4. How long has it been since you were in Venice?

    Circa 9 or 10 years.

5. Don't you know an English captain called Jackson, with whom you have recently sailed, as well as the merchant of the mentioned ship?

    Says yes he knows him.

6. Where have you been employed to the barque that has sailed under the aforementioned captain?
On the island of Barbados.

7. Who hired you?
Says the aforementioned captain and merchant.

8. How long have you been in Barbados?
Circa 8 to 10 days.

9. What is your religion?
Roman Catholic.

10. ~~Are you born as a white man?~~ 10. Are you born as a free man?
Says his mother has been a slave [and that] on his deathbed the patron has granted freedom to her and him, the detainee.

11. For which function were you hired on the barque?
As sailor and cook.

12. Were you the only one who has been hired?
Only one hired.

13. ~~What are the names of the two persons that were hired simultaneously?~~
13. Do you know a Ferdinandus da Costa and Joseph Pareijra?
Says to know them only by the name of Ferdinandus [Ferdinand] and Joseph.

14. Were they of Portuguese origin?
Says to have heard from them that they were Portuguese.

15. ~~How [unreadable] the Spaniard who the captain and merchant~~

   ~~Were they of white origin or Negros?~~

15. Where did you become acquainted with one another?
In Barbados.

16. How did you make a living after you left from Venice?
Says to have sailed the seas since his childhood.

17. How much did you earn on the barque [per month]?
    50 Barbadian shillings.

18. Have you been maltreated by the captain?
    Says he has no complaints against him nor against the merchant.

19. Have you ever been in a fight with the captain?
    Says no.

20. At what time did you discuss to attack the captain?
    Says that some Spaniard called Gousinh had been on board of the barque (and who has been left over here by the captain on his latter journey) [who] has told to Ferdinand and Pareijra and they subsequently to him, the detainee [added] that they had to beat the folk to death, and that he, the interrogated, replied on that why should you do that and you do not master any seamanship where would you end.

21. ~~Didn't you already discuss to kill the captain at the moment that you crossed the river for the first time?~~

21. Didn't Ferdinandus and Pareijra [Pareira] talk with you about the conspiracy afterward?
    Says yes when they were nearby the Suriname [River], and had postponed it until they would leave out of the Suriname again, although says he, the detainee, that he didn't want to have anything to do with it.

22. ~~How did you know that the Spaniard was making a conspiracy?~~

22. When the Spaniard stayed ashore, who was the first one that spoke about the conspiracy again?
    Says to know nothing about that.

    Didn't the Portuguese Ferdinandus come to you [to tell you he] wanted to commit the murder?
    Says Ferdinandus and Pareijra both came to me although he didn't want to.

Why didn't you warn the captain about the conspiracy when you were ~~still~~ ashore?
Says that he believed that he wouldn't execute the plan.

When one woke you up to commit the murder, why didn't you shout or make any noise?
Says that he didn't dare to shout out of fear, as the Negro Pareijra and Ferdinandus both had a machete.

Where were you with the barque when the attack and murder was committed?
Says somewhere beyond the river Suriname, on a corner he doesn't know by name.

What time did the murder happen?
The first night at eleven o'clock once they had sailed out of this river.

Weren't the captain the merchant and the writer sleeping in the cabin?
Says that the captain and merchant were sleeping in the cabin.

Who was the first to enter the cabin, to commit the murder?
~~Says no~~ the two Portuguese went into the cabin and that he, the interrogated, ~~had stayed on the spot where~~ didn't leave his place.

How did the captain and merchant left the cabin?
~~H.~~ Says [that he] has seen them ascend the quarter deck wounded.

After they came upstairs, who killed them?
Says Ferdinandus and Pareijra have beaten them to death.

[Lucas refused to answer the next 23 questions, which were similar to those answered by Da Costa.]

At what time did you break the caskets and goods open?
Three to four days after the murder.

Didn't you find any money among those goods?
Yes.

Was it gold or silver?
Says gold and silver.

[Lucas again refused to answer the remaining 19 questions, which were similar to those asked of Da Costa.]

NOTES

Works frequently cited are identified by the following abbreviations:

AHR: *American Historical Review*

"CREW TESTIMONY": "Testimony of William Blake, John Shaw, Josiah Jones, and Henry Deveries," 1 August 1743, Oud Archief Suriname: Raad van Politie, 1.05.10.02 (Processtukken betreffende criminele zaken), inv.nr. 796 (1743), Nationaal Archief, The Hague, the Netherlands

"CRIMINAL COMPLAINT": "Criminal Complaint against Ferdinandus Da Costa and Thomas Lucas," 3 August 1743, Oud Archief Suriname: Raad van Politie, 1.05.10.02 (Processtukken betreffende criminele zaken), inv.nr. 796 (1743), Nationaal Archief, The Hague, the Netherlands

"DA COSTA'S EXAMINATION": "Examinen en Ferdinandus da Costa," 24 July 1743, Oud Archief Suriname: Raad van Politie, 1.05.10.02 (Processtukken betreffende criminele zaken), inv.nr. 796 (1743), Nationaal Archief, The Hague, the Netherlands

EAS: *Early American Studies*

"INVENTORY": "Inventaris en Prisatie van de Barkentijn de Rijsende," Oud Archief Suriname: Notarissen Suriname tot 1828 (Inventarissen en Prisaties), 1.05.11.14, inv. nr. 176 (1743), f. 66–67, Nationaal Archief, The Hague, the Netherlands

"LUCAS'S EXAMINATION": "Examinen en Thomas Lucas," 25 July 1743, Oud Archief Suriname: Raad van Politie, 1.05.10.02 (Processtukken betreffende criminele zaken), inv.nr. 796 (1743), Nationaal Archief, The Hague, the Netherlands

MHS: Massachusetts Historical Society, Boston

MSA: Massachusetts State Archives, Boston

NA NETHERLANDS: Nationaal Archief, The Hague, the Netherlands

NAUK: National Archives United Kingdom, Kew

NEHGS: R. Stanton Avery Special Collections, New England Historical Genealogical Society, Boston

NEQ: *New England Quarterly*

ONCR: Old North Church Records Ms. N-2249, Massachusetts Historical Society, Boston

PEM: Phillips Library, Peabody Essex Museum, Salem, MA

SA: *Slavery & Abolition*

SCCP: Suffolk County (Massachusetts) Common Pleas Court Records,
Massachusetts State Archives, Boston

SCPR: Suffolk County (Massachusetts) Probate Records, Massachusetts State Archives, Boston

WMQ: *William and Mary Quarterly*

INTRODUCTION

1 See "Crew Testimony."

2 *New-York Weekly Journal*, 15 August 1743.

3 3 June 1743, Oud Archief Suriname: Gouvernementssecretarie, 1.05.10.01,
inv. nr. 3, NA Netherlands.

4 Ibid., 7 June 1743.

5 Ibid., 11 June 1743.

6 *New-York Weekly Journal*, 15 August 1743.

7 See "Crew Testimony."

8 Ibid.

9 *Boston News-Letter*, 4 August 1743.

10 Da Costa claims he dropped the axe "out of fright" from the actions of the
other two mutineers, but he probably did so in the chaos of the moment.
See "Da Costa's Examination."

11 "Crew Testimony"; *Boston News-Letter*, 4 August 1743.

12 "Da Costa's Examination."

13 "Crew Testimony."

14 For the fifteen enslaved Africans, see "Inventory."

15 *New-York Weekly Journal*, 15 August 1743.

16 "Da Costa's Examination."

17 See Wim Klooster, "Inter-Imperial Smuggling in the Americas, 1600–1800," in *Soundings in Atlantic History: Latent Structures and Intellectual Currents, 1500–1830*, ed. Bernard Bailyn and Patricia L. Denault (Cambridge, MA: Harvard University Press, 2009), 141–180.

18 Alan L. Karras, *Smuggling: Contraband and Corruption in World History* (Lanham, MD: Roman & Littlefield, 2010), 5.

19 Although introduced as a concept by Marxist theorist Cedric J. Robinson in the 1980s, the idea of racial capitalism has become increasingly important to scholars studying slavery and the rise of the modern capitalist economy. See Robinson, *Black Marxism: The Making of the Black Radical Tradition*, 2nd ed. (Chapel Hill: University of North Carolina Press, 2000), 2–3. For a further definition of the concept, see Robin D. G. Kelley, "What Did Cedric Robinson Mean by Racial Capitalism?," *Boston Review*, 12 January 2017, http://bostonreview.net. For the explicit connection between slavery and racial capitalism, see Walter Johnson, "To Remake the World: Slavery, Racial Capitalism, and Justice," *Boston Review*, 20 February 2018, http://bostonreview.net.

20 The best overview of the history of chocolate in the early modern Atlantic world is Marcy Norton, *Sacred Gifts, Profane Pleasures: A History of Tobacco and Chocolate in the Atlantic World* (Ithaca, NY: Cornell University Press, 2008).

21 G. A. R. Wood and R. A. Lass, *Cocoa*, 4th ed. (London: Blackwell, 2001), 1–2.

22 By the end of the seventeenth century, chocolate was, in the words of historian Marcy Norton, "approaching, if not quite obtaining, the status of [a] mass" commodity. See Norton, *Sacred Gifts*, 161.

23 In his 779-page tome about the identification and remediation of the myriad insects that attack cacao trees and pods, Oxford horticulturalist P. F. Entwistle notes that the "ecology of cocoa is more complex and subject to a greater range of variation than any other major crop." Entwistle, *Pests of Cocoa* (London: Longman, 1972), xxi.

24 See James Delburgo, "Sir Hans Sloane's Milk Chocolate and the Whole History of the Cacao," *Social Text* 29, no. 1 (Spring 2011): 71–101, for the early history of cacao in Jamaica and Great Britain.

25 For Raleigh's history and encounter with the region, see Walter Raleigh, *The Discouerie of the Large, Rich, and Bevvtiful Empyre of Guiana: With a Relation of the Great and Golden Citie of Manoa (Which the Spanyards Call El Dorado) and the Prouinces of Emeria, Arromaia, Amapaia, and Other Countries, with Their Riuers, Adioyning: Performed in the Yeare 1595*

(London: Robert Robertson, 1596) and Alan Gallay, *Walter Ralegh: Architect of Empire* (New York: Basic Books, 2019), chap. 24.

26 In recent years historians have become interested in the transfer of Suriname from the Dutch to the English. See Justin Roberts, "Surrendering Surinam: The Barbadian Diaspora and the Expansion of the English Sugar Frontier, 1650–75," *WMQ* 73, no. 2 (April 2016): 225–256, and Alison Games, "Cohabitation, Suriname-Style: English Inhabitants in Dutch Suriname after 1667," *WMQ* 72, no. 2 (April 2015): 195–242.

27 North American trade in seventeenth- and eighteenth-century Suriname is the subject of Karwan Fatah-Black, *White Lies and Black Markets: Evading Metropolitan Authority in Colonial Suriname, 1650–1800* (Boston: Brill, 2015).

28 Despite ever-present violence, smuggling, one of the themes of this book, was often nonviolent and smugglers used subterfuge, not force, to achieve their ends. See Karras, *Smuggling*, 7, for more on the relatively peaceful nature of smuggling.

29 For more on discussions of the morality of slavery and the slave trade in the eighteenth century, see Christopher Leslie Brown, *Moral Capital: Foundations of British Abolitionism* (Chapel Hill: University of North Carolina Press, 2006). The morality of smuggling and the ideological justifications for it can be found in Karras, *Smuggling*, 5–6; Michael Kwass, *Contraband: Louis Mandarin and the Making of a Global Underground* (Cambridge, MA: Harvard University Press, 2014), 287–304, and Tyson Reeder, *Smugglers, Pirates, and Patriots: Free Trade in the Age of Revolution* (Philadelphia: University of Pennsylvania Press, 2019), 3.

30 For more on the utility of court records in writing history despite their problems, see Edward Muir and Guido Ruggiero, eds., *History from Crime* (Baltimore: Johns Hopkins University Press, 1994), introduction.

31 In thinking about archives and their challenges, I draw from Sadiya Hartman, who notes that the archives of slave societies, but really anywhere in the eighteenth-century Atlantic world, were "produced by terror" and rest "upon a founding violence." Historians have to be careful when reading these narratives, or, in the words of historian Marisa J. Fuentes, they risk creating "historical narratives that reproduce . . . violent colonial discourses." See Hartman, "Venus in Two Acts," *Small Axe* 12, no. 2 (June 2008): 9–10, and Fuentes, *Dispossessed Lives: Enslaved Women, Violence, and the Archive* (Philadelphia: University of Pennsylvania Press, 2016), 5–6.

32 Gloria McCahon Whiting, "Race, Slavery, and the Problem of Numbers in Early New England: A View from Probate Court," *WMQ* 77, no. 3 (July 2020): 409.

33 Whiting responds directly to critics like Hartman and Fuentes by arguing that even when "shot through with violence," sources, such as the inventory or, in Whiting's (and other parts of this book's) case, probate records, documenting slavery "can move us toward visions of the past that foreground the actions and aspirations of people in bondage." Ibid., 428–429.

34 While scholars have studied smuggling in Britain's North American colonies extensively for more than a century, that literature has explored the topic from an institutional, often imperial, perspective with an emphasis on the volume of illegal trade, policies meant to curb smuggling, and the large-scale colonial defiance of these measures. See, for example, Charles McLean Andrews, *The Colonial Background of the American Revolution* (New Haven, CT: Yale University Press, 1924); Thomas C. Barrow, *Trade and Empire: The British Customs Service in Colonial America, 1660–1775* (Cambridge, MA: Harvard University Press, 1967); John W. Tyler, *Smugglers and Patriots: Boston Merchants and the Advent of the American Revolution* (Boston: Northeastern University Press, 1986); Gautham Rao, *National Duties: Custom Houses and the Making of the American State* (Chicago: University of Chicago Press, 2016).

Much of the older literature is Anglocentric, but more recently scholars have explored illegal trade with Britain's American colonies from the perspective of their foreign trading partners, such as Spanish America, the French Caribbean, and the Netherlands Antilles and Suriname. For illicit trade with Spanish America, see Adrian Finucane, *The Temptations of Trade: Britain, Spain, and the Struggle for Empire* (Philadelphia: University of Pennsylvania Press, 2016). Information on the illegal French trade can be found in Thomas M. Truxes, *Defying Empire: Trading with the Enemy in Colonial New York* (New Haven: Yale University Press, 2008). Illegal commerce with the Dutch has garnered much attention in recent years. See Wim Klooster and Gert Oostindie, *Realm between Empires: The Second Dutch Atlantic, 1680–1815* (Ithaca, NY: Cornell University Press, 2018), Wim Klooster, *Illicit Riches: Dutch Trade in the Caribbean, 1648–1795* (Leiden: KITLV Press, 1998), and Fatah-Black, *White Lies and Black Markets*.

One social and cultural history of smuggling in early America is Christian J. Koot, *Empire at the Periphery: British Colonists, Anglo-Dutch*

Trade, and the Development of the British Atlantic, 1621–1713 (New York: New York University Press, 2011). Scholars studying smuggling outside of the future United States have also started taking a similar social and cultural approach to the topic as this book. For two examples, see Kwass, *Contraband*, and Jesse Cromwell, *The Smugglers' World: Illicit Trade and Atlantic Communities in Eighteenth-Century Venezuela* (Chapel Hill: University of North Carolina Press, 2018).

Nevertheless, this book is not a revisionist account but rather is meant to provide a spotlight on key themes in the history and historiography of illicit trade and expand on the already robust literature. In the end, as one historian has argued in another context, individual stories like the mutiny on the *Rising Sun* can be used to "test and to refine standing generalizations" on smuggling in colonial America and the Atlantic world. See Richard D. Brown, "Microhistory and the Post-modern Challenge," *Journal of the Early American Republic* 23, no. 1 (Spring 2003): 13.

35 The idea of "entanglement" borrows from the work of Eliga H. Gould. See Gould, "Entangled Histories, Entangled Worlds: The English-Speaking Atlantic as a Spanish Periphery," *AHR* 112, no. 3 (June 2007): 764–786. While scholars have moved away from national histories in favor of more transnational approaches, much of popular literature remains American-centric and focused on the nation-state. More recently, however, there has been a movement to write "global" microhistories that seek to tell the history of early modern globalization through individual events, people, and communities. These histories deal with a wide array of issues in the early modern Atlantic and address early America's entanglement in a dynamic world of trade, circulation, and exploitation—the exact purpose of *Mutiny on the Rising Sun*. These new global microhistories have appeared as books and as articles in scholarly journals. For some of the most striking examples, see Linda Colley, *The Ordeal of Elizabeth Marsh: A Woman in World History* (New York: Anchor Books, 2008), and Randy J. Sparks, *The Two Princes of Calabar: An Eighteenth-Century Atlantic Odyssey* (Cambridge, MA: Harvard University Press, 2004). For articles, see John-Paul A. Ghobrial, "The Secret Life of Elias of Babylon and the Uses of Global Microhistory," *Past & Present* 222 (February 2014): 51–93, and Emma Rothschild, "Isolation and Economic Life in Eighteenth-Century France," *AHR* 119, no. 4 (October 2014): 1055–1082.

1. THE CAPTAIN

1   Three pieces of evidence support this assertion. First, two other members of the smuggling ring—Gedney Clarke and George Ledain—were from Essex County despite relocating elsewhere as adults. Second, in Jackson's probate inventory, he owned "one whole Right or Share in the New Township No. 2 on the East Side of the Connecticut River granted to Nath^el Harris Esq and others." Jackson possibly inherited this land claim in what is today Westmoreland, New Hampshire. The Massachusetts General Assembly granted this land as a reward in 1736 to veterans of the campaign that successfully captured Port Royal, Acadia (Annapolis Royal, Nova Scotia) in 1710. Numerous men from Essex County, including a few with the surname Jackson, received land grants from this allocation. See "Newark Jackson," docket 7944, SCPR, MSA. Nevertheless, Jackson speculated in real estate, and this could have been a one-off purchase. Third, as explored below, one of the first times Jackson appeared in Boston's court records, Benjamin Darling sued him for debt regarding some work he had done for Jackson. Darling was a Boston shipwright, but he had family in Salem and inherited land there. It is possible that when Jackson first arrived in Boston, he relied on others with connections to the North Shore to get himself situated. For Darling, see the Genealogical section of the *Boston Evening Transcript*, 26 September 1906.

2   *Boston News-Letter*, 8 July 1731.

3   Darling and Jackson, April 1735, *Suffolk Files* 39271, MSA.

4   John Adams, "2 January 1761," in *Diary & Autobiography of John Adams*, vol. 1: *Diary 1755–1770*, ed. L. H. Butterfield (1961; New York: Athenaeum, 1964), 187–188. For more on the idea "of Boston," especially how it related to the British soldiers who occupied the town in the late 1760s, see Serena Zabin, *The Boston Massacre: A Family History* (New York: Houghton Mifflin Harcourt, 2020), 101–102.

5   Alan Taylor, *American Colonies: The Settling of North America* (New York: Penguin, 2001), 177.

6   For more on Boston as a city-state, how its relationship with Britain changed over time, and the importance of maritime trade to its economy, see Mark Peterson, *The City-State of Boston: The Rise and Fall of an Atlantic Power, 1630–1865* (Princeton, NJ: Princeton University Press, 2019).

7   Adams, "16 January 1766," in Butterfield, *Diary & Autobiography*, 294.

8   Richard Pares, *Yankees and Creoles: The Trade between North America and the West Indies before the American Revolution* (Cambridge, MA: Harvard University Press, 1956), 24–36.

9   For intraregional competition and statistics on economic decline, see G. B. Warden, *Boston, 1689–1776* (Boston: Little, Brown, 1970), 103.

10 Gary Nash notes that in the 1730s "Boston was skidding on a downward slope that stretched indeterminately towards the future." Nash, *The Urban Crucible: Social Change, Political Consciousness, and the Origins of the American Revolution* (Cambridge, MA: Harvard University Press, 1979), 125.

11 A good example of a young, ambitious ship captain becoming prosperous is John Erving. Erving, born in Scotland in 1690, immigrated to Boston as a teenager. Throughout the 1730s and 1740s, he, like many other ship captains, transitioned from working on ships to a being a full-time, land-based merchant. By 1748, he was the "highest taxed citizen" of Boston and amassed enough wealth to be counted among the town's richest men. See Steven J. J. Pitt, "Building and Outfitting Ships in Colonial Boston," *EAS* 13, no. 4 (Fall 2015): 900.

12 Quoted in ibid., 886.

13 The only case is the aforementioned Darling and Jackson, April 1735, *Suffolk Files* 39271, MSA. Even this case ended up in arbitration, suggesting a desire of both parties to amicably resolve the issue. Jackson was the defendant in another debt suit in 1740, but that was when a merchant drew a bill of credit on his account to pay a shopkeeper. It is possible that Jackson was totally unaware of the bill or away from Boston when the transaction occurred. See *Barrett v. Jackson*, 1 January 1739/40, SCCP, 1740, 100, MSA and Jackson and Barrett, 12 August 1740, *Suffolk Files* 52272, MSA.

14 Pitt, "Building and Outfitting," 886.

15 There were two back-to-back cases, one for the costs of provisions and the other for back wages. See "Jackson v. Cunningham" and "Jackson v. Cunningham," 5 October 1742, 1741–1742, SCCP, 153–154, MSA. Jackson won both cases, but Cunningham appealed, and there are no records of the appeal or any subsequent decisions.

16 For more on these popular conceptions of sailors and their alleged danger, see Niklas Frykman, *The Bloody Flag: Mutiny in the Age of Atlantic Revolution* (Oakland: University of California Press, 2020), 3–4.

17 The quote, "Heeft geen klagte tegens hem als meede niet tegens den Koopman," comes from the testimony of Thomas Lucas and refers to both Jackson and Ledain. See "Lucas's Examination."

18 Jackson appears in these records fourteen separate times. For his 1736 voyage to the West Indies, Jackson appears in three different

newspapers, first as having declared his intentions to leave and then as being "Cleared Out" or actively leaving. Likewise, for three of those shipping lists, different newspapers printed the same port records. See *New England Weekly Journal*, 5 July 1731, *Boston News-Letter*, 8 July 1731, *Boston News-Letter*, 11 April 1734, and *New England Weekly Journal*, 15 April 1735, for duplicate records of Jackson in Boston. Philadelphia's *American Weekly Mercury* also reprinted shipping news from Boston containing Jackson's 1736 West Indies voyage. See *American Weekly Mercury*, 16 March 1736, which was based off those from the *Boston Evening Post*, 16 February 1736. Of the eleven unique records, six list Jackson by first and last name. The other five are probable matches based on known destinations from the confirmed entries and other known associations. For example, for his 1736 West Indian sojourn, the 20 January 1736 *New England Weekly Journal* reported a "Jackson" as "Outward Bound" with George Ledain, Newark Jackson's later super-cargo on the *Rising Sun*. Likewise, in the *Weekly Rehearsal*, another Boston newspaper, reported a "Jackson" as entering the port in March 1734. Less than a month later on 11 April 1734, however, the *Boston News-Letter* reported Newark Jackson entering from Lisbon, Portugal. It would have been impossible for Jackson to sail to Portugal and back in less than a month, meaning the *Weekly Rehearsal* article is not considered here.

19 *Weekly Rehearsal*, 30 October 1732.

20 *New England Weekly Journal*, 18 December 1732.

21 For London as the "central mart" for New England's global trade, see William B. Weeden, *Economic and Social History of New England*, vol. 2 (1890; New York: Hillary House, 1963), 617.

22 See T. H. Breen, "'Baubles of Britain': The American and Consumer Revolutions of the Eighteenth Century," *Past & Present*, no. 119 (May 1988): 73–104, for more on the manufactured goods purchased by colonial merchants in London. For credit, see 87.

23 This information can be extrapolated using the port records from Boston's newspapers and comparing it with average sea crossing times. A roundtrip voyage from Boston to London took about eight weeks of sailing time, but longer in the months of December, January, and February. Jackson left Boston on 18 December and would have reached London about five to six weeks later, in late January. He would have spent at least a few days, if not weeks, conducting business. He probably departed sometime in early to mid-February and arrived four to six weeks later or

in mid- to late March. Given that we have a record that Jackson returned to Boston from North Carolina on 9 April (*Weekly Rehearsal*, 9 April 1733) and the limitations of eighteenth-century sailing technology, it would have been near impossible to sail from London back to Boston in the middle of February, especially due to the winter weather in the north Atlantic, and then complete a roundtrip voyage to North Carolina. For a month-by-month breakdown of sailing times from Boston to London, see Ian K. Steele, *The English Atlantic 1675–1740: An Exploration of Communication and Community* (Oxford: Oxford University Press, 1986), 265 (Table 4.4).

24 In a world powered by wooden sailing ships, these goods, including pitch, turpentine, and tar, were cheap but vital necessities. All three helped waterproof ships. And all three came from pine trees. North Carolina had huge stands of longleaf pine (*Pinus palustris*), which were perfect for making naval stores. By the 1720s, North Carolina had a robust and extensive naval stores industry that formed the foundation of the colony's trading economy. See Justin Williams, "English Mercantilism and Carolina Naval Stores, 1705–1776," *Journal of Southern History* 1, no. 2 (May 1935): 169–185, and Bradford J. Wood, *This Remote Part of the World: Regional Formation in Lower Cape Fear, North Carolina, 1725–1775* (Columbia: University of South Carolina Press, 2004), 176–182. For a study of a New England merchant active in North Carolina's naval stores trade, see Virginia Bever Platt, "Tar, Staves, and New England Rum: The Trade of Aaron Lopez of Newport, Rhode Island, with Colonial North Carolina," *North Carolina Historical Review* 48, no. 1 (January 1971): 1–22.

25 Margaret Ellen Newell, *From Dependency to Independence: Economic Revolution in Colonial New England* (Ithaca, NY: Cornell University Press, 1999), 3.

26 As Jackson's activities suggest, economic historians estimate that the profits generated by the carrying trade were actually more valuable than all of New England's exported produce. See Taylor, *American Colonies*, 177.

27 *Weekly Rehearsal*, 9 April 1733.

28 *New England Weekly Journal*, 30 July 1733, and *Boston News-Letter*, 6 September 1733. Both records are of Jackson leaving Boston for Newfoundland.

29 For the relationship between New England and Newfoundland and how it changed over the course of the seventeenth century, see Peter E. Pope, *Fish into Wine: The Newfoundland Plantation in the Seventeenth Century* (Chapel Hill: University of North Carolina Press, 2004), 160.

30 An overview of New England–Newfoundland trade can be found in Ralph Greenlee Lounsbury, "Yankee Trade at Newfoundland," *NEQ* 3, no. 4 (October 1930): 607–626. Working with the estimates from other historians, John J. McCusker and Russell R. Menard estimate that by the 1770s New England's trade with Newfoundland was worth between 300,000 and 400,000 pounds per year. See McCusker and Menard, *The Economy of British America, 1607–1789* (Chapel Hill: University of North Carolina Press, 1986), 109.

31 For the illegal trade to Newfoundland, see Lounsbury, "Yankee Trade at Newfoundland," 612–614.

32 The British Royal Navy governed Newfoundland, but a fleet was present only from late spring in May or June through early September. At any other point in the year, there was next to no government except some locals appointed to maintain order. Most of the fishermen left by the early fall, and colonists largely remained indoors during the long, harsh winters, minimizing the need for a large government presence. Nevertheless, in the late summer and early fall, after the fleet left, Newfoundland was a free-for-all and a haven for contraband trading. It should be no surprise that one of Jackson's trading voyages to Newfoundland departed Boston in early September. See *Boston News-Letter*, 6 September 1733. For the Royal Navy in Newfoundland, see Jerry Bannister, *The Rule of the Admirals: Law, Custom, and Naval Government in Newfoundland, 1699–1832* (Toronto: University of Toronto Press, 2003).

33 In addition to this final voyage, Jackson left for North Carolina again in late October 1733.

34 For Boston's early trade with Spain, Portugal, and other ports in southern Europe, see Peterson, *City-State of Boston*, 38–41.

35 There is little work on the trade between New England and southern Europe in the eighteenth century (McCusker and Menard, *Economy of British America*, 311). There are some estimates on the volume of trade, which was quite considerable, based off a four-year period later in the century (1768–1772). See James F. Shepherd and Gary M. Walton, *Shipping, Maritime Trade, and the Economic Development of Colonial North America* (New York: Cambridge University Press, 1972), 40–41.

Despite the lucrativeness of this trade, however, it is unclear how much contact Jackson would have had with Lisbon's Portuguese merchants. By the time he arrived, English merchants dominated Lisbon's and, by extension, Portugal's foreign trade. In 1703, Britain and Portugal signed the Treaty of Methuen that created a formal military and economic alliance between the two nations. On the one hand, this treaty provided British naval protection for Portugal's overseas colonies and trade. It also helped secure Portugal from its aggressive neighbor, Spain. Protection, however, came at a high price. Portugal had to lift most of its tariffs on British manufactured goods and allow them to flow freely into the country, destroying domestic industries in Portugal. In addition, Portugal had to permit British merchants to live in the country. By the middle decades of the eighteenth century, these merchants dominated Portuguese overseas trade and were probably the men with whom Jackson conducted business. See L. M. E. Shaw, *The Anglo-Portuguese Alliance and the English Merchants in Portugal* (1998; New York: Routledge, 2017), chap. 3, and Xabier Lamikiz, *Trade and Trust in the Eighteenth-Century Atlantic World: Spanish Merchants and their Overseas Networks* (London: Boydell, 2010), 6–7.

36 *New England Weekly Journal*, 20 January 1736.

37 *Boston Evening Post*, 16 February 1736.

38 For sample cargoes, see Karwan Fatah-Black, *White Lies and Black Markets: Evading Metropolitan Authority in Colonial Suriname, 1650–1800* (Boston: Brill, 2015), 56–57.

39 "Gearriveerd Capitein Newark Jackson, voerende de scooner *Merry Chrismas*, komende van Boston met 1 paard," in 31 March 1736, Oud Archief Suriname: Gouvernementssecretarie, 1.05.10.01, inv. nr. 2, NA Netherlands.

40 For more on the 1704 statute and the horse export trade, see Johannes Postma, "Breeching the Mercantile Barriers of the Dutch Colonial Empire: North American Trade with Surinam during the Eighteenth Century," in *Merchant Organization and Maritime Trade in the North Atlantic, 1660–1815*, ed. Olaf Uwe Janzen (St. John's: International Maritime Economic History Association, 1998), 116–119, Table 2 (number of horses exported from New England to Suriname). Karwan Fatah-Black has found that many North American vessels entered Suriname without the requisite horses, which may have caused Postma to undercount the volume of North American trade to Suriname. See Fatah-Black, *White Lies and Black Markets*, 57.

41 Fatah-Black, *White Lies and Black Markets*, 53–54.

42 See Patrick Hutton, "The History of *Mentalités*: The New Map of Cultural History," *History and Theory* 20, no. 3 (October 1981): 237–259, for more on *mentalité*.

43 Jesse Cromwell, *The Smugglers' World: Illicit Trade and Atlantic Communities in Eighteenth-Century Venezuela* (Chapel Hill: University of North Carolina Press, 2018), 123.

44 Ibid., 168. As Alan Karras asserts, examining "smuggling allows [people] to understand the ways in which those who lived under a particular government, whether individually or collectively, understood that regime's role in their daily lives." The ability to disregard British authority when necessary suggests that, to Jackson at least, being British was more cultural and less tied to state power. See Karras, *Smuggling: Contraband and Corruption in World History* (Lanham, MD: Rowman & Littlefield, 2010), 3.

45 Pares, *Yankees and Creoles*, 117.

46 For more on Boston's strong localist traditions and desire for autonomy, see Peterson, *City-State of Boston*, 5–8.

47 "Pas verleend aan Capitein Neward Jakson, voerende de Bark Krismas, gaande na Nieuw Foundland," 26 May 1736, Oud Archief Suriname: Gouvernementssecretarie, 1.05.10.01, inv. nr. 2, NA Netherlands.

48 Johannes Postma, "Suriname and Its Atlantic Connections, 1667–1815," in *Riches from Atlantic Commerce: Dutch Transatlantic Trade and Shipping, 1585–1817*, ed. Johannes Postma and Victor Enthoven (Boston: Brill, 2003), 311.

49 It is estimated that Greenwood painted about 115 paintings during his time in Suriname. For more on his career there and the money he made, see Alan Burroughs, *John Greenwood in America, 1745–1752* (Andover: Addison Gallery of American Art, 1943), 13–14. One guinea was worth 21 shillings or 1.05 pounds sterling, thus the conversion rate.

50 John Greenwood Diaries, No. 2, 1752–1758, 110, Mss Collection BV Greenwood, John (artist), New-York Historical Society, New York.

51 Ibid., 113.

52 For more on planters and alcohol in the West Indies and their overindulgence more generally, see Richard S. Dunn, *Sugar and Slaves: The Rise of the Planter Class in the English West Indies, 1624–1713* (1972; Chapel Hill: University of North Carolina Press, 2001), 279–280.

53 John Greenwood Diaries, No. 2, 1752–1758, 35.

54 Ibid., 38.

55 Katelyn D. Crawford, "Painting New England in the Dutch West Indies: John Greenwood's *Sea Captains Carousing in Suriname*," in *The Eighteenth Centuries: Global Networks of Enlightenment*, ed. David T. Gies and Cynthia Wall (Charlottesville: University of Virginia Press, 2018), 184.

56 Ibid., 186–187.

57 Ibid., 184.

58 "Newark Jackson," docket 7944, SCPR.

59 *New England Weekly Journal*, 17 August 1736.

60 Karwan Fatah-Black describes a similar phenomenon used by North American ship captains in Suriname at the same time. They would claim to be headed to the Portuguese colony of Madeira and officials in Suriname likewise signed paperwork noting that as their intended destination. Like Jackson and Newfoundland, this gave captains cover when they returned to their home ports and allowed them to claim they were transshipping molasses to Madeira. In reality, they sold it at home. See Fatah-Black, *White Lies and Black Markets*, 59–61.

61 18 March 1737/8, "Naval Office Shipping Lists for Barbados," CO 33/16, NAUK. There is evidence to suggest that Jackson was on a smuggling run to Suriname when Barbadian officials created this record. Authorities claimed that the *Industry* was "not loaded" when it departed Barbados, nor did officials bother to list where Jackson was headed after leaving Barbados. One historian notes that the "practice was prevalent" for "customs officers to issue fictious clearance papers to sea-captains." Thus, a "very large but uncertain share of the exports" from North America recorded as landed in Barbados, like those Jackson carried, "were actually delivered in Santo Domingo or Surinam." See Frank Wesley Pitman, *The Development of the British West Indies, 1700–1763* (New Haven, CT: Yale University Press, 1917). Adding evidence for this assertion, in 1738 the customs collector for Barbados was Edward Lascelles, an allegedly corrupt and notoriously lax official who was himself involved in smuggling. Edward was the half brother of Henry Lascelles, and both would become close business partners with Gedney Clarke. For Edward Lascelles's career, including multiple investigations into his activities and the allegations of corruption, see S. D. Smith, *Slavery, Family, and Gentry Capitalism in the British Atlantic: The World of the Lascelles, 1648–1834* (New York: Cambridge University Press, 2006), 60–64, 70–72. As Jackson's final voyage in 1743 suggests, there is also the possibility that Jackson left the *Industry* and its cargo in Barbados to take command of a different ship to trade within the Caribbean.

62 For more information on Dowse and his career, see Leonard W. Labaree, ed., *The Papers of Benjamin Franklin*, vol. 3, *January 1, 1745, through June 30, 1750* (New Haven, CT: Yale University Press, 1961), 155–156n6.

63 Jackson was in the employ of George Ledain, a Boston ship captain and merchant, and Gedney Clarke, a Barbadian merchant, both featured in the

next chapter. Clarke, through his connections to the London merchant firm Lascelles & Maxwell, had access to gold from the Gold Coast of Africa (see chapter 3). It also seems the smuggling ring received payments in silver from planters purchasing slaves in Suriname.

64 Marjoleine Kars offers a succinct, effective definition of bills of exchange as "a complicated instrument somewhat comparable to a modern check, involving interest and subject to market fluctuations, drawn not on a bank, but on a merchant or private person." Bills of exchange were incredibly common in colonial commerce. They were subject to one's trust and reputation, meaning the more upstanding the firm drawn upon, the better. See Kars, *Breaking Loose Together: The Regulator Rebellion in Pre-revolutionary North Carolina* (Chapel Hill: University of North Carolina Press, 2002), 65.

65 Jackson was not the first chocolatier in Boston. A James Lubbock of Boston called himself a "Chocolate-Grinder" when he took out an advertisement for selling chocolate and grinding cacao in March 1727. Later that year, he took out a runaway advertisement for his enslaved man. See *New England Weekly Journal*, 20 March 1727 and 4 September 1727.

66 For more on the chocolate industry in early Massachusetts, see Anne Blaschke, "Chocolate Manufacturing and Marketing in Massachusetts, 1705–1825," in *Chocolate: History, Culture, and Heritage*, ed. Louis Evan Grivetti and Howard-Yana Shapiro (Hoboken, NJ: John Wiley, 2009), 345–358.

67 Breen, "'Baubles of Britain.'"

68 James F. Gay, "Chocolate Production and Uses in 17th and 18th Century North America," in Grivetti and Shapiro, *Chocolate*, 282–283.

69 *New England Weekly Journal*, 26 February 1740 and 25 March 1740.

70 "Newark Jackson," docket 7944, SCPR.

71 For more on chocolate consumption in eighteenth-century Britain, see Kate Loveman, "The Introduction of Chocolate into England: Retailers, Researchers, and Consumers, 1640–1730," *Journal of Social History* 47, no. 1 (Fall 2013): 27–46. Consumption patterns would have been similar across the empire and in Boston.

72 "Newark Jackson," docket 7944, SCPR.

73 Ibid.

74 Gay, "Chocolate Production," 283.

75 Jared Ross Hardesty, "'The Negro at the Gate': Enslaved Labor in Eighteenth-Century Boston," *NEQ* 87, no. 1 (March 2014): 72–98.

76 Deed for Pew 13, 29 May 1739, ONCR, box 19, folder 15; "List of Subscribers for Building Steeple, 1740," 15 April 1740, ONCR, box OS 1, folder 5, MHS.

77 For the location of pew 13, see "Pew Plans, 1723–1811," ONCR, box 20, folder 25, MHS.

78 There is evidence that Jackson was not a particularly dedicated Anglican. His probate inventory lists a number of books he owned. Many of these books were religious works. He owned a copy of Thomas Bradbury's two-volume *The Mystery of Godliness Considered*, a collection of sixty-one sermons, an edition of Lewis Bayly's *Practice of Piety*, and Robert Nelson's *Companion for the Festivals and Fasts of the Church of England*. Bradbury was one of the most prominent Congregationalists in eighteenth-century Britain, while Bayly, although from an earlier generation, was a Puritan and *Practice of Piety* was one of the most popular Puritan tracts of all time. Bradbury and Bayly were officially "dissenters" in the eyes of the Anglican Church. Meanwhile, Robert Nelson, although an Anglican, was a nonjuror, or an Anglican who supported the Stuart monarchy and opposed the Glorious Revolution. Jackson, then, owned books published by people who were very much outside the Anglican mainstream, which may suggest his own religious beliefs were not in line with those of Anglican Church. Thus, perhaps his association at Old North was more about social connections than religiosity.

There is a possibility that Jackson had evangelical leanings. What would later be known as Methodism started as an evangelical reform movement within the Anglican Church that drew heavily from Calvinist theology (like that of Bradbury and Bayly) and the nonjuroring tradition. Perhaps Jackson was a proto-Methodist. Equally likely, he inherited the Puritan/Congregational texts from a relative as many younger New Englanders converted to Anglicanism in the eighteenth century, or perhaps Jackson just liked to read religious texts from a variety of Protestant traditions and was an otherwise loyal Anglican. See "Newark Jackson's Inventory," docket 7944, SCPR; Nancy L. Rhoden, *Revolutionary Anglicanism: The Colonial Church of England Clergy during the American Revolution* (New York: Palgrave, 1999); and Geordan Hammond, *John Wesley in America: Restoring Primitive Christianity* (New York: Oxford University Press, 2014), chap. 1.

79 In defining social capital and social networks, sociologist Charles Kadushin follows the argument of Robert Putnam that social networks have value "because they allow access to resources and valued social attributes such as trust, reciprocity, and community values." See Kadushin, *Understanding Social Networks: Theories, Concepts, and Findings* (New York: Oxford

University Press, 2012), 164–165. For more on social capital formation, see Robert I. Rotberg, ed., *Patterns of Social Capital: Stability and Change in Historical Perspective* (New York: Cambridge University Press, 2001). Scholars of the early American republic have more directly engaged questions of social capital and social networking than those of the colonial era. See, for example, Hunter Price, "The Traveling Life of John Littlejohn: Methodism, Mobility, and Social Exchange from Revolutionary Virginia to Early Republican Kentucky," *Journal of Southern History* 82, no. 2 (2016): 237–268.

80 "Newark Jackson's Account," docket 7944, SCPR, MSA. For a list of some of the prominent merchants and their widows associated with King's Chapel (including Jackson's creditors), see Henry Wilder Foote, *Annals of King's Chapel from the Puritan Age of New England to the Present Day*, 2 vols. (Boston: Little, Brown, 1882), 1:549n2.

81 Daniel Vickers, "Competency and Competition: Economic Culture in Early America," *WMQ* 47, no. 1 (1990): 4.

82 Trevor Burnard, *Mastery, Tyranny, and Desire: Thomas Thistlewood and His Slaves in the Anglo-Jamaican World* (Chapel Hill: University of North Carolina Press, 2004), 38.

83 Vickers, "Competency and Competition," 4.

84 See, for example, Craig Muldrew, *The Economy of Obligation: The Culture of Credit and Social Relations in Early Modern England* (London: Macmillan, 1998). For the New England context, see W. T. Baxter, *The House of Hancock: Business in Boston, 1724–1775* (New York: Russel & Russel, 1965), chap. 2; James E. Wadsworth, ed., *The World of Credit in Colonial Massachusetts: James Richard and His Daybook, 1692–1711* (Boston: University of Massachusetts Press, 2017), 1–31; and Daniel Vickers, "Neighbors and Hedges: Shopkeeping in Early New England," in *Market Ethics and Practices, c. 1300–1850*, ed. Simon Middleton and James E. Shaw (New York: Routledge, 2018), 109–126.

85 The amounts from the previous two paragraphs are from "Newark Jackson's Account," docket 7944, SCPR, MSA.

86 *Boston Gazette*, 8 November 1743.

87 Burnard, *Mastery, Tyranny, and Desire*, 130.

88 Historian Trevor Burnard argues that slaves were not only laborers but also investments that generally increased in value over time and were readily salable to cover debts or quickly raise cash. See ibid., 55–58.

89 "Newark Jackson's Account," docket 7944, SCPR, MSA.

90 *Boston Gazette*, 8 November 1743.

2. THE CARTEL

1 *Boston News-Letter*, 4 August 1743.

2 Ibid. These were some of Ledain's clothes stolen and worn by the mutineers on the *Rising Sun*.

3 Other historians have likewise reconstructed early American smuggling rings. See, for example, Thomas M. Truxes, *Defying Empire: Trafficking with the Enemy in Colonial New York* (New Haven: Yale University Press, 2008) and Tyson Reeder, *Smugglers, Pirates, and Patriots: Free Trade in the Age of Revolution* (Philadelphia: University of Pennsylvania Press, 2019).

4 For more on the Jerseymen in Essex County, see David Thomas Konig, *Law and Society in Puritan Massachusetts: Essex County, 1629–1692* (Chapel Hill: University of North Carolina Press, 1979), 70–72, and Marsha L. Hamilton, *Social and Economic Networks in Early Massachusetts* (State College: Pennsylvania State University Press, 2009), 115–119.

5 *Vital Records of Newbury, Massachusetts to the End of the Year 1849*, vol. 2: *Marriages and Deaths* (Salem: Essex Institute, 1911), 12.

6 For more on the shipyard of Mary's father, see "Will of Isaac Adams," docket 6359, SCPR, MSA.

7 It is unclear when the children were born, but Mary Jr. later married Elijah Doubleday, the scion of another merchant family in the Suriname trade, and George Jr. joined the Royal Navy, where he served in the West Indies and died, most likely of disease, in 1749. Mary Jr.'s marriage can be found in Transcriptions of Marriage Records, box 18, folder 32, Old North Church Records Ms. N-2249, MHS. Evidence of George Jr.'s death can be found in "Letter of Administration, George Ledain," docket 9323, SCPR, MSA. George Jr. served on a succession of ships, including the *Rippon's Prize*, the *Enterprise*, and finally the *Cornwall*. The latter ship had been engaged in a number of operations in the West Indies, includ-ing capturing a fort in Saint Domingue in March 1748. Given the date of the probate administration document, 1 August 1749, however, the *Cornwall* was between campaigns. Disease stalked naval crews in the West Indies and resulted in high death rates, especially among sailors from Britain and the northern colonies. See Daniel A. Baugh, *British Naval Administration in the Age of Walpole* (Princeton, NJ: Princeton University Press, 1965), 217–218.

8 12 June 1731, "Naval Office Shipping Lists Bahamas," CO 27/12, NAUK.

9   4 April 1733 and 12 May 1733, Oud Archief Suriname:
Gouvernementssecretarie, 1.05.10.01, inv. nr. 1, NA Netherlands. Much like
Newark Jackson, George Ledain often spent more than a month in
Suriname at a time. His experiences would have been very similar to those
of Jackson.

10 8 November 1736 and 15 December 1736, Oud Archief Suriname:
Gouvernementssecretarie, 1.05.10.01, inv. nr. 2, NA Netherlands.

11 Ledain co-owned these vessels with Boston merchant Timothy Prout. See
15 April 1736 and 26 October 1737, "Naval Office Shipping Lists for
Barbados," CO 33/16, NAUK.

12 "Barkentijn off [*sic*] schoender" in "Inventory."

13 For more on topsail schooners and why they were used, see Phillip Reid,
*The Merchant Ship in the British Atlantic, 1600–1800: Continuity and
Innovation in a Key Technology* (Boston: Brill, 2020), 209, 260.

14 Joseph A. Goldenberg, *Shipbuilding in Colonial America* (Charlottesville:
University of Virginia Press, 1976), 98–99. The age of the ship can be
found in the same inventory as its description. See "Inventory."

15 S. D. Smith, "Gedney Clarke of Salem and Barbados: Transatlantic Super-
Merchant," *New England Quarterly* 76, no. 4 (December 2003): 505–506.

16 Ibid., 510.

17 For more on the Lascelles, see S. D. Smith, *Slavery, Family, and Gentry
Capitalism in the British Atlantic: The World of the Lascelles, 1648–1834*
(New York: Cambridge University Press, 2006). The marriage of Gedney
Clarke Jr. and Frances Lascelles can be found on 119–120.

18 There is an extensive correspondence, by the standards of Gedney Clarke at
least, between Clarke and the Lascelles regarding their partial ownership
of the *Rising Sun* and the insurance policy. See Simon D. Smith, ed.,
Lascelles and Maxwell Letter Books (1739–1769), Microfilm Edition, reel 1:
Lascelles and Maxwell Letter Book (September 1743–December 1746), 73–74,
80, 98, 149–150, 171, 178–179, 187–188, 197–198, 232, 271, 276, 300–301. For a
list of the underwriters, see Lascelles and Maxwell to Gedney Clarke, 14
July 1744, 178–179. Lascelles and Maxwell underwrote 500 pounds of the
total 1,500.

19 Smith, "Gedney Clarke," 511.

20 The Tothills can be found in Joyce D. Goodfriend, *Before the Melting Pot:
Society and Culture in Colonial New York City, 1664–1730* (Princeton, NJ:
Princeton University Press, 1992), 211.

21 Tothill married Elizabeth Shore in 1726. The marriage record did not note
Tothill was from elsewhere, suggesting he had already established himself

in Boston by that date. See City of Boston, ed., *Records Relating to the Early History of Boston: Boston Marriages from 1700 to 1751*, vol. 28 (Boston: Rockwell and Churchill, 1898), 135. Samuel Myles, an Anglican rector in Boston, married Tothill and Shore, demonstrating Tothill's membership and participation in the Church of England like Jackson, Ledain, Clarke, and other men involved with the smuggling ring.

22 The timeline for the death of his wife and his move to Suriname can be attributed to an advertisement from early June 1737 when Tothill advertised his Boston home for sale. See *Boston Gazette*, 6 June 1737.

23 There are some surviving pieces of evidence, beyond the mutiny, that relate to Tothill's activities as an agent. For a consignment of tropical goods from Suriname he sent to the Wendells, see Edward Tothill to John and Jacob Wendell, 6 February 1740, in *Quincy, Wendell, Holmes, and Upham Family Papers, 1633–1910*, Microfilm Edition, reel 23, MHS. His more general activities as an agent can be found in the bills of exchange recorded by colonial officials in Suriname. In November 1743, for example, Tothill provided salt cod to Plantation Boekesteijn. See 4 November 1743, Notarissen Suriname tot 1828 1.05.11.14, inv. nr. 759, f. 130, NA Netherlands.

24 Tothill married Sara van Hertsbergen shortly after arriving in Suriname in 1738. She seems to have died in childbirth, based on a will that refers to an unborn child, in September 1739. See "Testament of Sara van Hertsbergen," 14 September 1739, Notarissen Suriname tot 1828 1.05.11.14, inv. nr. 326, f. 71–72, NA Netherlands. He owned part of a plantation and the mansion house and warehouse at the time of his death in early 1749. See "Inventory of late Edward Tothill," 18/20 February 1749, Notarissen Suriname tot 1828 1.05.11.14, inv. nr. 187, f. 164–172, NA Netherlands.

25 Judicial Act, 13 August 1743, Notarissen Suriname tot 1828 1.05.11.14, inv. nr. 326, f. 179, NA Netherlands.

26 For "Edele Leeven," see "Inventory of late Edward Tothill," 18/20 February 1749, Notarissen Suriname tot 1828 1.05.11.14, inv. nr. 187, f. 164, NA Netherlands.

27 Historians have studied trade and merchant diasporas since the 1980s, but despite evidence of New England merchants living across the Americas and in Europe during the eighteenth century, there has not been an attempt to study them holistically or apply concepts such as "trade diaspora" to explain their activities. Rather, the idea of "trade diaspora" has largely been used by scholars of Africa and Asia looking to move away from Eurocentric explanations of the rise of global trade.

That is especially true for scholars studying the activities of Indian merchants in Central Asia during the early modern period. Those works inform my discussion of Tothill here. For the foundational work, see Philip Curtin, *Cross-Cultural Trade in World History* (New York: Cambridge University Press, 1984). The scholarship on Central Asia includes Stephen Dale, *Indian Merchants and Eurasian Trade, 1600–1750* (New York: Cambridge University Press, 1994) and S. C. Levi, *Indian Diaspora in Central Asia and Its Trade, 1550–1900* (Boston: Brill, 2002). The quote can be found in Levi, *Indian Diaspora*, 88.

28 For discussion of foreign merchants and moneylending, see Levi, *Indian Diaspora*, 1–2.

29 "Inventory of Edward Tothill," 9 August 1740, Notarissen Suriname tot 1828 1.05.11.14, inv. nr. 172, NA Netherlands. It was a significant sum of money. The average annual wage earned in the Netherlands for 1740 was 551 guilders; in other words, Tothill had lent out nearly eight times what a working person in the Netherlands would have made in a year. Information on wages in the Netherlands can be found in a website and database published online by the International Institute of Social History. See Jan Luiten van Zanden, "Prices and Wages and the Cost of Living in the Western Part of the Netherlands, 1450–1800" (International Institute of Social History), http://www.iisg.nl/hpw/brenv.php (website) and http://www.iisg.nl/hpw/brenv.xls (database).

30 Levi, *Indian Diaspora*, 1–2.

31 Edward Tothill to John and Jacob Wendell, 6 February 1740, in *Quincy, Wendell, Holmes, and Upham Family Papers, 1633–1910*, Microfilm Edition, reel 23, MHS.

32 For "goedvriend," see 7 July 1743, Oud Archief Suriname: Gouvernementssecretarie, 1.05.10.01, inv. nr. 3, NA Netherlands.

33 Xabier Lamikiz, *Trade and Trust in the Eighteenth-Century Atlantic World: Spanish Merchants and Their Overseas Networks* (London: Boydell, 2010), 150, 150n34.

34 For more on the Navigation Acts, see L. A. Harper, *The English Navigation Laws: A Seventeenth-Century Experiment in Social Engineering* (New York: Columbia University Press, 1939), and John J. McCusker and Russell R. Menard, *The Economy of British America, 1607–1789* (Chapel Hill: University of North Carolina Press, 1986), 46–50, 77–78.

35 Albert B. Southwick, "The Molasses Act—A Source of Precedents," *WMQ* 8, no. 3 (July 1951): 389.

36 Ibid., 390.

37 For more on "salutary neglect," see James A. Henretta, *Salutary Neglect: Colonial Administration under the Duke of Newcastle* (Princeton, NJ: Princeton University Press, 1972), 104.

38 Frank Wesley Pitman, *The Development of the British West Indies, 1700–1763* (New Haven, CT: Yale University Press, 1917), 206.

39 Southwick, "Molasses Act," 389.

40 For more on the West India interest and the Molasses Act, see Richard B. Sheridan, "The Molasses Act and the Market Strategy of the British Sugar Planters," *Journal of Economic History* 17, no. 1 (1957): 62–83, esp. 68–72.

41 One historian has called the ability of colonists to evade the Molasses Act as "persistent and general." Others note it was "neither clearly enforced nor obeyed." Thomas C. Barrow, *Trade and Empire: The British Customs Service in Colonial America, 1660–1775* (Cambridge, MA: Harvard University Press, 1967), 143, and McCusker and Menard, *Economy of British America*, 163.

42 McCusker and Menard, *Economy of British America*, 163–164.

43 For more on Dinwiddie and his activities as inspector general in Barbados, see Kenneth Morgan, "Robert Dinwiddie's Reports on the British American Colonies," *WMQ* 65, no. 2 (April 2008): 313–314. Even the Board of Trade and Plantations, the colonial governing body in London, and Commissioners of Customs found Dinwiddie's moves against Lascelles overzealous—although they did confirm them as true—and reprimanded him for heavy-handedness.

44 The consolidation of the sugar trade in Britain can be found in Sheridan, "Molasses Act," 69, 70.

45 For the importance of trust in business relationships during the time period, see Sheryllynne Haggerty, *"Merely for Money?" Business Culture in the British Atlantic, 1750–1815* (Liverpool: Liverpool University Press, 2012), 66–67.

46 Ledain purchased pew 7, which was kitty-corner to Jackson's pew 13. For Ledain, see Vestry Meeting, 13 May 1740, Vestry Meeting Minutes, vol. 2, ONCR, MHS.

47 "A List of Gentlemen Subscribers to the Steeple at Christ Church in Boston," Old North Accounts, vol. 15, 118, ONCR, MHS. Further proving their friendship, Tothill's name appears next to Ledain's in this list.

48 Vestry Meeting, 29 April 1742, Vestry Meeting Minutes, vol. 2, ONCR, MHS.

49 The church wardens sent a letter of thanks to Clarke. See Church Wardens to Gedney Clarke, n.d. [ca. 1745], "Old North Papers Relating to Christ Church Bells, 1745–1747," box 21, folder 3, ONCR, MHS.

50 For more on the relationship between social capital, slavery, and religion, see Nicholas M. Beasley, *Christian Ritual and the Creation of British Slave Societies,*

1650–1780 (Athens: University of Georgia Press, 2010), and Andrea Catherina Mosterman, *Spaces of Enslavement: A History of Slavery and Resistance in Dutch New York* (Ithaca, NY: Cornell University Press, 2021), chap. 5.

51 Petition of William Wingfield, Massachusetts Archives Collection, vol. 42, 113–114, MSA.

52 David Lowenthal, "Colonial Experiments in French Guiana, 1760–1800," *Hispanic American Historical Review* 32, no. 1 (February 1952): 23.

53 James Pritchard, *In Search of Empire: The French in the Americas, 1670–1730* (New York: Cambridge University Press, 2004), 201–208.

54 Deposition of Thomas Wilson, July 1742, *Suffolk Files* 55611, MSA.

55 Lowenthal, "Colonial Experiments," 25.

56 *American Weekly Mercury*, 11 August 1743.

57 Karwan Fatah-Black, *White Lies and Black Markets: Evading Metropolitan Authority in Colonial Suriname, 1650–1800* (Boston: Brill, 2015), 183.

58 The Society of Suriname was a joint venture funded by the city of Amsterdam, the Dutch West India Company, and the Van Aerssen van Sommelsdijck family. For more on the Society's structure and governance, see Wim Klooster and Gert Oostindie, *Realm between Empires: The Second Dutch Atlantic, 1680–1815* (Ithaca, NY: Cornell University Press, 2018), 60.

59 The Society of Suriname ultimately allowed this limited trade because of pressure from the planters and other colonists. Ever since the Dutch took control of the colony in 1667, residents had advocated for liberalizing commerce while conducting an illegal trade with foreign ships and merchants, who were largely from New England and Barbados. For more on the text of these laws and the pressure applied by colonists, see Fatah-Black, *White Lies and Black Markets*, 53–54

60 For more on New England's horse trade, especially with Suriname, see Deane Phillips, *Horse Raising in Colonial New England* (Ithaca, NY: Cornell University Press, 1922), 910. For a more modern account, see Johannes Postma, "Breeching the Mercantile Barriers of the Dutch Colonial Empire: North American Trade with Surinam during the Eighteenth Century," in *Merchant Organization and Maritime Trade in the North Atlantic, 1660–1815*, ed. Olaf Uwe Janzen (St. John's: International Maritime Economic History Association, 1998), 116–119.

61 For Ledain in Barbados, see "Naval Office Shipping Lists for Barbados," 15 April 1736 and 26 October 1737, CO 33/16, NAUK. His departure from Suriname can be found in 15 December 1736, Oud Archief Suriname: Gouvernementssecretarie, 1.05.10.01, inv. nr. 2, NA Netherlands.

62 Jesse Cromwell, *The Smugglers' World: Illicit Trade and Atlantic Commodities in Eighteenth-Century Venezuela* (Chapel Hill: University of North Carolina Press, 2018), 128. Thomas M. Truxes also provides an overview of the myriad strategies for smuggling. See Truxes, *Defying Empire*, chap. 3.

63 Besides Suriname, it was common for British merchants and ship captains to smuggle while conducting legal trade in the Spanish colonies, especially after Britain received the *asiento*, a contract for a monopoly on slave trading to Spanish America, in 1713. This parallel trade was one of the leading causes of a war between Britain and Spain in 1739. See Adrian Finucane, *The Temptations of Trade: Britain, Spain, and the Struggle for Empire* (Philadelphia: University of Pennsylvania Press, 2016), 124. There is also a question of how smugglers conducted this parallel trade. In the Americas, it was most likely conducted openly once a ship had cleared the port. Nevertheless, studies have shown how in Europe those involved in the transportation of goods, such as carters, and those who helped store goods while in transit, such as innkeepers and tavern owners, built special compartments and hiding spaces for contraband. It is possible these existed on ships as well. See Michael Kwass, *Contraband: Louis Mandarin and the Making of the Global Underground* (Cambridge, MA: Harvard University Press, 2014), 94–97.

64 Cromwell, *Smugglers' World*, 128. In Europe, the nobility and clergy would often assist smugglers and help them flout local laws. See Kwass, *Contraband*, 97–100.

65 Fatah-Black, *White Lies and Black Markets*, 58–61.

66 Cromwell, *Smugglers' World*, 128.

67 For more on this practice, see ibid., 128–129.

68 3 June 1743, Oud Archief Suriname: Gouvernementssecretarie, 1.05.10.01, inv. nr. 3, NA Netherlands.

69 Ibid., 7 June 1743.

70 Ibid., 10 June 1743.

71 Ibid., 11 June 1743.

72 For the *Rising Sun*'s departure, see *Boston News-Letter*, 4 August 1743 and *New-York Weekly Journal*, 15 August 1743. A description of how smuggling functioned can be found in Fatah-Black, *White Lies and Black Markets*, 133.

73 It seems not only that the smuggling ring purchased these tools from Britain and dispatched them to Suriname, but that some were manufactured in the colonies. Besides his wife Amey, Newark Jackson's other executor was Thomas Greenough, an "instrument maker" in Boston

renowned for making navigational tools. See Jackson's Inventory, docket 7944, SCPR. For Greenough, see Silvio A. Bedini, *Early American Scientific Instruments and Their Makers* (Washington, DC: Smithsonian Institution, 1964), 85–92.

74 These items are enumerated in *Clarke v. Wingfield* and *Ledain v. Wingfield*, 6 July 1742, SCCP, 1742, 111, MSA.

75 *Ledain v. Wingfield*, 6 July 1742, SCCP, 111. Wingfield probably purchased other commodities as well, but was accused of swindling Ledain and Clarke only out of the cacao. As mentioned, chocolate was largely drank in the eighteenth century, meaning chocolate consumption in England should be compared to tea and coffee, which it lagged behind. While gaining in popularity, it was still largely consumed by the wealthy, while middling people occasionally partook. Much of that had to do with the fact that, compared to tea and coffee, "chocolate-drinking was more expensive; chocolate made less liquid per pound that tea or coffee; and chocolate was more complex to prepare than the other" beverages. See Kate Loveman, "The Introduction of Chocolate into England: Retailers, Researchers, and Consumers, 1640–1730," *Journal of Social History* 47, no. 1 (Fall 2013): 40.

76 See, for example, "Ledger of Imports and Exports, 1739," 33, CUST 3/39, NAUK.

77 "Petition of William Wingfield," Massachusetts Archives Collection, vol. 42, 113, MSA.

78 For the final verdict in arbitration, see "Wingfield & Clarke," August 1742, *Suffolk Files* 55890, MSA. In arbitration, each party in the lawsuit chose an advocate and the court appointed the third. Representing the interests of Clarke and Ledain was John Wendell who was Edward Tothill's kinsman and Clarke's friend.

79 Petition of William Wingfield, Massachusetts Archives Collection, vol. 42, 113–114, MSA.

80 Ibid.

81 See Haggerty, *"Merely for Money?,"* 102, for a discussion of reputation, its centrality to business relationships in the British Atlantic, and the way gossip could ruin one's reputation.

82 Deposition of Thomas Wilson, July 1742, *Suffolk Files* 55611, MSA.

83 Ralph Davis, *The Rise of the English Shipping Industry in the Seventeenth and Eighteenth Centuries* (London: Macmillan, 1962), 129–130.

84 Edward Bromfield to Gedney Clarke, 6 February 1743/4, Bromfield Family Collection, 1729–1844, vol. 1: Letter Book, 1742–1744, Mss. 664, NEHGS.

3. THE CARGO

1 For the inventory with the enslaved people, see "Inventory."

2 "13 slaeven soo jongens als meijsjes," in ibid.

3 "Neger" in ibid.

4 "Inventaris van Edward Tothill," 18/20 February 1749, Notarissen Suriname tot 1828 1.05.11.14, inv. nr. 187, f. 171, NA Netherlands.

5 S. D. Smith, "Gedney Clarke of Salem and Barbados: Transatlantic Super-Merchant," *New England Quarterly* 76, no. 4 (December 2003): 511–512. Clarke personally funded an army to help quell a massive slave rebellion in Berbice in 1763. See Marjoleine Kars, *Blood on the River: A Chronicle of Mutiny and Freedom on the Wild Coast* (New York: New Press, 2020).

6 "Inventory of William Wingfield," docket 15678, SCPR, MSA.

7 *Boston Gazette*, 8 November 1743.

8 *Boston Weekly Post-Boy*, 19 May 1740.

9 Wingfield departed Boston on 11 June 1740. See *Boston News-Letter*, 12 June 1740; *Ledain v. Wingfield*, 6 July 1742, SCCP, 1742, 111, MSA.

10 Historians call this trade the intercolonial or inter-American slave trade. The foundational work is Gregory E. O'Malley, *Final Passages: The Intercolonial Slave Trade of British America, 1619–1807* (Chapel Hill: University of North Carolina Press, 2014). In the British Empire, much of this intercolonial slave trading was legal. After the War of Spanish Succession, the British acquired the *asiento*, a contract to provide slaves to Spanish America. The South Sea Company, a British company chartered in part to service the *asiento*, operated a robust legal slave trade from Jamaica to parts of Spanish America. See O'Malley, *Final Passages*, chap. 6 and Adrian Finucane, *The Temptations of Trade: Britain, Spain, and the Struggle for Empire* (Philadelphia: University of Pennsylvania Press, 2016). Nevertheless, much like smuggling more generally, this legal trade opened the door for illicit slave trading in Spanish America. The activities of the illegal slave trade are often difficult to track, although historians have attempted. Scholars of Dutch America, especially those studying the Dutch island of Curaçao, have done some of the most important work on this topic. See, for example, Linda M. Rupert, *Creolization and Contraband: Curaçao in the Early Modern Atlantic World* (Athens: University of Georgia Press, 2012).

11 Clarke appears in the Fairfax family account books. See Fairfax Family Ledger, 1742, 1748, 1763, & 1772, George Washington's Mt. Vernon, Mt. Vernon, VA, 30–46. William Fairfax had a daughter from his first marriage, Anne, who married Lawrence Washington, the brother of George

Washington. Thus, George Washington and Gedney Clarke were related by marriage. When Washington visited Barbados in 1751–1752, the only time he ever left what became the United States, he stayed with Clarke and most likely contracted smallpox in his household. See George Washington, *George Washington's Barbados Diary, 1751–52*, ed. Alicia K. Anderson and Lynn A. Price (Charlottesville: University of Virginia Press, 2018).

12 The rebellion was known as the Stono Rebellion. For more on it and the aftermath, see Peter Charles Hoffer, *Cry Liberty: The Great Stono River Slave Rebellion of 1739* (New York: Oxford University Press, 2010).

13 Pringle was the brother of Andrew Pringle, a London merchant and business associate of the Lascelles. Andrew was also one of the insurance underwriters for the *Rising Sun*.

14 Robert Pringle to Gedney Clarke, 4 May 1744, in Walter B. Edgar, ed., *The Letterbook of Robert Pringle Volume Two: October 9, 1742–April 29, 1745* (Columbia: University of South Carolina Press, 1972), 685–686.

15 Robert Pringle to Gedney Clarke, 29 June 1744, in ibid., 715–716.

16 As with most parts of Gedney Clarke's life, we have only letters to him, not from him, about the slave trade to South Carolina. It is difficult to gauge how Clarke reacted to this information, thought about the slave trade to South Carolina, or the exact nature of his relationship with men like Pringle. That said, Clarke's partners in the slave trade to South Carolina changed over time. In the 1740s, he continued trading with Pringle, but by the 1750s he had also begun a business partnership with Henry Laurens, one of the leading slave traders in South Carolina. There is a robust correspondence between Clarke and Laurens throughout the 1750s. Much like Pringle, Laurens offered Clarke information on market conditions, instructing him when to dispatch captives. See, for example, Henry Laurens to Gidney Clarke, 1 January 1756, in Philip M. Hamer, George C. Rogers Jr., and Peggy J. Wehage, eds., *The Papers of Henry Laurens*, vol. 2: *November 1, 1755–December 31, 1758* (Columbia: University of South Carolina Press, 1970), 57–58.

17 For more on Clarke's activities in Dutch Guiana, see Bram Hoonhout, *Borderless Empire: Dutch Guiana in the Atlantic World, 1750–1800* (Athens: University of Georgia Press, 2020), 168–169. For the bigger picture of the relationship between these colonies and the British ones, see Wim Klooster and Gert Oostindie, *Realm between Empires: The Second Dutch Atlantic, 1680–1815* (Ithaca, NY: Cornell University Press, 2018), 51–52.

18 A number of historians have written about the floating factory scheme, often from the perspective of different London merchants invested in

the venture. One of the investors was Thomas Hall, a wealthy London merchant who made a significant portion of his wealth in the East India trade. See Conrad Gill, *Merchants and Mariners of the 18th Century* (London: Edward Arnold, 1961), chap. 8, for a history of the floating factory from Hall's perspective. There is a considerable trove of documents regarding the floating factory housed at the United Kingdom National Archives in Kew due to the number of lawsuits regarding the scheme. See Chancery Court Records, C 103/130, NAUK. For "floating factories" more generally, see Anne Ruderman, "Intra-European Trade in Atlantic Africa and the African Atlantic," *WMQ* 77, no. 2 (April 2020): 232–233. Special thanks to Anne Ruderman for sharing her work and photographs from C 103/130.

19 Gill, *Merchants and Mariners*, 92. There is evidence that Lascelles ordered all ships to head to Barbados first regardless of market conditions. In March 1740, Lascelles wrote a business associate in Barbados to have him notify any slave ships dispatched from the factory to resupply in Barbados and immediately head for Jamaica. See Henry Lascelles to Richard Morecroft, 28 March 1740, in S. D. Smith, ed., *Lascelles & Maxwell Letterbooks, 1739–1769*, reel 2: *Pares Transcripts* (Wakefield, UK: Microfilm Academic, 2003), f. 33. For Henry Lascelles's investment in the floating factory, see S. D. Smith, *Slavery, Family, and Gentry Capitalism in the British Atlantic: The World of the Lascelles, 1648–1834* (New York: Cambridge University Press, 2006), 74–76.

20 For an example of a slave ship that sailed from the coast of Africa southeast to São Tomé and then caught the South Equatorial Current across the Atlantic, see Robert Harms, *The Diligent: A Voyage through the Worlds of the Slave Trade* (New York: Basic Books, 2001), 302. The *Diligent* was a French slave ship headed for Martinique, but Dunning's ship would have taken a similar course.

21 The history of Anomabu can be found in Randy J. Sparks, *Where the Negroes Are Masters: An African Port in the Era of the Slave Trade* (Cambridge, MA: Harvard University Press, 2014). For more on the floating factory as the only source of European trade, see Paul E. Lovejoy, "The African Background of Venture Smith," in *Venture Smith and the Business of Slavery and Freedom*, ed. James Brewer Stewart (Amherst: University of Massachusetts Press, 2010), 42.

22 For more on the "military revolution" on the Gold Coast, see Vincent Brown, *Tacky's Revolt: The Story of an Atlantic Slave War* (Cambridge,

MA: Harvard University Press, 2020), 97–99. Fante's response to the Akyem attack can be found in Lovejoy, "African Background," 42.

23 Venture Smith, *A Narrative of the Life and Adventures of Venture, a Native of Africa: But Resident above Sixty Years in the United States of America. Related by Himself* (New London, CT: C. Holt, 1798), 5.

24 Ibid., 5–8.

25 Ibid., 8. For the argument it was an Akyem army, see Lovejoy, "African Background."

26 Smith, *Narrative of the Life*, 11.

27 Ibid., 11.

28 Ibid., 13.

29 Lovejoy, "African Background," 42 ("panyarring"), 46 (continued conflict between Akyem and Fante).

30 Smith, *Narrative of the Life*, 13.

31 Lovejoy, "African Background," 42.

32 Smith, *Narrative of the Life*, 13.

33 See Stephanie E. Smallwood, *Saltwater Slavery: A Middle Passage from Africa to American Diaspora* (Cambridge, MA: Harvard University Press, 2007).

34 Smith, *Narrative of the Life*, 13.

35 It is unclear exactly how long the *Charming Susanna* took to cross the Atlantic. Likewise, there is a discrepancy on the number of captives on board. Smith alleged 260, while the official record of the voyage on the Slave Voyages Database claims 85. See www.slavevoyages.org, Voyage ID 36067.

36 Smith, *Narrative of the Life*, 13.

37 This number is an estimate determined based on many factors, many of them covered below, including the size of the *Rising Sun* and the nature of the inter-imperial slave trade in the Americas. As historian Greg O'Malley has demonstrated, the average number of captives on board intercolonial slaving voyages that left the British Empire was sixty-eight. This figure, however, is skewed upward by the large slaving vessels that departed Jamaica for Spanish colonies. Likewise, those vessels to Spanish America, because the slave trade was legal, would have been overcrowded with enslaved people and carried little other cargo. The *Rising Sun*, however, also carried various trade goods from New England, thus cutting down on the space for captives. See O'Malley, *Final Passages*, 62–63.

   Moreover, the values of the ship, captives, and insurance policy allow us to calculate the number of captives. The men who took the inventory calculated that the ship, the captives, and some of the personal effects of the crew were worth 4,990 Suriname guilders. A Suriname guilder was worth 0.8333 of a Dutch guilder, meaning the ship, captives, and personal property were worth 4,158 Dutch guilders. While currency conversion is difficult for the eighteenth century, one historian estimates that early in the eighteenth century, 100 Dutch guilders was worth 9 British pounds sterling, a ratio of slightly more than 11:1. Converted to pounds sterling using this measurement, the ship and cargo were worth 375 pounds sterling (rounded up). When broken out alone, Dutch authorities apprized the ship as worth 1,850 Dutch guilders, or 167 pounds sterling (rounded up). The 13 enslaved children were worth 2,170 Suriname guilders or 1,808 Dutch guilders (rounded down). Each child was worth 139 Dutch guilders. The two men were valued at 300 Suriname guilders apiece or 250 Dutch guilders (rounded up). The children were worth 13 pounds sterling and the young men 23 pounds sterling (both rounded up) apiece when converted.

These converted figures allow us to calculate the potential number of enslaved people on board the *Rising Sun*. The Lascelles underwrote the *Rising Sun* and its cargo for 1,500 pounds sterling, suggesting the value of ship and its cargo. Despite being seaworthy, the *Rising Sun* had been damaged in the mutiny and was probably worth closer to 300 pounds when it departed. The cargo was thus ensured at 1,200 pounds. The ship did have other goods on board and, based off the Wingfield case, was probably worth 200–300 pounds. That left 900 pounds to cover the captives. The average price of an able-bodied enslaved male in the British Caribbean during early 1740s was around 28 pounds sterling. Nevertheless, we know these were recent arrivals from Africa, that there were enslaved children on board, and even the young men were not that highly valued. The average price of an enslaved person on the *Rising Sun* was probably closer to 20 pounds. That means there would have been, depending on the number of women and children, both valued less than men, between 45 and 50 people on board.

See "Inventory" for the Dutch valuations of the ship and captives. The Lascelles insurance policy can be found in Lascelles and Maxwell to Gedney Clarke, 14 July 1744, in S. D. Smith, ed., *Lascelles & Maxwell Letterbooks, 1739–1769*, reel 1: *Lascelles and Maxwell Letter Book (September 1743–December 1746)* (Wakefield, UK: Microfilm Academic, 2003), 178–179. For currency conversion, see "The Marteau Early 18th-Century Currency Converter: A Platform of Research in Economic

History," www.pierre-marteau.com. One scholar has found the early eighteenth-century conversions between Dutch guilders and British pounds sterling compiled by Marteau stayed fairly constant throughout the century. See Alexander J. P. Raat, *The Life of Governor Joan Gideon Loten (1710–1789): A Personal History of a Dutch Virtuoso* (Hilversum: Verloren, 2010), 598n50. Slave prices can be found in David Eltis, Frank D. Lewis, and David Richardson, "Slave Prices, the African Slave Trade, and Productivity in the Caribbean, 1674–1807," *Economic History Review* 58, no. 4 (November 2005): 679 (Table 2).

38 Olaudah Equiano, *The Interesting Narrative of the Life of Olaudah Equiano, or Gustavus Vassa, the African* (London, 1789), "yard," 86, "fortnight," 90.

39 See Smallwood, *Saltwater Slavery*, 189–190, on the bonds made by captives on board slave ships.

40 Quoted in O'Malley, *Final Passages*, 43.

41 For more on the destructiveness of the inter-American slave trade to enslaved communities and families, see ibid., 41–46.

42 Dutch authorities describe the ship and give the most detail about it in "Inventory." For information on schooners, their average size, and the difference between North American and West Indian schooners, see Joseph A. Goldenberg, *Shipbuilding in Colonial America* (Charlottesville: University of Virginia Press, 1976), 78.

43 O'Malley, *Final Passages*, 49.

44 Ibid., 50–51. While we do not have the details of the *Rising Sun*, there is information on other New England schooners available, especially from a couple decades later. In the mid-1760s, the British Navy purchased some schooners from Marblehead, Massachusetts, to serve as customs collectors off the coast of North America. The smallest of these, the *Sultana*, was nearly 53 tons and had a hold height of 8.3 feet. The *Rising Sun* was slightly bigger than the *Sultana*, suggesting a slightly larger cargo hold. See Rif Winfield, *British Warships in the Age of Sail 1714–1792: Design, Construction, Careers and Fates* (Barnsley: Seaforth Publishing, 2007), 297.

45 Paramaribo is roughly 650 nautical miles from Bridgetown, and eighteenth-century schooners could move five to seven knots per hour. That said, the ship had to battle against the South Equatorial Current as it sailed southeast from Barbados and then fight against the current of the Suriname River to reach Paramaribo. Both of those, depending on other conditions such as wind and tides, may have extended the voyage by a few days. Governor Jan Jacob Mauricius noted that the *Rising Sun* arrived on 3 June 1743 (New Style) or 23 May 1743 in the British Empire. That means

Jackson, Ledain, and the captives departed Barbados between 16 and 18 May 1743. See 3 June 1743, Oud Archief Suriname: Gouvernementssecretarie, 1.05.10.01, inv. nr. 3, NA Netherlands.

46 Smith, *Narrative of the Life*, 14.

47 For more on the relative comfort of the intercolonial slave trade for captives compared to the transatlantic, see O'Malley, *Final Passages*, 53–55.

48 Ibid., 56.

49 This information comes from the Slave Voyages Database (www.slavevoyages.org), which provides an account of most known slaving voyages from Africa between the fifteenth and nineteenth centuries. Each voyage is assigned an identification number. For the four voyages referenced here, see 10643, 10767, 10977, and 11010 (the *Surinaamse Galei*). These ships likewise seemed to have trouble selling their cargo. The *Surinaamse Galei*, for example, arrived on 2 June 1743 (New Style) and did not depart until 26 July, suggesting issues selling all the captives and acquiring a return cargo. Even more dramatic, the *Gulde Vrijheid* (10643) arrived on 30 May and did not depart until 20 August. There was, in general, a sharp uptick in slavers arriving to Paramaribo in 1743 compared to the two years prior. See Karwan Fatah-Black, "Paramaribo as Dutch and Atlantic Nodal Point, 1650–1795," in *Dutch Atlantic Connections, 1680–1800: Linking Empires, Bridging Borders*, ed. Gert Oostindie and Jessica V. Roitman (Boston: Brill, 2014), 56 (Figure 2.1). For more on the Dutch slave trade to Suriname, see Johannes Postma, *The Dutch in the Atlantic Slave Trade, 1600–1815* (New York: Cambridge University Press, 1990).

50 This preference was changing in Suriname as traders moved away from auctions to individual sales in the 1740s. See Postma, *Dutch in the Atlantic Slave Trade*, 170.

51 Cornelis Ch. Goslinga, *A Short History of the Netherlands Antilles and Surinam* (The Hague: Martinus Nijhoff, 1979), 100.

52 Klooster and Oostindie, *Realm between Empires*, 126–128.

53 Ibid., 87 (Table 12).

54 Ibid., 131–132.

55 Justin Roberts, "The Development of Slavery in the British Americas," in *The World of Colonial America: An Atlantic Handbook*, ed. Ignacio Diaz-Gallup (New York: Routledge, 2017), 135.

56 Natalie Zemon Davis, "Judges, Masters, Diviners: Slaves' Experience of Criminal Justice in Colonial Suriname," *Law and History Review* 29, no. 4 (2011): 930.

57 Klooster and Oostindie, *Realm between Empires*, 139–140.

58 Although his work is about the British West Indies, an excellent account of the impact of disease on slave societies in the Caribbean is Richard B. Sheridan, *Doctors and Slaves: A Medical and Demographic History of Slavery in the British West Indies, 1680–1834* (New York: Cambridge University Press, 1985).

59 Roberts, "Development of Slavery," 138.

60 Ibid., 139.

61 "Inventory of Edward Tothill," 9 August 1740, Notarissen Suriname tot 1828 1.05.11.14, inv. nr. 172 f. 78–79, NA Netherlands.

62 An inventory of Mopentibo was taken in 1739. See "Plantage Mopentibo," 26 March 1739, Notarissen Suriname tot 1828 1.05.11.14, inv. nr. 171 f. 49–59.

63 A number of Highlanders founded estates in Suriname following the Dutch acquisition in 1667. For more, see David Alston, "Scottish Slave Owners in Suriname, 1651–1863," *Northern Scotland* 9, no. 1 (2018): 17–43 and David Worthington, "Sugar, Slave-Owning, Suriname and the Dutch: Imperial Entanglement of the Scottish Highlands before 1707," *Dutch Crossing: Journal of Low Countries Study* 44, no. 1 (2020): 3–20.

64 Will of Henry McIntosh, 10 November 1725, Bristol County Probate Records vol. 5, 193–194, MSA.

65 "Plantage Fairfield," 22 July 1740, Oud Archief Suriname: Notarissen Suriname tot 1828, 1.05.11.14, inv. nr. 172 f. 39–49, NA Netherlands. In that same year, Isaac Royall had inherited his father's estate, including a large mansion house, slave quarters, and farm in Medford, Massachusetts. Until he departed the colonies as a Loyalist, Royall was the single largest slave owner in Massachusetts. In addition to his holdings in Massachusetts and his partial ownership of Fairfield through his wife, Royall also owned plantations in the British colony of Antigua. His house in Medford is now a site of interpreting Royall's relationship and connections to slavery. For more on Royall, see Alexandra Chan, *Slavery in the Age of Reason: Archaeology at a New England Farm* (Knoxville: University of Tennessee Press, 2007), and C. S. Manegold, *Ten Hills Farm: The Forgotten History of Slavery in the North* (Princeton, NJ: Princeton University Press, 2010). See https://royallhouse.org for the historical site.

66 A Dutch acre was nearly double the size of an English one. See Patrick Neill, *Journal of a Horticultural Tour through Some Parts of Flanders, Holland, and the North of France in the Autumn of 1817* (Edinburgh: Bell & Bradfute, 1823), 176.

67 The amount of land under use versus unused was calculated by examining the inventory. "Plantage Fairfield," 22 July 1740, Oud Archief Suriname:

Notarissen Suriname tot 1828, 1.05.11.14, inv. nr. 172 f. 39–49, NA
Netherlands.

68 John Gabriel Stedman, *Narrative of a Five Years Expedition against the
Revolted Negroes of Surinam*, ed. Richard Price and Sally Price (Baltimore:
Johns Hopkins University Press, 1988), 480, emphasis original.

69 A. Reyne, "Geschiedenis der Cacaocultuur in Suriname," *De West-Indische
Gids* 6 (1924/1925): 195.

70 "Plantage Fairfield," 22 July 1740, Oud Archief Suriname: Notarissen
Suriname tot 1828, 1.05.11.14, inv. nr. 172 f. 45, NA Netherlands. Chocolaet
was valued at 400 guilders. Although not as much as the plantation's
enslaved carpenters and masons, he was still worth the same as coopers
and other skilled slaves.

71 Stedman, *Narrative*, 480.

72 Reyne, "Geschiedenis der Cacaocultuur," 195.

73 Stedman, *Narrative*, 480.

4. THE CREW

1 The documents directly related to the mutiny never give McCoy's first
name. The deposition from the surviving crew and the excerpts from
Blake's journal refer to him only as the "Merchant's Clerk." His surname
comes from the summary of the case written by Dutch authorities and the
questions they asked Ferdinand da Costa and Thomas Lucas. The Dutch
documents refer to him as "Makaij," which would be Anglicized as McKay
or McCoy. See *Boston News-Letter*, 4 August 1743 and "Criminal
Complaint," which contains the testimony of both the crew and the
mutineers. Nevertheless, in the probate records of Massachusetts, there
are two administrative documents and an inventory for a John McCoy
(also spelled MacCoy, MacCay, and McCay in the various documents)
dated December 1743. The documents described McCoy as a mariner and
noted that he died intestate. These suggest a man who, while married, had
not become an independent ship captain or merchant nor had taken into
account the possibility of an early death. Likewise, in the inventory,
McCoy owned a significant amount of cocoa, illustrating his affiliation
with the smuggling ring. See "John McCoy's Inventory," 13 December 1743,
docket 8002, SCPR, MSA.

2 *New-York Weekly Journal*, 15 August 1743.

3 This narrative has been pieced together from the excerpts of Blake's
journal and the court records, especially the testimony of the crew. See
Boston News-Letter, 4 August 1743 and, including the quote, "Crew

Testimony." The court record includes both the original English testimony and a translation. Despite Blake's name appearing first, the first part of the document was Shaw's recollections before switching to those of Blake.

4 "Lads," *Boston News-Letter*, 4 August 1743. Names of the two men are from "Crew Testimony."

5 The idea of sailors as wage laborers in class conflict with their employers comes from Marcus Rediker, *Between the Devil and the Deep Blue Sea: Merchant Seamen, Pirates, and the Anglo-American Maritime World, 1700–1750* (New York: Cambridge University Press, 1986).

6 Nine crew members, including Jackson, was probably about the right size for the *Rising Sun*. As noted, it was a large schooner between 60 and 90 tons. One historian calculated that for London ships headed to the West Indies in the late 1730s, the average tonnage per crew member was 10.4. While the *Rising Sun* was not making a labor-intensive transatlantic journey, it would have nevertheless needed additional crew members to manage the enslaved people on board. See Ralph Davis, *The Rise of the English Shipping Industry in the Seventeenth and Eighteenth Centuries* (London: Macmillan, 1962), 59.

7 "Crew Testimony."

8 There was a John Skinner born in Marblehead, Massachusetts, in 1733. Given Jackson, Ledain, and Clarke's connections to Essex County and the boy's age in 1743, it is possible that this John Skinner was the same who perished on board the *Rising Sun*. Nevertheless, a genealogical listing notes beside this John Skinner's birth that "a" John Skinner later married in 1763. There were many John Skinners on Massachusetts's North Shore. See John Ward Dean, ed., *The New England Historical and Genealogical Register*, vol. 54 (1900), 419.

9 For more on the types of New England boys who entered maritime service as cabin boys, see Barry Levy, *Town Born: The Political Economy of New England from the Founding to the Revolution* (Philadelphia: University of Pennsylvania Press, 2009), 217–218.

10 Lucas noted being the cook when Dutch authorities interrogated him. See "Lucas's Examination." Cabin boys would also be put in "command" of a ship that was in port when the rest of the crew went on shore for recreation or to conduct business. Given the presence of enslaved people on the *Rising Sun*, however, it is doubtful that Skinner would have been left to watch the vessel on his own. See Davis, *Rise of the English Shipping Industry*, 113.

11 Levy, *Town Born*, 219.

12 McCoy's probate records describe him as a mariner. See "John McCoy's Inventory," 13 December 1743, docket 8002, SCPR, MSA.

13 Large numbers of Scots and Scots-Irish, Protestants of Scottish descent who had colonized Ireland in the seventeenth century, migrated to the American colonies in the eighteenth century. Some of the earliest of these migrants arrived in Boston, but then moved to the Merrimack River Valley in northern Massachusetts and New Hampshire. The mouth of the Merrimack is in Newburyport, Massachusetts, George Ledain's hometown, creating the possibility of interaction between the merchant and New England's Scots community. For more on the Scots-Irish in New England, see A. L. Perry, *Scots-Irish in New England* (Boston: J.S. Cushing, 1891). More modern accounts of Scots-Irish immigration to America are James G. Leyburn, *The Scotch-Irish: A Social History* (Chapel Hill: University of North Carolina Press, 1962), and Patrick Griffin, *The People with No Name: Ireland's Ulster Scots, America's Scots Irish, and the Creation of a British Atlantic World, 1689–1764* (Princeton, NJ: Princeton University Press, 2001). For the settlement of people with the surname McCoy in New Hampshire, see D. Hamilton Hurd, *History of Merrimack and Belknap Counties, New Hampshire* (Philadelphia: J. W. Lewis, 1885), 443, and Edward L. Parker, *The History of Londonderry, Comprising the Towns of Derry and Londonderry, N. H.* (Boston: Perkins and Whipple, 1851).

14 Boston Record Commissioners, eds., "City Document No. 150: Boston Marriages from 1700 to 1751," in *Documents of the City of Boston for the Year 1898*, vol. 3 (Boston: Municipal Printing Office, 1899), 339. The spelling of McCoy's name is all over the place, and in this record it is the phonetic "MaCay." His wife Jean's maiden name was "MaCoy."

15 "John McCoy's Inventory," 13 December 1743, docket 8002, SCPR, MSA.

16 James B. Bell, ed., *The Colonial Records of King Chapel, 1686–1776*, vol. 2 (Boston: Colonial Society of Massachusetts, 2019), 678.

17 Historian Daniel Vickers describes activities such as going to sea as "by-employments," or the types of extra work mostly young men performed to make extra money and find financial independence from their parents. Over the course of the eighteenth century, however, many of these by-employments became increasingly commonplace and workers became reliant on them as a source of income as the rural economy faltered. For how common young New England men going to sea was by the 1730s and 1740s, see Vickers, *Farmers and Fishermen: Two Centuries of*

Work in Essex County, Massachusetts, 1630–1850 (Chapel Hill: University of North Carolina Press, 1994), 251.

18 Levy, *Town Born*, 210.

19 The note about the mutiny occurring during the captain's watch can be found in "Crew Testimony."

20 Marcus Rediker describes the ways that mutinies "provided perhaps the most clear-cut examples of the way class lines were drawn on board the ship." It was common for a certain part of the crew to start a mutiny with the intent of winning other members over to their cause. See Rediker, *Between the Devil and the Deep Blue Sea*, chap. 5, quote 233.

21 In the correspondence between Lascelles and Maxwell and Gedney Clarke, they speak of the need to reward John Shaw for his loyalty, but never mention Blake, suggesting that Clarke did not discuss Blake or he was dead. See Lascelles and Maxwell to Gedney Clarke, 19 November 1743, in S. D. Smith, ed., *Lascelles & Maxwell Letterbooks, 1739–1769*, reel 1: *Lascelles and Maxwell Letter Book (September 1743–December 1746)* (Wakefield, UK: Microfilm Academic, 2003), 74.

22 Rediker, *Between the Devil and the Deep Blue Sea*, 84.

23 These parts of the copied log first appeared in the *Boston News-Letter*, 4 August 1743.

24 Margaret E. Schotte, *Sailing School: Navigating Science and Skill, 1550–1800* (Baltimore: Johns Hopkins University Press, 2019), 8–9.

25 Blake noted that they dropped the soldiers stationed on board the *Rising Sun* "below at the New Fort at the River called Cottica." The fort, Fort New Amsterdam, sits at a point where the Commewijne River flows into the Suriname River. *New-York Weekly Journal*, 15 August 1743.

26 Davis, *Rise of the English Shipping Industry*, 112.

27 Shaw served on board the *Charming Rebecca* under William Wingfield as a "Sailer." See "Deposition of Thomas Wilson," in Wingfield & Le Dain, July 1742, *Sufflok Files* 55611, MSA.

28 This account of Shaw's behavior can be found in ibid.

29 "Severall Voyages" and "knew the Land" in "Crew Testimony"; "pretty good Dutch," in *Boston News-Letter*, 4 August 1743.

30 Lascelles and Maxwell to Gedney Clarke, 19 November 1743, in Smith, *Lascelles & Maxwell Letterbooks*, 74.

31 "Da Costa's Examination."

32 Steven J. J. Pitt, "Building and Outfitting Ships in Colonial Boston," *EAS* 13, no. 4 (Fall 2015): 886. Pitt chalks merchant intervention up to nepotism,

but it could also be a form of patronage and/or a desire to exert control over the captain.

33 For "Portuguese Negroes," see *New-York Weekly Journal*, 15 August 1743 and "Extract of a Letter from Surinam, dated Aug. 15, 1743," *Gentleman's Magazine and Historical Chronicle* 13 (November 1743): 609. An example of "mulattoes" (*mulatten* in Dutch) can be found in 7 July 1743, Oud Archief Suriname: Gouvernementssecretarie, 1.05.10.01, inv. nr. 3, NA Netherlands.

34 "Synde beide Negers" in "Criminal Complaint."

35 The testimony of da Costa and Lucas is in the form of a question and answer, so authorities asked da Costa if he was born a white man, and he replied in the affirmative. "Bent gij een blanke van geboorten" and "Jaa" in "Da Costa's Examination."

36 "Moijta" in "da Costa's Examination."

37 See David Northup, *Africa's Discovery of Europe*, 3rd ed. (New York: Oxford University Press, 2013), 7, for Lisbon's black population.

38 Information on Lusophone sailors of color in the Brazilian slave trade can be found in Mary Ellen Hicks, "The Sea and the Shackle: African and Creole Mariners and the Making of a Luso-African Atlantic Commercial Culture, 1721–1835" (PhD diss., University of Virginia, 2015), esp. chap. 3.

39 "Lucas's Examination."

40 Much of the scholarship on sub-Saharan African slavery in the Italian city-states focuses on the era of the Renaissance (late fourteenth century through early seventeenth). Nevertheless, the literature acknowledges that it is "reasonable to assume that Black slaves remained a fixture of elite Venetian households well into the eighteenth century." See E. Natalie Rothman, "Contested Subjecthood: Runaway Slaves in Early Modern Venice," *Quaderni Storici* 47, no. 140 (August 2012): 439n13. For domestic servitude and manumission, see Sally McKee, "Domestic Slavery in Renaissance Italy," *SA* 29, no. 3 (September 2008): 312. Manumission was so commonplace in Venice that one historian notes it "was a stage or an event in their life course through which Venetian slaves could expect to pass." Kate Lowe, "Visible Lives: Black Gondoliers and Other Black Africans in Renaissance Venice," *Renaissance Quarterly* 66, no. 2 (Summer 2013): 421. One of the few books to examine slavery in Italy after the seventeenth century is Giulia Bonazza, *Abolitionism and the Persistence of Slavery in Italian States, 1750–1850* (New York: Palgrave Macmillan, 2019).

41 The manumission of mother and son also suggests that the man who enslaved Lucas's mother was also his father. See "Lucas's Examination."

42 See, for example, Pablo E. Perez-Mallaina, *Spain's Men of the Sea: Daily Life on the Indies Fleets in the Sixteenth Century* (Baltimore: Johns Hopkins University Press, 1998).

43 For Lucas's long career at sea, see his answer to inquiry 16, "Zegt van sijn jeugt aff aen, ter zee gevaren," in "Lucas's Examination."

44 See "Da Costa's Examination."

45 Rediker, *Between the Devil and the Deep Blue Sea*, 156–157.

46 For more on the wages of black sailors, see W. Jeffrey Bolster, *Black Jacks: African American Seamen in the Age of Sail* (Cambridge, MA: Harvard University Press, 1997).

47 See "Da Costa's Examination" and "Lucas's Examination." In March 1743, 130 Barbadian pounds was worth 100 pounds sterling, meaning a Barbadian pound was worth roughly three-fourths of a pound sterling; 55 Barbadian shillings was 2 pounds 5 shillings Barbadian or 2 pounds 2 shillings and 6.5 pence in pounds sterling, while 50 Barbadian shillings was 1 pound 18 shillings and about 6 pence sterling. See John J. McCusker, *Money and Exchange in Europe and America, 1600–1775* (Chapel Hill: University of North Carolina Press, 1978), 243. These were on the high end of wages for sailors and probably due, in part, to the short duration of the voyage, lasting no more than a month. Rediker, *Between the Devil and the Deep Blue Sea*, 122–123.

48 See Emma Christopher, *Slave Ship Sailors and Their Captive Cargoes, 1730–1807* (New York: Cambridge University Press, 2006), 17.

49 For more on Barbados's domestic sailing fleet, see Mary Draper, "Timbering and Turtling: The Maritime Hinterlands of Early Modern British Caribbean Cities," *EAS* 15, no. 4 (Fall 2017): 769–800.

50 Rediker notes that during war, sailor's wages were 27.7 percent higher than during peacetime. Rediker, *Between the Devil and the Deep Blue Sea*, 123.

51 Marcus Rediker, *The Slave Ship: A Human History* (New York: Penguin, 2007), 229.

52 See Hicks, "Sea and the Shackle," 6–7.

53 Rediker, *Slave Ship*, 251–253.

54 "Da Costa's Examination."

55 The information regarding who knew each other, wages, and jobs comes from the trial records: "Criminal Complaint." For more on Bridgetown, see Mary Draper, "The 'Metropolis of the Island' and the 'Thames of the West Indies': Early Modern Bridgetown, Barbados, 1627–1766" (PhD diss., University of Virginia, 2013). The sum of 55 Barbadian shillings was over

two pounds sterling, which meant Jackson offered wages that were competitive with most other merchant sailors during wartime.

56 Johannes Postma, *The Dutch in the Atlantic Slave Trade, 1600–1815* (New York: Cambridge University Press, 1990), 263.

57 Jackson's Inventory, docket 7944, SCPR, MSA.

58 There is a possibility that one other purpose of the smuggling ring was to bring hard currency back into the economies of Barbados and Massachusetts. In addition to procuring captives, the floating factory also purchased large amounts of gold on the Gold Coast and shipped it to Barbados before sending it to London, suggesting Clarke and Edward Lascelles dabbled in the specie market. See Conrad Gill, *Merchants and Mariners of the 18th Century* (London: Edward Arnold, 1961), 93–94. Likewise, Tothill's kinsmen and Clarke's friend Jacob Wendell was one of the backers of a scheme called the Silver Bank in Boston. By the late 1730s, paper currency issued by New England colonies had become nearly worthless. Since the colonies needed a medium of exchange, there were all sorts of plans to ensure that they could print paper money that was worth something. One scheme was the Land Bank, which backed paper currency with the value of land. There was widespread opposition to this project, and a group of leading New England merchants, who were largely Anglican and based in Boston, devised the idea of a bank that issued paper currency redeemable in silver. The problem, however, was where to obtain specie. Foreign trade was an option. A list of merchants backing the Silver Bank, including Wendell, can be found in Andrew MacFarland Davis, ed., "List of Subscribers to the Silver Bank," in *Publications of the Colonial Society of Massachusetts*, vol. 4 (Boston: Colonial Society of Massachusetts, 1910), 196–200. For more information on currency issues in Massachusetts, see Elizabeth E. Dunn, "'Grasping at the Shadow': The Massachusetts Currency Debate, 1690–1751," *New England Quarterly* 71, no. 1 (March 1998): 54–76, and Rosalind Remer, "Old Lights and New Money: A Note on Religion, Economics, and the Social Order in 1740 Boston," *WMQ* 47, no. 4 (October 1990): 566–573.

59 Rediker, *Slave Ship*, 218, 247–250.

60 See "Zegt dat den Bootsman toen gesegt heeft, dat hij Bootsman, Cap[itei]n was, en dat hij depos[an]t daar op heeft geantwoord wij sijnen allemaal Cap[itei]n" in "Da Costa Examination."

61 In 1717, the province of Venezuela, and by extension Orinoco, became part of the Viceroyalty of New Granada.

62 Bram Hoonhout and Thomas Mareite, "Freedom at the Fringes? Slave Flight and Empire-Building in the Early Modern Spanish Borderlands of Essequibo–Venezuela and Louisiana–Texas," *SA* 40, no. 1 (March 2019): 65–67.

63 This assessment of the mutineers' prospects in Orinoco is based off the cultures of smuggling present in colonial Venezuela. See Jesse Cromwell, *The Smugglers' World: Illicit Trade and Atlantic Communities in Eighteenth-Century Venezuela* (Chapel Hill: University of North Carolina Press, 2018). Nevertheless, it is doubtful if Orinoco would have been as welcoming as they thought. While the captives, manufactured goods such as cloth, and sugar may have been salable, it is questionable if the cacao and ship would have been. And while the colony welcomed outsiders, they were often runaways, who were then made wards of local missions and other institutions. It is hard to know what would happen to three men arriving under suspicious circumstances and asserting their right to free trade and independence. There was a logic to their choice in destination, but it was not a particularly sound one.

64 The references to the "Spaniard" can be found in "Da Costa's Examination" and "Lucas's Examination." The Spaniard's name comes from Thomas Lucas's testimony. "Gousinh" was most likely "Gausin" or "Gousin," which are Catalan surnames. Ferdinand da Costa claimed that Jackson "set him ashore" ("dat den Capn wel gedaan had van hem aen de wal te hebben gelaten watt"), while Thomas Lucas said the Spaniard "has been left here [Paramaribo] by the captain" ("en die den Capn bij bij sijne laatste rijse hier gelaten heeft"). It is odd that the mutineers used euphemisms for selling the man into slavery. Part of it could be due to translation issues. The mutineers spoke to the court in Portuguese. Their testimony came through a translator—Moses Bassano Jr., most likely one of the Suriname's many Portuguese Jewish residents—who would have been rapidly translating from Portuguese to Dutch as the clerk scribbled the answer. Likewise, it is entirely possible that Jackson did nothing more than "set him ashore." Jackson and Ledain were not the ones who physically sold the captives. Rather, they entrusted them to the care of Edward Tothill, who was responsible for selling them. While some ship captains doubled as merchants, with a supercargo on board, Jackson had to ensure only that the captives arrived safely and, like any other cargo, ended up in the proper hands.

65 There are a few explanations for this omission. First, much of the day-to-day documentation about the ship has disappeared. The mutineers

destroyed Jackson's log and the schooner's bill of lading, which may have discussed the Spaniard. Likewise, the only extracts of mate William Blake's diary that survive are those starting on 31 May, the day before the mutiny. Blake may have made reference to Gousinh, but the full diary no longer exists. Second, the court wanted to establish guilt, not motive. Thus, the crew's testimony directly related to the actual events of the mutiny. Finally, the crew probably could not even communicate with Gousinh and may have known only the most basic information about him. Unlike the mutineers, who were fluent in multiple languages and could probably speak Spanish (or at least as Portuguese speakers understand it), the rest of the crew were Anglophones and probably unable to communicate.

66 For more on the causes of the war, see Adrian Finucane, *The Temptations of Trade: Britain, Spain, and the Struggle for Empire* (Philadelphia: University of Pennsylvania Press, 2016), 124–134.

67 See ibid., 135–140, for the course of the war.

68 Julian Gwyn, *The Enterprising Admiral: The Personal Fortune of Admiral Sir Peter Warren* (Montreal: McGill-Queen's University Press, 1974), 19.

69 Clarke's investments in privateering and naval prize cargoes can be found in Smith, *Slavery, Family, and Gentry Capitalism*, 113–114. Warren had a correspondence with Clarke about the prizes and also used his naval ships to move rum and other tropical produce for Clarke. See Peter Warren to Gedney Clarke, 2 June 1746, in Julian Gwyn, ed., *The Royal Navy and North America: The Warren Papers, 1736–1752* (London: Naval Records Society, 1973), 250–251.

70 For more on "Spanish Negroes," see Charles R. Foy, "Ports of Slavery, Ports of Freedom: How Slaves Used Northern Seaports' Maritime Industry to Escape and Create Trans-Atlantic Identities, 1713–1783" (PhD diss., Rutgers University, 2008), chap. 4, esp. 230–234. The number of "Spanish Negroes" captured and condemned as slaves is unclear. Foy calculates nearly 500 during the period of his study (1713–1783), with the largest number, 95, being sold during the War of Jenkins' Ear. See ibid., Appendix C. That said, Foy calculates the number of Spanish Negroes only in the North American colonies, and really only the northern port cities, suggesting a significantly higher number when the southern and West Indian colonies are included. Jamaica, for example, had the largest admiralty court in British America and would have assessed far more prize cargoes than those of North America. Barbados and Antigua also had active admiralty courts.

5. ENDINGS

1 This was Blake's term for Da Costa in his log. See *Boston News-Letter*, 4 August 1743.

2 "Da Costa's Examination."

3 For the reference to fabrics on the *Rising Sun*, see 23 July 1743, Oud Archief Suriname: Gouvernementssecretarie, 1.05.10.01, inv. nr. 3, NA Netherlands.

4 About the only clue on quantity comes from a warrant selling some of these goods shortly after the mutiny where he enumerated seventeen barrels of sugar, nine of cacao, and one of coffee. "Edward Tothill," 13 August 1743, Notarissen Suriname tot 1828 (Judicial Acts), 1.05.11.14, inv. nr. 326, f. 199.

5 See Marcus Rediker and Peter Linebaugh, *The Many-Headed Hydra: Sailors, Slaves, Commoners, and the Hidden History of the Revolutionary Atlantic* (Boston: Beacon, 2001), chap. 5, for a discussion of solidarity between sailors.

6 There is an extensive literature on free people of African descent owning enslaved people in the Americas. See, for example, Zephyr L. Frank, *Dutra's World: Wealth and Family in Nineteenth-Century Rio de Janeiro* (Albuquerque: University of New Mexico Press, 2004), and Marisa Fuentes's discussion of Rachel Pringle Polgreen, a free mixed-race brothel owner who lived in Barbados, in *Dispossessed Lives: Enslaved Women, Violence, and the Archive* (Philadelphia: University of Pennsylvania Press, 2016), chap. 2.

7 In his interrogation, when asked if he thought they had reached the Orinoco, Da Costa replied "yes" ("jaa"). "Da Costa's Examination."

8 "Hem vrij de kop konden afkappen," in ibid.

9 *New-York Weekly Journal*, 15 August 1743. The house was about sixty miles upriver. In the Guiana colonies, the coastal plain was prone to flooding when the rivers rose with the tide. For that reason, settlements were often established far inland. New Amsterdam, the capital of Berbice, for example, was fifty-six miles inland.

10 *Boston News-Letter*, 4 August 1743.

11 Dutch authorities were well aware of this "deception" and discussed it in some of the documents relating for the case. For an example of this "deception" ("misleijding"), see Request van Jan Heijse, 15 August 1743, Oud Archief Suriname: Raad van Politie, 1.05.10.02, inv.nr. 25, f. 34, NA Netherlands.

12 Ibid. and *New-York Weekly Journal*, 15 August 1743.

13 See 21 July 1743, Oud Archief Suriname: Gouverneursjournalen, 1.05.03, inv. nr. 199, f. 242, NA Netherlands. His first name, Jan, comes from a later

petition to receive compensation. Likewise, Dutch documents called him "Heijser" or "Heijssen," but he signed documents "Heijse." See Petition of Jan Heijse, 15 August 1743, Oud Archief Suriname: Raad van Politie, 1.05.10.02, inv.nr. 326, f. 68–70, NA Netherlands.

14 Dutch officials rarely note what Amerindian groups they encountered. Moravian missionaries, however, who moved into the Courantyne River region in the 1750s, noted the presence of both Kali'na and Arawak. Given Heijse later hired fifty warriors to assist him, he probably worked with a mix of both groups. See Felix Stähelin, *Die Mission der Brüdergemeine in Suriname und Berbice im achtzehnten Jahrhundert* . . . (Herrnhut: Verlag der Vereins für Brüdergeschichte in Kommission der Unitätsbuchhandlung in Gnadau, 1914), 2:163. Special thanks to Marjoleine Kars for this information.

15 See Marjoleine Kars, *Blood on the River: A Chronicle of Mutiny and Freedom on the Wild Coast* (New York: New Press, 2020), 37–48; Neil Whitehead, "The Conquest of the Caribs of the Orinoco Basin, 1498–1771" (PhD diss., Oxford University, 1983), chap. 4; and Bram Hoonhout and Thomas Mareite, "Freedom at the Fringes? Slave Flight and Empire-Building in the Early Modern Spanish Borderlands of Essequibo–Venezuela and Louisiana–Texas," *SA* 40, no. 1 (March 2019): 65. For the guns, see Bram Hoonhout, *Borderless Empire: Dutch Guiana in the Atlantic World, 1750–1800* (Athens: University of Georgia Press, 2020), 37.

16 Hoonhout, *Borderless Empire*, 35.

17 Just a few months prior to the arrival of the *Rising Sun*, for example, Governor Mauricius noted the presence of an interpreter, Hendrik Hart, at Courantyne. See 29 March 1743, Oud Archief Suriname: Gouverneursjournalen, 1.05.03, inv. nr. 199, f. 127. For an overview of the postholder system, see Hoonhout, *Borderless Empire*, 35–37.

18 "Da Costa's Examination."

19 *New-York Weekly Journal*, 15 August 1743.

20 "Da Costa's Examination."

21 *New-York Weekly Journal*, 15 August 1743.

22 Heijse named the soldiers in his petition for compensation. See Request van Jan Heijse, 15 August 1743, Oud Archief Suriname: Raad van Politie, 1.05.10.02, inv.nr. 25, f. 53–54, NA Netherlands.

23 Ibid.

24 "Da Costa's Examination."

25 Ibid. This comes from Da Costa's testimony, and he may have been trying to save himself by making it seem like he encouraged surrender. Lucas,

unfortunately, stopped answering questions by the time his interrogation reached this point.

26 Ibid.

27 *Boston News-Letter*, 4 August 1743.

28 For the arrival of the crew in Paramaribo, see 7 July 1743, Oud Archief Suriname: Gouverneursjournalen, 1.05.03, inv. nr. 199, f. 227, NA Netherlands.

29 *New-York Weekly Journal*, 15 August 1743.

30 This sequence of events was related in *Boston News-Letter*, 4 August 1743.

31 This report no longer exists. For mention of the document, see 7 July 1743, Oud Archief Suriname: Gouverneursjournalen, 1.05.03, inv. nr. 199, f. 227 and 7 July 1743, Oud Archief Suriname: Gouvernementssecretarie, 1.05.10.01, inv. nr. 3, NA Netherlands.

32 *Boston News-Letter*, 4 August 1743.

33 The Dutch had an excellent catalog of and familiarity with the various flora and fauna living in Suriname, especially insects. Indeed, it was one of the first American colonies to have its insects systematically studied, by a German woman named Maria Sibylla Merian who resided in Suriname from 1699 to 1701. She later published her findings, making her one of the first women to publish in science. For her work, see Maria Sibylla Merian, *Metamorphosis Insectorum Surinamensium. Ofte Verandering der Surinaamsch Insecten* (Amsterdam, 1705). For more on Merian, see Natalie Zemon Davis, *Women on the Margins: Three Seventeenth-Century Lives* (Cambridge, MA: Harvard University Press, 1997), part 3.

34 Edward Bancroft, *An Essay on the Natural History of Guiana in South America* . . . (London, 1769), 18.

35 *Pennsylvania Gazette*, 25 August 1743.

36 Heijse described his concerns and how much he paid the Amerindians in a petition to Suriname's Council of Policy. See Petition of Jan Heijse, 15 August 1743, Oud Archief Suriname: Raad van Politie, 1.05.10.02, inv.nr. 326, f. 68–70, NA Netherlands.

37 21 July 1743, Oud Archief Suriname: Gouverneursjournalen, 1.05.03, inv. nr. 199, f. 242, NA Netherlands. Interestingly, Mauricius noted that the mutineers were also executed on this day, but seems to have gone back and noted this in his journal. The mutineers were not executed until 5 August NS.

38 Kars, *Blood on the River*, 244.

39 Ibid., 245.

40 For Suriname's large Portuguese Jewish population, see Aviva Ben-Ur, *Jewish Autonomy in a Slave Society: Suriname in the Atlantic World, 1651–1825* (Philadelphia: University of Pennsylvania Press, 2020).

41 Reference to the process for the British crew can be found in "Crew Testimony."

42 "Antwoord, off ik ja en off ik neen segt, daar sal mij overkomen het geene de heeren sullen goed vinden" in "Da Costa's Examination."

43 At the beginning of their interrogations, the record noted that Da Costa confessed freely, but never mentioned Lucas. Then, when ordering their executions, the clerk noted, in the plural, "prisoners' confession" ("confessie van de gedetineerdens"). This confession may have been extracted when Da Costa and Lucas were sat together. See "Criminal Complaint." There is also the possibility that the Raad Fiscaal had Lucas tortured to extract his confession. While most European nations had outlawed the use of torture in judicial proceedings and it had decreased in frequency in the Netherlands by the 1740s, it was not unheard of. Likewise, torture remained common in Suriname, especially for enslaved people accused of crimes. Colonial officials subjected them with little regard to their humanity or care that confessions from torture were largely useless. See Natalie Zemon Davis, "Judges, Masters, Diviners: Slaves' Experience of Criminal Justice in Colonial Suriname," *Law and History Review* 29, no. 4 (2011): 962–963n86.

44 "Die ter bevijliging van de zeevaart ten rigoreuste moeten gestraft" in "Criminal Complaint."

45 For more on Black executioners in Suriname and other slave societies, see Davis, "Judges, Masters, Diviners," 970, and Kars, *Blood on the River*, 243.

46 Descriptions of the execution can be found in "Extract of a Letter from Surinam, Dated Aug. 15, 1743," *Gentleman's Magazine and Historical Chronicle* 13 (November 1743): 609, and 5 August 1743, Oud Archief Suriname: Gouverneursjournalen, 1.05.03, inv. nr. 199, f. 260, NA Netherlands.

47 Historian Peter Linebaugh refers to this as "thanatocracy," or the use of mass state violence and executions to maintain order. In his accounting, it was central to the rise of capitalism in the eighteenth and nineteenth centuries. See Linebaugh, *Red Round Globe Hot Burning: A Tale at the Crossroads of Commons & Closure, of Love & Terror, of Race & Class, and of Kate & Ned Despard* (Berkeley: University of California Press, 2019), sec. B.

48 *Boston News-Letter*, 4 August 1743.

49 Ibid.

50 *Boston Evening Post*, 1 August 1743; *Boston Gazette*, 2 August 1743; and
 Boston News-Letter, 4 August 1743. It is hard to tell the effect Tothill's letter
 had on Boston's reading public. Certainly, the form of the story, a summa-
 rized or reprinted letter, would not have been surprising. Printers
 extracted many of the articles they placed in eighteenth-century newspapers from private correspondence. It was a common, popular narrative
 style. See Andrew Pettigree, *The Invention of News: How the World Came
 to Know about Itself* (New Haven, CT: Yale University Press, 2014), 322.
51 *Boston News-Letter*, 11 August 1743, and *Boston Post-Boy*, 15 August 1743.
52 *Boston News-Letter*, 29 September 1743.
53 *American Weekly Mercury*, 11 August 1743, and *Pennsylvania Gazette*, 11
 August 1743.
54 *Pennsylvania Gazette*, 25 August 1743.
55 See *London Daily Post and General Advertiser*, 30 September 1743, and
 Country Journal or The Craftsman, 1 October 1743.
56 To compare the terminology used, see *Boston News-Letter*, 4 August 1743,
 and *New-York Weekly Journal*, 15 August 1743.
57 *New-York Weekly Journal*, 15 August 1743.
58 This testimony is different from that offered on 1 August (NS) during the
 trial of the mutineers, which is much shorter, meant only to establish guilt,
 and signed by all four surviving sailors. For the comparison, see "Crew
 Testimony."
59 See *Boston Gazette*, 2 August 1743, *Boston News-Letter*, 4 August 1743, *Boston
 Post-Boy*, 15 August 1743, and *Boston News-Letter*, 29 September 1743,
 respectively, for these descriptions.
60 See, for example, *London Evening Post*, 5 November 1743, *Daily Gazetteer*, 5
 November 1743, *Newcastle Weekly Courant*, 5 November 1743, *Ipswich
 Journal*, 12 November 1743, and *Universal Spectator and Weekly Journal*, 12
 November 1743.
61 The story of the execution originally printed in Boston on 29 September
 first appeared in London's *General Evening Post* on 22 November.
62 "Extract of a Letter from Surinam, dated Aug. 15, 1743," *Gentleman's
 Magazine and Historical Chronicle* 13 (November 1743): 609.

6. AFTERMATHS

 1 "Die een goed vriend van den vermoorden koopman was geweest, en mijn
 Commiseraties voor de weduwe imploreerde," in 7 July 1743, Oud Archief
 Suriname: Gouverneursjournalen, 1.05.03, inv. nr. 199, f. 228, NA
 Netherlands.

2 8 July 1743 and 9 July 1743, Oud Archief Suriname: Gouverneursjournalen, 1.05.03, inv. nr. 199, f. 228–230, NA Netherlands. Mauricius listed the names of the crewmen hired in the margins of folio 230.

3 21 July 1743, Oud Archief Suriname: Gouverneursjournalen, 1.05.03, inv. nr. 199, f. 242–243, NA Netherlands.

4 "Geen hesitatie kan overblij-ven of de Bark moet geconsidereerd worden als een Engelsch schip, ende goederen, als aan groot Brittannische onderdaanen toebehoorende," in ibid., f. 243–244.

5 Ibid., f. 243.

6 Ibid., f. 244.

7 Ibid., 22 July 1743, f. 244.

8 Ibid., 23 July 1743, f. 245.

9 "Request van Jan Heijse," 15 August 1743, Oud Archief Suriname: Raad van Politie, 1.05.10.02, inv.nr. 25, f. 53–54, NA Netherlands.

10 Both the request for a formal letter and the decision to sell can be found in ibid., f. 245.

11 A document regarding the sale of some of the goods on the *Rising Sun* refer to Halewijn's "conditions" ("Conditien" in the document) placed on the sale of these goods. Those conditions were the enforcement of the colony's trade laws. To ensure that these were enforced, anyone taking the goods out of the Raad Fiscaal's custody had to produce shipping documents, which presumably included the ship's destination. See "Edward Tothill," 13 August 1743, Oud Archief Suriname: Notarissen Suriname tot 1828, 1.05.11.14, inv. nr. 326, f. 179, NA Netherlands.

12 The document does not explicitly state these goods were from the *Rising Sun*, but they were in the custody of the Raad Fiscaal and there were certain conditions placed on their sale. Moreover, Samuel Dowse was the brother of Joseph Dowse, Newark Jackson's business partner and co-owner of the *Industry*. He may have been purchasing some of those goods to take home to Amey Jackson. See ibid. and Thomas Bellows Wyman, *The Genealogies and Estates of Charlestown in the County of Middlesex and Commonwealth of Massachusetts, 1629–1818*, vol. 1 (Boston: David Clapp and Son, 1879), 306. For a direct mention of the Samuel and Joseph Dowse's relationship, see the bill of exchange in 6 December 1741, Notarissen Suriname tot 1828, 1.05.11.14, inv. nr. 759, f. 87, NA Netherlands.

13 Mauricius noted that Moulder's ship, the *Johanna Wilhelmina*, departed Suriname on 10 October (NS) with a cargo of sugar, coffee, and cacao. Interestingly, the governor did not list Moulder's destination (he also did not list where Moulder arrived from earlier in the year). This record does

raise the possibility that Dowse entrusted Moulder with his cargo. More likely, however, since Moulder traded in these commodities and probably had them on board his ship, it created the paper trail necessary for Dowse to hold onto the goods from the *Rising Sun*. See 10 October 1743, Oud Archief Suriname: Gouverneursjournalen, 1.05.03, inv. nr. 199, f. 321, NA Netherlands.

14 Petition of Edward Tothill, 15 August 1743, Oud Archief Suriname: Raad van Politie, 1.05.10.02, inv.nr. 326, f. 58–59, NA Netherlands.

15 "Request van E. Tothil," 15 August 1743, Oud Archief Suriname: Raad van Politie, 1.05.10.02, inv. nr., inv.nr. 25, f. 54–55, NA Netherlands.

16 See "Inventory."

17 30 August 1743, Oud Archief Suriname: Gouverneursjournalen, 1.05.03, inv. nr. 199, f. 281–282, NA Netherlands. John Tufton Mason was a Boston merchant active in the Suriname trade. Around this same time, the British government gave him entail rights to a significant amount of land in the colony of New Hampshire. He benefitted immensely from the sale of this land, became a grandee and power broker in the province, and was something of a merchant adventurer later in life. See Otis Grant Hammond, "The Mason Title and Its Relations in New Hampshire and Massachusetts," *Proceedings of the American Antiquarian Society* 26 (April 1916): 245–263, and David Dewar, "The Mason Patents: Conflict, Controversy, and the Quest for Authority in Colonial New Hampshire," in *Constructing Early Modern Empires: Proprietary Ventures in the Atlantic World, 1500–1750*, ed. L. H. Roper and Bertrand Van Ruymbeke (Boston: Brill, 2007), 269–300.

18 Heijse later noted maintaining the ship as one of his expenses when requesting compensation for his services. That would have included feeding the enslaved people. See "Request van Jan Heijse," 15 August 1743, Oud Archief Suriname: Raad van Politie, 1.05.10.02, inv.nr. 25, f. 53–54, NA Netherlands.

19 Ibid., 21 July 1743, f. 242.

20 James B. Bell, ed., *The Colonial Records of King Chapel, 1686–1776*, vol. 2 (Boston: Colonial Society of Massachusetts, 2019), 678.

21 Lascelles and Maxwell to Gedney Clarke, 19 November 1743, in S. D. Smith, ed., *Lascelles & Maxwell Letterbooks, 1739–1769*, reel 1: *Lascelles and Maxwell Letter Book (September 1743–December 1746)* (Wakefield, UK: Microfilm Academic, 2003), 74–75.

22 Vlaggen Island, also known as Flag Island or Fort Island, sits at the mouth of the Essequibo River. It was home to Fort Zeelandia, the center of Dutch

administration in the colony. The fort flew a giant Dutch flag, thus the name. For Shaw, see Great Britain, *British Guiana Boundary. Arbitration with the United States of Venezuela: Appendix to the Case on Behalf of the Government of Her Britannic Majesty*, vol. 7 (London: Harrison and Sons, 1898), 197.

23 See "Crew Testimony."

24 For more on Clarke's investments in the Dutch Guianas, see Bram Hoonhout, *Borderless Empire: Dutch Guiana in the Atlantic World, 1750–1800* (Athens: University of Georgia Press, 2020), 168–173, and S. D. Smith, *Slavery, Family, and Gentry Capitalism in the British Atlantic: The World of the Lascelles, 1648–1834* (New York: Cambridge University Press, 2006), 105–107.

25 The increase in land prices was due to the *negotiates* system, which pooled private capital to provide mortgages for plantations in Suriname, Essequibo, Demerara, and Berbice. The height of the system was in the 1760s, and the infusion of cheap credit caused the number of plantations in Demerara and Essequibo to nearly double. Land prices also skyrocketed. In Demerara, for example, land that would have cost two or three guilders per acre in the 1750s rose to between thirty and thirty-six guilders per acre a decade later. By 1771, land could sell for upward of sixty guilders per acre. It was a speculative bubble as commodity prices could not support the amount of money lent. For John Shaw, on the ground witnessing this firsthand, he probably understood what was going on and sold his land at a much higher value than he paid for it. See Hoonhout, *Borderless Empire*, 138–139.

26 In the same letter where Lascelles and Maxwell discussed John Shaw, they also noted that they believed Clarke would receive the full amount from the insurance he purchased "at least after a deduction of the value in your hands on the sales of the Scooner and Negroes." Since the insurers would not cover the property that made it into Clarke's hands—the schooner and the captives—he would have to sell them on his own. See Lascelles and Maxwell to Gedney Clarke, 19 November 1743, in Smith, *Lascelles & Maxwell Letterbooks*, 74.

27 For Frank, see Jackson's inventory and the account of his estate from 1745, Newark Jackson, docket 7944, SCPR, MSA. One pound in Massachusetts currency was worth slightly more than 18 percent of a British pound sterling in 1743. Depreciating currency was a serious issue at the time and may help explain why the *Rising Sun* had so much gold and silver on

board. See John J. McCusker, *Money and Exchange in Europe and America, 1600–1775* (Chapel Hill: University of North Carolina Press, 1978), 149.

28 For the business relationship between Clarke, Robert Hooper, and Hooper's colleague Joseph Swett, see Smith, *Slavery, Family, and Gentry Capitalism,* 100–101.

29 Robert Hooper to Gedney Clarke, 5 March 1743, *Swett and Hooper Letter Book, 1740–1747,* Fam. Mss. 986, PEM.

30 Robert Hooper to Gedney Clarke, 17 August 1743, ibid.

31 Robert Hooper to Gedney Clarke, 8 November 1743, ibid.

32 Robert Hooper to Gedney Clarke, 4 March 1744, ibid. He also requested an enslaved teenage boy for his business partner, Joseph Swett. See Robert Hooper to Gedney Clarke, 2 March 1744, ibid.

33 These goods can be found in Jackson's probate inventory. See Jackson's Inventory, docket 7944, SCPR, MSA.

34 More than 1,200 of Boston's 16,382 residents in 1742 were widows. Considering women made up more than half the population, it works out to about 15 percent. See Boston Record Commissioners, *A Report of the Record Commissioners of the City of Boston, Containing the Records of Boston Selectmen, 1736 to 1742,* vol. 15 (Boston: Rockwell and Churchill, 1886), 369–370.

35 Jackson's Will, docket 7944, SCPR, MSA. Considering Jackson had been to Suriname and the West Indies before 1738, it raises the possibility that he may have become gravely ill while on an earlier voyage and decided to file a will. He likewise had his first child in 1738, which made the matter of inheritance more complicated. A will could clarify some of those issues.

36 See "Richards to Richards," 21 February 1771, *Suffolk Deeds,* 118:207–208, MSA. There is a reference to an abutting property belonging to "the land of the heirs or Assigns of Newark Jackson decd."

37 Amey Jackson owned the pew through 1748, when her name disappeared from the receipt book. See "Old North Pew Tax Receipt Book, 1744–1750," Old North Church Records Ms. N-2249, box OS 1, folder 8, MHS.

38 See Boston Record Commissioners, *A Report of the Record Commissioners of the City of Boston, Containing Boston Marriages From 1752 to 1809,* vol. 30 (Boston: Rockwell and Churchill, 1903), 9.

39 Amey Jr. possibly married Abraham Miller in 1758. She would have been sixteen, which was young, but given the family's financial problems and Amey Sr.'s remarriage, there was probably a desire to marry her off. Nevertheless, this could be Amey Sr. marrying again, although a David

Gardner does not appear in any of Boston's death records in the interven-
ing years. See ibid., 29.

40 *Vital Records of Newburyport, Massachusetts to the End of the Year 1849*, vol.
1 (Salem: Essex Institute, 1911), 403.

41 See Sara T. Damiano, "'To Well and Truly Administer': Female
Administrators and Estate Settlement in Newport, Rhode Island, 1730–
1776," *NEQ* 86, no. 1 (March 2013): 92. Massachusetts followed similar
practices to Rhode Island. Special thanks to Sara Damiano for explaining
a widow's role in settling an intestate estate and sharing her article.

42 Ledain's Administration, docket 7936, SCPR, MSA.

43 *Boston Weekly Post-Boy*, 24 October 1743.

44 Edward Bromfield to Gedney Clarke, 13 December 1743, Bromfield Family
Collection, 1729–1844, vol. 1: Letter Book, 1742–1744, Mss. 664, NEHGS.

45 "En mijn Commiseraties voor de weduwe imploreerde," in 7 July 1743, Oud
Archief Suriname: Gouverneursjournalen, 1.05.03, inv. nr. 199, f. 227, NA
Netherlands.

46 Petition of Edward Tothill, 15 August 1743, Oud Archief Suriname: Raad van
Politie, 1.05.10.02, inv.nr. 326, f. 58–59, NA Netherlands.

47 Ledain's Power of Attorney, docket 7936, SCPR, MSA.

48 Lascelles and Maxwell to Gedney Clarke, 14 July 1744, in Smith, *Lascelles &
Maxwell Letterbooks*, 178–179.

49 The Lascelles state this fact in a letter to Clarke. See Lascelles and Maxwell
to Gedney Clarke, 10 September 1744, ibid., 198.

50 Lascelles and Maxwell to Gedney Clarke, 23 December 1743, ibid., 80.

51 Lascelles and Maxwell to Gedney Clarke, 4 April 1744, ibid., 149.

52 Lascelles made a mistake here. He believed that the Raad Fiscaal
impounded and sold most of the goods from the *Rising Sun*. Since the
"Fiscal," as Lascelles called him, ensured the legal sale of the goods,
they would move on Dutch ships and most likely be sent to
Amsterdam. Lascelles made this arrangement with Couderc in
November 1743, however, months after Tothill had found other ways to
sell the cargo through both legal and illegal channels. See Lascelles
and Maxwell to Gedney Clarke, 19 November 1743, ibid., 74.

53 Lascelles and Maxwell to Gedney Clarke, 23 December 1743, ibid., 80.

54 Lascelles and Maxwell to Gedney Clarke, 15 June 1745, ibid., 276.

55 Lascelles and Maxwell to Gedney Clarke, 5 October 1745, ibid., 300.

56 Edward Bromfield to Gedney Clarke, 8 January 1743/4, Bromfield Family
Collection, 1729–1844, vol. 1: Letter Book, 1742–1744, Mss. 664, R. Stanton
Avery Special Collections, NEHGS. Despite his earlier complaints,

Bromfield continued working as an intermediary with Clarke to settle Ledain's account.

57 Lascelles and Maxwell to Gedney Clarke, 5 October 1745, in Smith, *Lascelles & Maxwell Letterbooks*, 301.

58 For the dispute, see Steven J. J. Pitt, "Building and Outfitting Ships in Colonial Boston," *EAS* 13, no. 4 (Fall 2015): 903–904. Pitt mistakes Edward Bromfield for his son Henry, who would have been only sixteen at the time of the dispute in 1743–44. The Bromfield Letter Books are confusingly all labeled "Bromfield, Henry" despite the earliest being Edward's.

59 Swett and Hooper to Gedney Clarke, 7 November 1743, *Swett and Hooper Letter Book, 1740–1747*, Fam. Mss. 986, PEM.

60 Clarke continued supporting his kin in Salem, including paying for his mother's funeral and offering business opportunities to his nephews. Some moved to Barbados. See Smith, *Slavery, Family, and Gentry Capitalism*, 121. He also maintained a close friendship and conducted some business with the Wendells, although that also resulted in a commercial dispute in the late 1750s. See, for example, Gedney Clarke to Jacob Wendell, 13 June 1747 (friendship), reel 24, and "Charles Apthorp, attorney for Gedney Clarke," 4 November 1758 (dispute), reel 26, *Quincy, Wendell, Holmes, and Upham Family Papers, 1633–1910*, Microfilm Edition, Call No. P-347, MHS.

61 For more on the rift and separation between the North American and West Indian colonies, see Trevor Burnard, *Jamaica in the Age of Revolution* (Philadelphia: University of Pennsylvania Press, 2020), 207.

62 Trevor Burnard, *Planters, Merchants, and Slaves: Plantation Societies in British America, 1650–1820* (Chicago: University of Chicago Press, 2015), 121–122.

63 During the 1740s, Demerara and Essequibo produced over 45,000 pounds of cacao. That was almost nine times as much as the two colonies produced the previous decade, suggesting how much British merchants invested. Nevertheless, in the 1740s, the colonies produced over 10 million pounds of sugar, demonstrating how cacao was still a supplemental crop. See Eric Willem Van Der Oest, "The Forgotten Colonies of Essequibo and Demerara, 1700–1814," in *Riches from Atlantic Commerce: Dutch Transatlantic Trade and Shipping, 1585–1817*, ed. Johannes Postma and Victor Enthoven (Boston: Brill, 2003), 350 (Table 12.6).

64 Anne Blaschke, "Chocolate Manufacturing and Marketing in Massachusetts, 1705–1825," in *Chocolate: History, Culture, and Heritage*, ed. Louis Evan

Grivetti and Howard-Yana Shapiro (Hoboken, NJ: John Wiley, 2009), 346–347.

EPILOGUE

1 "Mission Statement," Old North Foundation, https://oldnorth.com.
2 His name, according to retired vicar and former executive director of the Old North Foundation Steve Ayres, was "picked somewhat out of a hat." Egan Millard, "Iconic Boston Church Reckons with Its Links to Slavery," *Episcopal News Service*, 8 November 2019, www.episcopalnewsservice.org.
3 Khari Thompson, "Old North Church Will Remove Name of Parishioner Involved with Slave Trade," *WBUR*, 14 November 2019, www.wbur.org.
4 Quoted in Brian MacQuarrie, "Old North Church, a Cherished Symbol, Opens Up about Its Link to Slavery," *Boston Globe*, 26 October 2019, www.bostonglobe.com.
5 See Eliga H. Gould, "Entangled Histories, Entangled Worlds: The English-Speaking Atlantic as a Spanish Periphery," *AHR* 112, no. 3 (June 2007): 764–786.

APPENDIX I

1 Johannes Postma calculated that 1,654 captives arrived in Suriname between 1740 and 1744, compared to 1,926 from 1735 to 1738 and 1,965 from 1730 to 1734. See Postma, *The Dutch in the Atlantic Slave Trade, 1600–1815* (New York: Cambridge University Press, 1990), 186t (1730–1734 and 1735–1738 figures), 212t (1740–1744 figures).
2 Richard B. Sheridan, *Sugar and Slavery: An Economic History of the British West Indies, 1623–1775* (Kingston: Canoe Press, 1974), 140–141.
3 S. D. Smith, *Slavery, Family, and Gentry Capitalism in the British Atlantic: The World of the Lascelles, 1648–1834* (New York: Cambridge University Press, 2006), 107–108.
4 Bram Hoonhout, *Borderless Empire: Dutch Guiana in the Atlantic World, 1750–1800* (Athens: University of Georgia Press, 2020), 168–169.
5 See the lists of cargo in *Clarke v. Wingfield* and *Ledain v. Wingfield*, 6 July 1742, SCCP, 1742, 111, MSA.
6 For more, see Robin Pearson and David Richardson, "Insuring the Transatlantic Slave Trade," *Journal of Economic History* 79, no. 2 (June 2019): 417–446.
7 The correspondence regarding the insurance policy can be found in Simon D. Smith, ed., *Lascelles and Maxwell Letter Books (1739–1769)*, Microfilm Edition, reel 1: *Lascelles and Maxwell Letter Book (September*

1743–December 1746), 73–74, 80, 98, 149–150, 171, 178–179, 187–188, 197–198, 232, 271, 276, 300–301. For a list of the underwriters, see Lascelles and Maxwell to Gedney Clarke, 14 July 1744, 178–179. Lascelles and Maxwell underwrote 500 pounds of the total 1,500.

8 Lascelles and Maxwell to Gedney Clarke, 19 November 1743, ibid., 74.

9 Trevor Burnard, *Jamaica in the Age of Revolution* (Philadelphia: University of Pennsylvania Press, 2020), 180.

10 "Barkentijn off [*sic*] schoender" in "Inventory."

11 For more on topsail schooners and why they were used, see Phillip Reid, *The Merchant Ship in the British Atlantic, 1600–1800: Continuity and Innovation in a Key Technology* (Boston: Brill, 2020), 209, 260.

12 Joseph A. Goldenberg, *Shipbuilding in Colonial America* (Charlottesville: University of Virginia Press, 1976), 98–99.

13 Mary Ellen Hicks, "The Sea and the Shackle: African and Creole Mariners and the Making of a Luso-African Atlantic Commercial Culture, 1721–1835" (PhD diss., University of Virginia, 2015), 6–7.

14 Marcus Rediker, *The Slave Ship: A Human History* (New York: Penguin, 2007), 229.

15 Ibid., 251–253.

APPENDIX II

1 An identical version of this article appeared in the *Boston Gazette* the following day on 2 August 1743.

2 Inserted with a caret (^) in the manuscript.

INDEX

Figures and notes are indicated by f and n following the page number.

ABOUT THE AUTHOR

JARED ROSS HARDESTY is Associate Professor of History at Western Washington University. He is the author of *Unfreedom: Slavery and Dependence in Eighteenth-Century Boston* and *Black Lives, Native Lands, White Worlds: A History of Slavery in New England*.